MISCELLANEOUS

WRITINGS

OF

F. W. GRANT.

VOL. I.

WIPF & STOCK · Eugene, Oregon

Wipf and Stock Publishers
199 W 8th Ave, Suite 3
Eugene, OR 97401

Miscellaneous Writings of F. W. Grant, Volume 1
By Grant, F. W.
Softcover ISBN-13: 978-1-7252-7571-3
Publication date 3/30/2020
Previously published by Loizeaux Bros., 1917

CONTENTS.

VOL. I.

THE REDEMPTION FROM "VANITY."
SOME THEMES OF THE SECOND PART OF ROMANS.
RE-TRACINGS OF TRUTH.
REASONS FOR MY FAITH AS TO BAPTISM.
HOUSEHOLD BAPTISM.—A REVIEW OF OBJECTIONS.
THE CHURCH'S PATH.
DR. WALDENSTROM AND NON-VICARIOUS ATONEMENT.
FRUIT OR ROOT; THOUGHTS ON JOB'S DITCH.
CREATION IN GENESIS AND IN GEOLOGY.

VOL. II.

THE PROPHETIC HISTORY OF THE CHURCH. (ON REV. 2 & 3.)
CHRISTIAN HOLINESS; ITS ROOTS AND FRUITS: A REVIEW OF DR. STEELE'S "ANTINOMIANISM REVIVED."
THE HOPE OF THE MORNING STAR. WITH A REVIEW OF THE OBJECTIONS TO AN IMMEDIATE EXPECTATION OF THE LORD'S RETURN.
LIVING BY THE WELL.

VOL. III.

THE MYSTERIES OF THE KINGDOM OF HEAVEN.
NOTES ON THE EPISTLE TO THE HEBREWS.
BUT ONE THING NEEDFUL.
THE ONE ONLY NAME.
FOUR LECTURES—1. THE MEDIATOR. 2. "OUTSIDE THE CAMP." 3. CONFLICT AND PROGRESS. 4. "FROM THE TOP OF THE ROCKS."
THE SALVATION ARMY AND ITS LESSONS.
THE SWALLOW'S NEST.
"REMEMBER YOUR GUIDES;" A MEMORIAL OF THE MINISTRY OF F. W. GRANT BY S. RIDOUT.
FROM AMAM TO BIZIOTHIAH.

The Redemption from "Vanity."

THE great wheel of the world goes round,
   And nothing is at a stay;
The generations come and pass,
As shadows move upon the grass,
   More permanent than they.

A transient ill, a fleeting good,
   A hope that is attained, and gone—
On all, the penalty alike,
Of passing with the hours that strike,
   As the great world moveth on.

And the flowers that cluster over it
   Are crushed and buried beneath;
For life sports with its strength above,
And we dare to smile, and we dare to love,
   But ever below is death.

And we cry, O God, but our joys are sweet:
   And why doth the wheel go round?
And why must that which is high be low?
And how canst Thou have ordained it so?
And where—this throbbing movement through—
   Oh, where can rest be found?

But yet, though the wheel be high, look up:
   For a Form, and a Human Form
Sitteth in peace above it still,
And guideth it with a perfect will,
   Through brightness and through storm.

A Form, and a Human Form is there,
  Whom the wheel, with spirit instinct, obeys—
The chariot-wheel of destiny—
For a purpose fixed and firm has He,
  And the end shall be only praise.

For it bringeth low all human pride,
  And humbleth into dust the Dust,
And thou seest not the other side—
  For there we see not, but we trust—
Where the wheel revolveth into day,
And the cycle of life comes to its stay.

The Dead and Risen, He knoweth it all,
  And therefore His face is bright and still
With the joy to which He alone can guide
The souls for whom He has stooped and died
  In the might of His perfect will.

And the wheel of the world is His chariot-wheel;
  For His triumph it moveth on:
And we catch from His glorious face to-day
The peace of its promise all the way,
  Till the goal of His rest be won.

F. W. G.

Some Themes of the Second Part of Romans.

I.—"In Adam" and "in Christ" (chap. v. 12–21).

MY desire is to take up and discuss as simply as possible, and yet as fully as may be necessary, some of the leading truths of the epistle to the Romans. My aim is not controversy, as I trust, but edification; yet on this very account I shall seek to remember all through the need of those who have been exercised by questions which have of late arisen. Exercise is not to be deprecated. It is well to be made thus to realize how far we have really learned from God, and our need of being taught in His presence that which cannot be shaken. There is an uneasy dishonoring fear in the hearts of many as to submitting all that they have apparently learned, through whomsoever or in what way soever learned, to be afresh tested by what seems "novel" and in some measure in conflict with it. But it will only be found, by those who in patience and confidence in God allow every question to be raised that can be raised, and seek answer to it from Him through the Word, how firm His foundation stands, and how that which seems at first to threaten more or less the integrity of our faith only in result confirms it. Difficulties are cleared away, things obscure made to take shape and meaning, the divine power of the Word to manifest itself, Christ and His grace to be better known. Much too that we looked at or were prepared to look at as fundamental difference in another's view turns out to be only the emphasizing (though perhaps the *over*-emphasizing) of what was really defective in our own. And so "by that which *every* joint supplieth, according to the effectual working in the measure of every part," there is made "increase of the body to the edifying of itself in love."

Let us now look at what is surely the key-note to the interpretation of what is known to many as the second part of Romans (ch. v. 12–viii.), the two contrasted thoughts, "in Adam" and "in Christ." This is what we start with in chap. v. 12–21, though as yet we have neither term made use of. Indeed the first term occurs but once in Scripture, and that not in Romans, but in 1 Cor. xv, where the first Adam and the last are put in emphatic contrast.

The statements of chap. v. 12–21 are the exposition of the doctrine:—

"By one man sin entered into the world, and death by sin; and so death passed upon all men, for that all have sinned."

"If through the offense of one the many be dead."

"The judgment was by one to condemnation."

"By one man's offense death reigned by one."

"By the one offense toward all men to condemnation." (*Greek.*)

"By the one man's disobedience the many were made sinners."

"Sin hath reigned in death." (*Greek.*)

These are the statements as to the first man and the consequences of his sin. They show that his sin has affected not himself alone, but many with him; that it brought in death as a present judgment upon a fallen race, and tending to merge in final condemnation.

Two things as to present fact: a race of sinners;

death as God's judgment-stamp upon this race. The final outlook or tendency for all, utter condemnation.

The first man was thus in a very real way the representative of his race; not indeed by any formal covenant for his posterity, of which Scripture has no trace; but by his being the *divinely constituted head of it*. As the father of men, he necessarily stood as charged with the interests of his posterity; from his fall, a corrupt nature became the heritage of the race, and thus death and judgment their appointed lot, the final issue no uncertain one. Thus in a real way he represented them before God; but, as I have said, not by any formal covenant on their behalf. His representative-character was grounded in what men call natural law, which is nothing but divine law, and which is both evident in nature and asserted in the plainest possible way in Scripture. "Who can bring a clean thing out of an unclean? not one," expresses the law. "What is man, that he should be clean? and he that is born of a woman, that he should be righteous?" "Behold, I was shapen in iniquity; and in sin did my mother conceive me." The Lord's words in the gospel fully and emphatically confirm these sayings of saints of old: "That which is born of the flesh is flesh." What men now call, The principle of "heredity," is thus affirmed, and it is the whole scriptural account of the matter. The theories of a covenant with Adam for his posterity, and the imputation of his sin to them, are simply additions to Scripture, and as such, not only needless, but an obscuring of the truth, as all mere human thoughts of necessity are.

"By one man sin entered into the world, and

death by sin; and so death passed upon all men, for that all have sinned."* Such is the apostle's statement here. It speaks of death as with every individual the result of his own sins, although his being made (or "constituted") a sinner was the result of Adam's disobedience (*v.* 19). I know it has been argued that this could not apply to infants, who if they sinned could only have done so in Adam. But the apostle is not speaking of infants, nor did their case need to be considered here. Sinning in Adam is not a doctrine of Scripture, and it is not allowable to insert words of such a character and importance in this place. The apostle is addressing himself to believers, to show the application of the work of Christ to such, as delivering them from all that attached to them by nature or practice. From this the case of infants may be easily inferred, but it is not his object to speak of it, and it cannot be shown that he does so at all.†

Sin, then, came in through Adam. The nature of man was corrupted; by his disobedience the many were made sinners: and thus death introducing to judgment was the stamp of God upon the fallen condition. Adam was the representative of his race by the fact that he was the head of it, and thus, as it is put in 1 Corinthians xv. 22, "in Adam all die."

This expression, though found but once, is of great significance, because it is contrasted with

---

*The marginal reading, "*in whom* all have sinned," will hardly be now justified by any scholar.

†For those "that had not sinned after the similitude of Adam's transgression" (*v.* 14) are not infants, as many have supposed, but those who had not sinned against positive law as Adam had. For Adam's law in its nature could not be that of his posterity, who, until Moses, had none. The words "from Adam to Moses" show what is meant.

and throws light upon another expression which is of the highest importance to us, and which the following chapters of Romans use repeatedly. "For as in Adam all die, even so *in Christ* shall all be made alive." We are now prepared to understand how "in Adam all die." In his death was involved and insured the death of all men. As head of the race, his ruin and death was theirs, and so "in him," their representative, they die. "In Adam" speaks of place,—of representation; as the apostle argues as to Levi and Abraham (Heb. vii. 9, 10): "And as I may so say, Levi also, who receiveth tithes, *paid tithes in Abraham; for he was yet in the loins of his father when Melchisedek met him.*" We too were in the loins of Adam when he fell and sentence of death was passed upon him; and in him we die. Thank God, we have heard the voice of Another, Head and Representative too of His race, which says, "Because I live, ye shall live also." (Jno. xiv. 19.) In Adam we die: in Christ we live.

As in Adam, then, we are completely ruined. We are "constituted sinners"—sinners by constitution. Death and judgment are our appointed lot. This is what has to be met in our behalf, if Christ comes in for us. It is not enough for Him to be a new head and fountain of life for us from God. He must not only be our new Representative in life, but our Representative in death, and under curse also, taking the doom of those whose new Head He becomes. Hence comes a distinction which we must bear in mind. In life, He is our Representative that with Him we may live and inherit the portion He has acquired for us: in death, He is our Representative that we may *not* die, because already dead with Him. This last is *substitution*. He dies for us, and He alone: in life He lives for us, and (blessed be God!) lives *not* alone.

Now let us look at the apostle's statements. And first,—

Adam "is the figure of Him that was to come." (*v*. 14.)

Thus it is that in 1 Cor. xv. 22 "in Christ" is set over against "in Adam," and that in ver. 45 again "the last Adam" is seen in essential contrast to the "first:" "The first Adam was made a living soul; the last Adam was made a quickening Spirit."

But what, then, does a "last *Adam*" mean? The head of a new race. And thus "if any man be *in Christ*"—set over against "in Adam" in the verse already looked at,—"it is a *new* creation." (2 Cor. v. 17, *Gr*., comp. marg. Rev. Vers.) The first Adam was the head of the old creation; the last Adam is the Head of the new. "In Christ" means to belong to the new creation and the new Head.

I merely link these terms together now. I do not propose to examine here what exactly the new creation is. The term is not used in Romans, though in Galatians (its kindred epistle, though wider in scope,) it is. But it should be obvious that the first Adam, as "the figure of Him that was to come," figures Christ as "the last Adam," the representative Head of a new race. As such, the apostle compares the results of the obedience of the One to "the many" who stand in Him, with the results of the first man's *dis*obedience to "the many" who fell with him.

But we must pause before proceeding with this, to make it perfectly clear to any who have a doubt that Scripture speaks of the last Adam as really the Head of a race. Spite of the term "last Adam," some *have* doubt of this. They say, "We are never called children of *Christ*, but of God;" which is true, because it is divine life that is communicated, and "children of Christ" would imply only human life. "The last Adam is made a quickening Spirit" surely proves, however, that in this character He quickens (or gives life), while at the same time it shows the character of the life communicated; for "that which is born of the Spirit is spirit." And this action of the last Adam we find imaged by the Lord in resurrection breathing upon His disciples when He says, "Receive ye the Holy Ghost." The first Adam was but a "living soul" into whose nostrils God breathed the breath of life, that he might become so. The last Adam breathes upon others; He is a quickening Spirit, not merely a living soul.

Isaiah also, foreseeing the glory of the Lord, declares, "When Thou shalt make His soul an offering for sin, *He shall see His seed*" (liii. 10). And again, in words which are quoted and applied to Christ by the apostle, "Behold, I and the children which God hath given Me" (ch. viii. 18; Heb. ii. 13).

There is surely no more need to prove that Christ as last Adam, like him whose antitype He is, is the Head of a race. It is the key to all that follows in Romans v. and the two next chapters, where "in Christ" as Corinthians gives it, is in contrast, yet antitypical correspondence, with "in Adam."

Now, as in Adam's case we have traced the results of the disobedience of the one to the many, let us trace the results of the obedience of the new Representative-Head to the many connected with Him.

> "Much more the grace of God, and the gift by grace, which is by one man, Jesus Christ, hath abounded unto many."

> "The free gift is of many offenses unto justification."

> "They which receive abundance of grace and of the gift of righteousness shall reign in life by one, Jesus Christ."

> "By the one righteousness toward all men to justification of life." (*Gr.*)

> "By the obedience of the one shall the many be made righteous."

These are the statements corresponding to, yet contrasted with, the former ones which we considered. One thing we must remember in considering them, that these two accounts do not exhibit a mere balance of results. "*Not* as the offense so also is the free gift" (*v.* 15). If righteousness be shown in dealing with sin, the "free gift," while of course it must be righteous, absolutely so, is yet measured only by the grace that has given Christ for us. Hence His work by no means merely cancels the results of sin, but lifts us into a place altogether beyond what was originally ours. Let us see what we have here, although even here the tale is not fully told.

First, we have "life;" and this in the next chapter (*v.* 23) is expanded into "*eternal* life in Christ Jesus our Lord." It is not merely life from another source, but life of an entirely new character and quality; not a restoration of the failed and forfeited life, but a life infinitely higher—a divine life. There is but one life which is eternal, and "in Christ Jesus our Lord" declares its source to be in a divine Person, and now become man. Nor only so, for the force of the expression is precise. It is not correctly given in our common version, but in the revised it is, as I have quoted it. It is "in," not, as the common version, "through;" and "Christ Jesus," not "Jesus Christ." Such differences, minute as they may seem, are in Scripture never without significance. "Jesus Christ" is the Lord's personal name emphasized; "Christ Jesus" emphasizes His official title. It speaks of a place now taken through His work accomplished. In the eleventh verse it should read similarly, "alive to God in Christ Jesus." Again we have it in the eighth chapter, "no condemnation to them which are in Christ Jesus;" and in the second verse, "life in Christ Jesus." Elsewhere we have "sanctified" and "saints in Christ Jesus," "created in Christ Jesus," "of Him are ye in Christ Jesus," and so repeatedly. Except once—Peter (1 Pet. v. 10), no inspired writer uses this order of words, but only Paul. "In Jesus," or "in Jesus the Christ," we are never said to be, but only "in Christ," or "in Christ Jesus." The special force ought to be therefore clear.

Our life, then, is not only in Him, but in Him as now having accomplished His work and gone up to God. There, as Peter on the day of Pentecost bears witness, He is made Lord and Christ (Acts ii. 36), actually reaching the place which was His already by appointment, but to be reached only in one way. The last Adam becomes Head of the race after His work of obedience is accomplished, as the first Adam became head when his work of *dis*obedience was accomplished. And as in the one case, so in the other, the results of the work become the heritage of the race. The head of the race represents the race before God. The ruin of the head becomes the ruin of the race. If the head stands, so does the race.

In either case, the connection of the head and the race is by life and nature, a corrupt nature being transmitted from the fallen head, a divine life and nature, free from and incapable of taint, from the new head, Christ Jesus. Death and judgment lay hold upon the fallen creature; righteousness characterizes the possessor of eternal life.

But here there is another need to be met; for these possessors of righteousness in a new life are by the old one children of Adam, and under wrath and condemnation because of manifold sins. Christ, the Son of the Father, is not stooping to take up unfallen beings, and bring *them* into a new place of nearness to God, but He is taking up sinners. For these, then, He must provide, along with a new life, a righteousness which shall justify them from all charge of sin. They must not only be delivered from inward corruption by a principle of righteousness imparted; they must be delivered from guilt also by a righteousness *imputed*. There must be a "justification of life,"—that is, a justification belonging to the life communicated: "by one righteousness toward all men,"—God's grace offering itself for acceptance by all,—"unto justification of life."

Here, then, comes in, not representation simply, but *substitution*,—representation under penalty for those who had incurred the penalty. He who is our Representative-Head in life must be our Substitute in death also. He must be "obedient unto death," standing in our place, that we may stand in His,—in the place He has won and taken for us with God.

His obedience avails for much more than negatively to justify from all charge of sin: it has its own infinite preciousness before God, in virtue of which we have a *positive* righteousness measured by this. *He* "of God is made unto us righteousness" (1 Cor. i. 30). We "receive *abundance* of the gift of righteousness," as the passage before us says, and "shall reign in life by One, Jesus Christ."

Thus are the effects of the fall for us removed, and we stand in a new place under a new Head. We are in Christ, not Adam; and this, as we have seen, speaks of place in a representative,—that by virtue of headship of a race. Our connection with Christ is now, as formerly it was with Adam, by the life which we receive from Him, and of which we partake in Him,—that is, by belonging to the race of which He is head. This and its consequences are unfolded further in the following chapters, to which this doctrine of the two Adams is the key.

II.—Justification and Dead to Sin.

The doctrine of justification is developed mainly in the first part of Romans, but extends, in a certain very important application of it, into the sixth chapter, while the latter part of the fifth, which we were last considering, connects it with the doctrine of the two Adams therein given. It is as in Christ we find it, accompanying the new life by which we are made of His race as last Adam:— "justification of life." For this reason a glance back will be here in place.

The truth is developed in this epistle in the order of application to the soul's need. And the first part accordingly begins with that which is its first conscious need, the guilt of sins committed; the second part takes up what is a later discovery and distress, the sin inherent in a fallen nature. The first of these is met by the application of the blood of Christ, justification by His blood. The second is met by the application of the death of Christ: "our old man is crucified with Christ;" "he that is dead is justified from sin" (vi. 6, 7, *marg.*).

These are two different applications of the same work of Christ, which avails in all its fullness for every believer. No one can be justified by the blood of Christ who is not at the same time justified by the death of Christ. The blood is already the sign of death having taken place, and only as that could it avail for us. It is only as that that it could put away our sins, so as to give us effectual peace with God at all.

Justification is the act of divine righteousness. It is for this reason that the righteousness of God is so prominent in the first part of Romans, while it is not found at all in the second part. Righteousness is that quality in God which has of necessity to say to sin, and on account of which the soul conscious of its guilt trembles to meet Him. No one, whatever be his guilt, is afraid of God's love; but how great soever that love may be, the awakened conscience at once begins to realize that it is *righteousness* must have to say to sin. The glory of the gospel is this, that it takes up just this character of God to put it on the side of the believer in Jesus, so as to make it his very boast and confidence. "I am not ashamed of the gospel [the glad tidings]," says the apostle; "for it is the power of God unto salvation to every one that believeth." And how this power? "For therein"—in these glad tidings to guilty men,—"the *righteousness* of God is revealed, by faith, to faith" (chap. i. 16, 17, *Rev. Vers.*). It is the revelation of divine righteousness in a gospel to the guilty, faith alone being required to receive the gospel, it is this which is the power of God for the deliverance of souls.

In the third chapter it is more fully made known as divine righteousness declared by the cross "in the passing over of the sins done aforetime, in the forbearance of God" (iii. 25, *R.V.*), and at this time, "that He might be just and the justifier of him that believeth in Jesus" (*v.* 26). The righteousness of God is that, then, which makes *Him* righteous in pronouncing righteous the believer in Jesus. This righteousness of God becomes as it were a house of refuge with its door open "unto all," and its protecting roof, impervious to the storm, "*over**

---

* $ἐπι$, "over," or "on." There is indeed a question of reading here, and some would leave out "and over all;" but we need not consider this now.

all them that believe,"—over all that have fled to the cross for refuge (*v.* 22).

It is the righteousness of God which repels every charge against the believer in Jesus. His justification is an act of righteousness, for the blood that is before God is the token of the death of his Substitute in his behalf. The penalty of his sins has been endured by Another, who, if "delivered for our offenses," "was raised again for our justification." This is the public sentence of it which declares on God's part His acceptance of the work. The *ground* is the blood; the *sentence* is the resurrection of our Surety. This sentence is God coming in to manifest Himself for us on account of the work of Christ accomplished. Faith rests in Him who raised up Jesus our Lord from the dead.

This might seem all that is needed. Assuredly the work of Christ meets every need, and His resurrection is the token of complete acceptance. What is needed is not in fact something more than this, but the fuller bringing out of what is involved in it; that in our Substitute we have therefore passed away as on the footing of the first man, identified with Adam, and are in Christ on the footing of the Second Man, alive in Him to God. For faith, therefore, I am dead to sin; because He died to it, and cannot live in what I am, —though for faith only,—dead to. This approves the *holiness* of the doctrine, as the seventh and eighth chapters show its *power*. It answers the moral question with which the sixth chapter opens.

Let us notice the way the doctrine is unfolded. The objection is started, "If then grace abounds over sin, then the more our sin the more His grace. Shall we then continue in sin, that grace may abound?" To which he answers, "We are dead to sin, how can we live in it?" This is conclusive against the abuse of the doctrine, although it is only for faith that we are dead: for then *faith* in it must tend to holiness, and not unholiness. The truth is ever according to godliness.

But how then are we dead to sin? He bids them think of what was involved in their baptism. Baptized to Christ Jesus,—again the order of words whose significance we have seen before,— we were baptized to His *death:* to have our part in this, according to the ordained testimony of it upon earth. Burial is just putting a dead man into the place of death: "we are therefore *buried* with Him by baptism into death." Our place in natural life is ended: upon earth we have but our part in the death of Jesus. But He is risen; the glory of the Father necessitated His resurrection from among the dead, and this is to give its character to the new life in which henceforth we are to walk; "for if we have come to be identified*[with Him] in the likeness of His death, we shall be also on the other hand in the likeness of His resurrection." That is, if our baptism—the "likeness of His death"—have real meaning with us, we shall be, in the character of our walk, in the likeness of His resurrection.† One thing will be the result of the other; "knowing this, that our old man"—all that we were in that old fleshly life—"is crucified

---

* I follow the London New Translation. "United," which the Revised Version gives, does not give the full force. It is literally "*grown together*" (not "planted") so as to be one. "With Him" is evidently to be understood.

†Observe the $\gamma\varepsilon\gamma\acute{o}\nu\alpha\mu\varepsilon\nu$, "we have become," in contrast with the $\dot{\varepsilon}\sigma\acute{o}\mu\varepsilon\theta\alpha$, "we shall *be*,"—not "become." But this is only moral "likeness," not the full being "risen with Him" of Ephesians and Colossians.

with Him, that the body of sin might be destroyed,"—"nullified," rather, "brought practically to nothing,"—"that henceforth we should not serve sin."

The "knowing this" connects with the sentence before, and confirms the meaning of "the likeness of His resurrection" as a present moral result. Our old man received its sentence of shame and condemnation from God, (for this is what the cross means,) where Christ died for us. We know and have accepted its setting aside thus.

But here we must inquire the exact force and meaning of "our old man." Many take it as the expression of the "natural corruption or unholy affections of men," or "the old nature." But Scripture has a different term for the old nature, and for the principle of evil in it. It speaks of the "flesh," and of "sin in the flesh." Between person and nature there is an essential and important difference; and if we are to take the inspired words as a perfect guide, (which we surely are,) "the old *man*" is person, and not nature. The importance lies in this, that responsibility (because the real *activity*) belongs to the person, not the nature. It is not *nature* that acts, although it may give character to the actions; and we as Christians are exhorted not to "walk after the flesh, but after the Spirit:" practically—though with an important difference too, which we may by and by consider,—not after the old nature, but after the new. The responsible person is distinguished as such from *both* natures,* which are together in him.

---

* "Nature" (from *natus*, "born,") means the character derived from birth; and we are born, and born again. The man of Romans vii. 17, 18, although new born, and able to distinguish himself from "the sin that dwelleth in" him, still must say, in his "flesh dwelleth no good thing."

So, in full accordance with this, we read of "the flesh with its affections and lusts," and even of "the *works* of the flesh" (Gal. v. 24, 19),—*i. e.*, fleshly works; but "*doings*" ($\pi\rho\acute{\alpha}\xi\varepsilon\iota\varsigma$) are attributed to the "old man" only (Col. iii. 9).

Moreover, the old man is never said to be in the Christian, but always to have been "put off," as in Ephesians iv. 22, *Gr.*, Colossians iii. 9, or as here, "crucified with Christ" (vi. 6); while the flesh, on the contrary, (though he is not in it,) is always recognized as in him.*

The "old man" is not, therefore, "the flesh"—the old nature, but the person *identified with the nature.* It is myself as I was under the old head,—as a living responsible child of Adam. It is as such the Lord stood for me upon the cross, and dying, ended for me the whole standing and its responsibilities together. He died for *me*, not for the old man, to restore it, but for me, that as the sinner that I was, I might find, in nature and activities together, my rightful condemnation in the cross, and have my place in Himself before God, and not in Adam. Responsibility *as a Christian* of course only here begins, but as a child of Adam it is over. My Substitute has died, and death ends the whole condition to which responsibility attaches. Eternal judgment is only for the deeds *done in the body;* and, my Substitute having died, I have died with Him—have passed out of the whole sphere of accountability in this respect.

We see how well it may be said, "Much more,

---

*Galatians v. 24 may be objected to this, where it is said that "they that are Christ's *have crucified* the flesh with its affections and lusts." But this is not the same thing with Romans vi. 6. *There*, it is "with Christ,"—the effect of His cross: *here*, it is *they that are Christ's* have done it, as accepting in heart and mind their place as His.

then, being now justified by His blood, *we shall be saved* from wrath through Him." Every thought that might raise a question is indeed for the once-justified one completely gone; and, in Christ, we live because He lives.

And what is the consequence of this crucifixion of the old man? It is that "he that is dead is justified from sin." So the Greek, and the Revised Version rightly now. We see how truly it is a question of person and personal standing all through here. Justification is of course that, but it is a justification more complete than in the first part of the epistle. No lust, no sin of thought, no evil passions, belong to a dead man—to a corpse. And this shows in how far we are dead to sin. Nothing of all this can be imputed to one dead with Christ. "Now if we be dead with Christ, we believe that we shall also live with Him." The life now begun is as much involved in and dependent upon His life as the death we have been considering is involved in His death. Changeless, eternal, past the power of death it therefore is: "knowing that Christ being raised from the dead dieth no more: death hath no more dominion over Him; for in that He died, He died unto sin once; but in that He liveth, He liveth unto God."

He has died to sin, but what sin? In Him there was none, but on the cross—standing there for us—He had to say to it, and as "made sin for us" died. But thus He has passed away from it forever, to live ever to Him now from whose blessed face, when bearing the burden of it, it had necessarily separated Him. For us He died, and died to sin: this death and this deliverance by death belong to us. But in Him also we live, in the life He lives,

SECOND PART OF ROMANS.

a life wholly to God. "Even so reckon yourselves dead indeed unto sin, and alive unto God in Christ Jesus" (v. 11, R. V.).

We are to "reckon" this so, not feel, find, or experience. It is not a matter of feeling or experience that Christ has died to sin. By faith we know it, and by faith also that He lives to God beyond the power of death. It is a most certain fact; but faith alone can apprehend it; and faith alone can apprehend our death with or our life in Him.

But here let us pause a little to consider some things that have been in dispute of late, and their application to what is before us. Is it condition, or standing, to be in Christ before God? or is it perhaps both together? The doctrine already considered, if it be clearly according to the Word, will enable us, surely, conclusively to settle this.

What is meant by "standing"? Clearly it is the same as position or place,* but in a certain aspect which makes it practically somewhat narrower. The last words are not found in Scripture in the present application, and in the New Testament in any real application to what we call *Christian* standing, the former possibly three times.† Two passages say it is *in grace* we stand; one speaks of standing "faultless in the presence of His glory." In Romans v. 1 it is "*this* grace," referring, not necessarily to what has gone before, but to present known grace—the free and absolute

---

*The same verb, ἵστημι, in certain tenses means "to stand," and in certain others, transitively, "to *make* to stand: to set, or set up, establish, etc."

†Rom. v. 1; 1 Pet. v. 12; Jude 24. In the last case it is in the transitive form, "*present*," or "*make* you stand." We must not confound with these such passages as Rom. xi. 20; 1 Cor. xv. 1; 2 Cor. i. 24; Col. iv. 12, etc., the force of which is really different. The text in Peter is doubtful: many read "stand," not "ye stand."

favor of God. Further than this, if we insist on the direct use of the word, Scripture does not carry us.

But the force of the word is simple, and its legitimate application does not seem hard to reach. As I have said, "standing" is position in a certain aspect, namely, in view of its *capability of being maintained*. Thus it is used often for continuance, as in opposition to falling: "If a kingdom is divided against itself, that kingdom cannot *stand*."—"I *continue* [or 'stand'] unto this day." "Standing" is used, therefore, of position where there might be question of such continuance; and the question before God being as to the claim of His righteousness being met, and the claim of His righteousness being the demand of His throne, I believe "*position before the throne*" would fitly express what would be meant by "standing."

It does not follow that this will be negative merely, however,—a mere question of guilt. For the throne of God is surely as much that which appraises righteousness as guilt; nay, it is this which involves the other. Our standing before God is much—how much!—more than as justified from sins or sin; it is "the abundance of the gift of righteousness,"—the *best* robe for the Father's house.

But we do not ordinarily,—and I think, rightly—speak of standing as sons, or as members of the body of Christ. The terms of the throne we do not apply to the family, or to Church-relationship. Standing is what we call a forensic term, and does not convey the whole truth of our position.

Now if we speak of condition, it is simple that this may refer to either a fixed or a variable state. If born again, *that* is a condition which abides unchangeable, while there are states, as of feeling, etc., which may change in the lapse of a few moments.

In the application of this to what we have before us, what does this speak of? standing, or state, or both—"dead to sin, and alive unto God in Christ Jesus"?

Now being "dead" is state—the state of one who has died. I have died with Christ to sin, as real a fact as can be; and though He lives, and death has no more dominion over Him, yet *as to sin* He remains still separated from it by death, *to it* still and ever dead: and this is my condition too as dead with Him. Though faith alone can realize it, it is a state in which I am unchangeably. So also, and of course, as to being "alive unto God:" that is unmistakably a condition contrasted with the other.

But what is implied in being "dead to sin"? The apostle answers, "Being *justified* from it." "Our *old man* is crucified with Christ." It is I myself as one standing on the old ground,—myself as *identified* with the old nature and its fruits alike —who have come to an end, and come to an end in deserved judgment: crucified; yes, and crucified *with Christ*. It is Christ who has stood for me, died for me: the old *standing* is gone. In this "dead to sin," condition and standing are inseparably united.

What then about the other side? If the old condition and standing are removed together, what replaces these? A new condition—"alive unto God; inseparably connected with a new standing—"*in Christ Jesus.*" This, and this alone, is the complete answer. I have before remarked upon the order of the words. "In Christ," in contrast with "in Adam," speak of a new Head of a new race, who is at the same time the Representative of it, as Adam of his. "In Adam" we die: "in Christ we live,"—our life bound up with His life: "Because I live, ye shall live also."—"If we be dead with Christ, we believe that we shall also live with Him." This life is already begun: by faith we know, and reckon it so. We are "dead indeed unto sin, and alive unto God in Christ Jesus."

This gives us the new standing, and the positive righteousness which is ours before God. As Head of His race, He stands before God in the perfection of the work He has accomplished, in the value of that matchless obedience, raised from the dead by the glory of the Father. "Of Him are ye in Christ Jesus, who is made unto us wisdom from God,—even righteousness." This is not merely guilt removed; it is the *best* robe in the Father's house.

III.—"IN THE FLESH" AND "IN THE SPIRIT."

THE doctrine of chap. vii. 1–6, which is the key to all that follows, is that of the fourth verse—that "ye are become dead to the law by the body of Christ, that ye should belong to another, even to Him who is raised from the dead, that we should bring forth fruit to God." It is the same doctrine of our being dead with Christ, dead in His death, but differently applied.

First of all, as a fundamental necessity for holiness, the spirit of *lawlessness* is met by the doctrine that we are dead to *sin*. Here, as a step further in the same direction, the spirit of *legality* is met by the doctrine that we are dead to the *law*. In either case it is holiness—fruit-bearing—that is in question; not justification from sins, and peace with God, which the former part of the epistle has already answered. Here, it is "that we may bring forth *fruit*," "that we may *serve* in newness of spirit."

The sixth chapter deals with the objections of unbelief, whether outside or inside the profession of Christianity. The seventh chapter deals with the objections of earnest but self-occupied hearts, ignorant of God's way of liberty and power. The objections in the one case are of those who have *no* experience, as we may say; the objections in the other are drawn *from* experience, but yet unenlightened by the Word. In the one case, the apostle can appeal *to* the experience of men who had found no fruit in things of which now they were ashamed (vi. 21); in the other, he appeals *from* experience to the truth of the place which

God had given them, and which faith, and only faith, could receive.

We are not now to look at the whole argument, (for argument it is,) but at two pregnant expressions, which must be understood, rightly to apprehend it. "For, *when we were in the flesh*, the motions of sins, which were by the law, did work in our members to bring forth fruit unto death." "But *ye are not in the flesh, but in the Spirit*, if so be that the Spirit of Christ dwell in you; now if any man have not the Spirit of Christ, he is none of His."

What is it, then, to be in the flesh, and what to be in the Spirit,—these two evidently contrasted and mutually exclusive conditions? In the one, (if Christ's,) we are not; in the other we are. In the one, we "cannot please God;" in the other, if we live, we have yet to walk in order to please Him (Gal. v. 25).

Turning to the doctrine of the seventh chapter, it would seem the simplest thing possible to define what is meant by being "in the flesh." To be in the flesh is to be just a *living man*. We have it twice applied in the natural sense—Gal. ii. 20, Phil. i. 22. Here in Romans it is the condition of one who has not *died with Christ*. It is as "dead . . . . . . by the body of Christ" that the apostle can say with all Christians, "*When* we were in the flesh" (vii. 4, 5).

Condition and standing, as we have seen, are here inseparable. Condition is, in the context of the passages before us, the thing most dwelt upon; but it is *the condition of one in the standing*, and of no other. "When we were in the flesh, the motions of sins, which were by the law, did work in our members to *bring forth fruit unto death*." This is what we find in the sixth chapter: "What fruit had ye *then* in those things whereof ye are now ashamed? for the *end of those things is death*. But *now*, being freed from sin, and made servants to God, ye have your fruit unto holiness, and the *end everlasting life*." The man in the flesh is one on the road to death.

Again in the eighth chapter: "For they that are after the flesh do mind the things of the flesh, and they that are after the Spirit the things of the Spirit; for the mind of the flesh is *death*, but the mind of the Spirit is life and peace. For the mind of the flesh is *enmity against God*, for it is not subject to the law of God, neither indeed can be: so then they that are in the flesh *cannot please God*." (viii. 5–8.)

They that are in the flesh are thus in a state of spiritual death, going on to eternal death. They are "after the flesh"—characterized by and identified with it. They are mere natural men: flesh, as born of flesh.

Here, then, was no fruit, while we were in this condition. The law is what applies to it, but is no remedy for it. "The law was not made for a righteous man, but for the lawless and unruly, for the ungodly and sinners, for the unholy and profane" (1 Tim. i. 9, *R.V.*). Moreover, "the law is not of faith:" faith is not its principle (Gal. iii. 12); and "as many as are of the works of the law are under the curse" (*v.* 10). To be "under the law" and "under grace" are things exclusive of one another (Rom. vi. 14).

It is true that God had once a people under law, for His own purposes of unfailing wisdom. As the "ministration of death" and "of condemnation"

(2 Cor. iii. 7, 9), it was a "schoolmaster" under which in Israel even saints were "kept, shut up unto the faith which should afterward be revealed" (Gal. iii. 23, 24). The wholesome lessons of man's natural helplessness and hopelessness were taught by it, God saving of course all the time by a grace which He could not yet declare openly. But to believers it was necessarily bondage, "added" only "till the Seed should come to whom the promise was made," and when "faith came," as God's openly acknowledged principle, they were "no longer under the schoolmaster" (*v.* 19, 25). We are henceforth disciples of Christ and not of the law, although we have the good of the tutorship under which others were of old.

For the child of God, from the first moment of his being that, "faith" and "grace,"—the opposites of law,—are God's linked principles of unfailing blessing. The ministry of the new covenant is the "ministration of life" and "of righteousness" (2 Cor. iii. 6, 9). "The gift of God is eternal life in Christ Jesus our Lord,"—a new standing and a new condition. The power of His death attaches to the gift of His life, and he who lives in Him has died with Him. This is death to sin and to law* alike.

The law was in Israel, then, that to which man was linked, a link from which fruit was looked for, nay, demanded. In fact, only "passions of sins" were "by the law" (*v.* 5), the full account of which the apostle gives afterward (*vv.* 7–13). The law is not merely the ministration of condemnation; it is

---

*It may be urged that God never put the Gentile under law at all, and this is true. The apostle addresses himself especially to Jewish converts. Yet the practical freedom is the same for all. And the Gentile needs the apprehension as well as the Jew, as we are witness to ourselves.

SECOND PART OF ROMANS.

also "the strength of sin" (1 Cor. xv. 56). "Sin shall not not have dominion over you, because ye are not under the law, but under grace" (vi. 14).

Death to the law is therefore absolutely necessary for fruitfulness. The death of Christ is the believer's effectual divorce, that he may be free to be linked with Christ raised up from the dead, that thus there may be fruit.

But here, the doctrine goes beyond that of the sixth chapter. For the figure is that of marriage, —of union; and a divorce from the law must have come first in order that we may be united to Christ. We cannot be *dis*united by what unites us to another. It is not, therefore, by life in Christ that we are *united* to Christ, nor is this what could be figured by marriage. For this, we must go on to what really unites Christians to their Lord,—the gift of the Spirit. It is the contrast of chap. viii. 9 to which this brings us. "In the flesh," the link is with law; the fruit, the passions of sins; the end, death. "In the Spirit," we are linked with Christ, the fruit is holiness, the end everlasting life. "If ye *through the Spirit* mortify the deeds of the body, ye shall live."

I pass over the experience of the seventh chapter entirely now to consider the statement of chap. viii. 9, "But ye are not in the flesh, but in the Spirit, if so be that the Spirit of God dwell in you;" to which is emphatically added, "Now if any man have not the Spirit of Christ, he is none of His."

It seems unaccountable how any one, except by some preoccupation of the mind, should see in this the statement that we only cease to be in the flesh by the indwelling of the Spirit. To take the figure already used by the apostle: one alive in the flesh is married to the law; if by the Spirit he is now married to Christ,—does he die to the law by the new marriage? must he not be dead to the law to be *free* for the new marriage? Surely it is as clear as noonday that a new marriage cannot dissolve an old one, but that the old, as long as it existed, would forbid the new!

On the other hand, what more simple than to argue that if you are in the new bond (the Spirit), you are not in the old one (the flesh), without at all implying that the new bond had *destroyed* the old? It only shows, and that conclusively, that the *old does not exist*.

The "old man"—what for a Christian is now such—is a man in the flesh, as the sixth chapter has already shown us. He is the man "corrupt according to the deceitful lusts," and "they that are in the flesh cannot please God." Is it in such the Spirit comes to dwell? They may think so who suppose the indwelling of the Spirit to be only tantamount to being born again; but Scripture is of course clear that it is "*having believed*, ye were sealed with that Holy Spirit of promise" (Eph. i. 13, *R. V.*), the very form of expression showing that it is that which began at Pentecost (Acts i. 4, 5) that is referred to, and not the common possession of believers of all time.

God's order is, first, new birth, then sealing; first, the preparing of the house, and then dwelling in the house prepared; not simply a new life for us, but a divine Person dwelling in us: and this is the testimony to the perfection of the work now accomplished for us, for *God's seal can only be set on perfection.* Having believed, we have already seen that we are in the value of Christ's work before God, sin and flesh completely gone from before Him, ourselves dead to sin, alive to God in Christ. It is here the Spirit of God can seal us, and unite us to Christ as His. And where one is found upon whom the value of that work is, there is but one thing for which He waits, and that is the *acknowledgment* of Christ as Lord and Saviour, before He takes possession of His dwelling-place, and unites that soul to Christ on high.

Hence, *among those owning Christ* it can be said, "If any one have not the Spirit of Christ, he is none of His." The seal of the Spirit is Christ's mark upon His own; therefore among those professing to be His, if the mark is not, it is a false profession.

Thus there is no thought in the New Testament of a class of believers in Christ who have not,—or may not have,—the Holy Ghost. It is in vain to seek elsewhere for a class of persons the existence of which the apostle here denies. To the Corinthians he writes in the most general way, so as to include *all* bowing really to the name of Jesus,—"To the Church of God which is at Corinth, to them that are sanctified in Christ Jesus, called saints, *with all that* in every place *call upon the name of Jesus Christ our Lord*, both theirs and ours." And what does he ask of all these? "*Know ye not that your body is the temple of the Holy Ghost, which ye have of God*, and ye are not your own?" (1 Cor. i. 2; vi. 19.) Surely, this is the prescience of the divine Word, to settle all controversy. Who will say, in face of this, that one who in heart calls on the name of Jesus Christ his Lord has not the Holy Ghost?

But then Romans viii. 9 becomes simplicity itself, and the many questions raised receive their absolute settlement. Our eyes have not to roam over christendom, lamenting that in so few of Christ's people the work of God is no more than half accomplished. That there is so little *manifestation* we may still lament, as even at Corinth the apostle could, and we may urge upon men still, with the apostle to the Galatians, "If we live in the Spirit, let us also walk in the Spirit" (v. 25), for these still are different things.

Does it make less of the gift that it is so little realized? or would it be more honoring to God to suppose that He has not bestowed it, where there is so little manifestation of it? Surely, surely, it is no such thing. Let the grace, and the responsibility of the grace, be pressed upon Christians; for it is faith that works for God, not doubt. Oh for a voice of power to cry in the ears of slumberers, "Know ye not that your body is the temple of the Holy Ghost, which ye have of God, and ye are not your own?" Ye belong to Christ—ye are Christ's, and the seal of God is upon you. Lord, wake up Thy beloved people to the apprehension of Thy marvelous gift!

RE-TRACINGS OF TRUTH:

IN VIEW OF

QUESTIONS WHICH HAVE BEEN LATELY RAISED.

I. THE PRESENT OUTLOOK ACCORDING TO SCRIPTURE.

IN looking out upon the features of our own times, and even in proportion to our personal interest in them, we are apt to project our own personalities upon them. That a sanguine person will take a hopeful view, where a desponding one will only see gloom and shadow, no one needs to be informed. But every idiosyncrasy, whatever it may be, is quite apt to make its mark upon the canvas of the picture. Hence the taking of one in a manner perfectly trustworthy is a thing as rare as it is desirable. How thankful should we be, therefore, for the briefest testimony of Scripture as to the character of the times through which we are passing, when it is the pathway for our feet that is in question, and our responsibility to God presses upon us at each step we take!

Such guidance we have, through the tender mercy of our Great Shepherd, in the seven epistles of the book of Revelation; every one traced by His own hand, and our attention called to every address, as in no other part of the word of God: he that hath an ear being bidden to hear what the Spirit saith unto the churches! We are not going to dwell upon this now: the application has been long familiar to those for whom I am specially writing; but I would nevertheless press upon my readers the main points of that to Philadelphia, which (to myself at least) seems ever of more commanding interest as the time goes on, and the features of the last days develop themselves before our eyes.

There can scarcely be much difficulty in discerning what Philadelphia stands for. If the "woman Jezebel" makes popery absolutely plain in Thyatira, Sardis, having a name to live, though dead, yet with a remnant undefiled, marks out as clearly the state-churches of the Reformation. Philadelphia, following this, with its "brotherly love," as simply speaks of the movement to find and to separate the true Church out of this world-mass. Such has been more or less the character of many "revivals" since the Reformation, when there was sought a true "communion of saints" and subjection to the word of Christ, rather than the state-upheld creed. Laodicea nevertheless closes the series here; a picture, alas, less and less hard to be read at present, of a church made more and more popular to please the masses, and lukewarm as to the Christ outside. But we have to do now with Philadelphia.

Here, if "brotherly love" characterizes the assembly, that which the Lord specially commends is classed under three heads: first, that they keep Christ's word; secondly, they have not denied His name; thirdly, they have kept the word of His patience. Their danger is that, having but "a little strength," they may not hold fast that which they have; the overcoming will, therefore, be in holding fast.

Of necessity the stream will be against them: that is no more than is implied in every phase in which men are found cleaving to God. The world is against God; and, the world having come into the church, the stream here is against God also. Where shall we find a haven of rest outside of it all? Not in any earthly refuge anywhere. Philadelphia is no place of rest, but the centre of a battle-field; and the cry of "overcome" is found here as elsewhere. Our rest is only in the glorious Leader, who covers our head in the day of battle, and in the power of the Holy Spirit who can make something out of things that are not, and out of weakness make us strong. Our trust cannot be in the attainment of an ecclesiastical position, though a right one,—in principles of truth, although divine; through all this the enemy made his way at the beginning, when things were almost in their first freshness; no! we need tireless energy to resist fresh inroads; never more likely to be successful than when we are beginning to believe that the battle is over, and that our victories are to be now only in the quiet harvest-field,—in the ingathering of souls from the seed sown by the evangelist, or the recovery of the people of God themselves out of the superstition and error that have inwrapped them. Then indeed it may be that, while we are congratulating ourselves that we are leaders of the blind, lights of those who sit in darkness, instructors of the foolish, teachers of babes, the pit of darkness may be opening at our feet, to ingulf us all.

A terrible thing it is, in fact, to think of that actual chasm which swallowed up the church of the apostles' days—the church of Peter and John and Paul—and left only as the successor of this the legal, hierarchical, ritualistic church of the so-called "fathers," of which one well-known to us has said, "It is quite certain that neither a full redemption, nor, though the words be used once or twice, a complete possessed justification by faith, as Paul teaches it, a perfecting for ever by its one offering, a known personal acceptance in Christ, is ever found in any ecclesiastical writings after the canonical scriptures, for long centuries." In what, then, were *they* inferior to us, those men to whom apostles and prophets preached, —what have we that they had not, which is to assure us that we are not in danger of making such shipwreck of the faith as it is certain they did? What but the most foolish self-confidence could say, with such a warning before our eyes, that we were in none?

Nor can we seriously consider the epistle to Philadelphia in connection with the character of the present times, without realizing that Satan's batteries to-day are turned upon the very central points of Philadelphian position; and that we are contemplating the beginning of an apostasy from the Christian faith which will be more complete than any which have preceded it? What is the so-called "higher criticism," spite of its lamblike speech where the flock of Christ perchance may be alarmed, but the most thorough attack that can be imagined upon the Word of Christ? He Himself was hardly beyond His times in matters of criticism; and grounded His triumphant argument against the scribes as to David's Son being David's Lord upon a mere mistake as to the authorship of the hundred and tenth psalm! But, in fact, who knows if the evangelists have rightly reported Him? or who knows anything that the critics may please to question? Judgment is removed from the power of the common man: we have no more our Bibles with the appeal to every man's heart and conscience; you must have trained specialists to settle the facts! and what they will leave you after they have completed their dissections is but the fragments of a corpse without voice or life!

Look again at the denial of Christ's Name! Was there ever a day in which heresies affecting His Person or work more abounded? or the tendency to leave out any particular demand for orthodoxy as to either, so long as people accept Him as their Leader in some way not to be too severely criticized. If you should have mistaken the Son of the Father for a mere servant of the Father's house, eternity will make that right, of course, and it is hoped that the mistake will not prove very serious! After all, the Fatherhood of God and the brotherhood of man are the broad lines upon which religions are to be reconstructed today; and we need not fear but that they will be found to run on into eternity.

This, it will be said, is outside the sphere of Philadelphia; but it is what infects the air which day by day we breathe, and Satan is the "prince of the power of it." There are plenty of modifications of such principles to ensnare those for whom the full poisonous dose would be too large; and what is even more to be noted is that there are apt to be contradictories and opposites of them, born, indeed, of reaction, which by this opposition may deceive the earnest-hearted. For the serpent's lie is scarcely ever the mere negative of truth; and he is apt himself to have an alternative to it, planned directly to catch the opposers. And he who goes by the safe-seeming rule of steering as far as possible from Scylla may find the enemy's Charybdis lying before him on the other side. With God is perfect guidance; but even with the word of God before our eyes, how far from it may we swerve through the self-will to which we are so prone!

I have no desire to conceal the thought that prompts me in writing the present series of papers, which is to examine in the light of Scripture principles and doctrines which are being put forth at the present time among those who, I believe, have truly filled a position answering to what the Spirit of God has characterized as Philadelphian, and which are but the enemy's wile to seduce them from it. Nay, I fear, in the wide-spread acceptance which they are certainly gaining, the loss of that precious deposit of truth which the grace of God had committed to their trust. This is, to me, much more than any ecclesiastical position, however true, which owes its value so largely to the truth to which it witnesses. I therefore desire to take up, with whatever ability the Lord may give, the main points that are in question; in which I shall be in large measure but retracing the outline of truths once familiar, once how precious!—only necessarily to put them in connection and comparison with what is now presented for truth, and not without the hope of some fresh light being elicited by the discussion; which is what God would surely overrule all our differences for. We shall try to look at the moral bearing of things; as indeed the one who is very much the cause of the present inquiry rightly presses: without this they cannot get their just value for our souls; and this is what, speaking for myself once more, I can say I desire. Oh that the value of God's truth may be more realized by us all! It is inestimable, as that which alone can form in us the mind of Christ; and as this, one cannot help contending for it, though it is no wonder if one's motives should be challenged, and one should be treated as a mere "accuser of the brethren." Protestations are of no avail in such a case; specially as those who charge this are not those most likely to seek to satisfy themselves if there may be a cause. One may be well content if there be some who go far enough with me to discern its gravity.

I do not propose, however, to try and establish any specific charges, or make any quotations from any one with regard to what we shall consider. I prefer to leave every one to make for himself the personal application, and thus to eliminate as far as possible the distressing personal element. Let the inquiry be strictly a scriptural one; though it must be along lines which are marked out by what has called forth these papers. Then, if after all one is only fighting a nightmare of the imagination, we shall still not have made, I trust, a wholly useless survey of some important truths. If, on the other hand, it should be found that there is some serious question raised with regard to views that are really current and finding acceptance with many at the present time, then let my readers, without regard to persons, take it into the court of their own conscience, with God alone as the Judge of all, and argue it out there, with all that could distract them put aside. Truth carries its own authority with it for the true; although that in no wise means the setting aside of needed exercise, and the absolute subjection of one's mind to Scripture where Scripture has plainly spoken. And indeed we have little truth, of any spiritual importance, outside of that which Scripture has given to us. We shall by the course pursued be as far as possible delivered from the collision of opinion as to what Mr——has said, or what he means by what he has said, and fasten our minds upon the one question of any prime importance, "What saith the Lord?"

There is, however, one question with which I shall now conclude. Looking again at the epistle to Philadelphia, and referring to the first two points in the commendation there, they are plainly these: "Thou hast kept My word, and not denied My Name." Serious, then indeed, would be the issue which raised question as to both of these! If there were admittedly a question as to the Person of the Lord plainly raised, and permitted to go at least without any public settlement of it; the thing dropped, perhaps, yet the offending expressions never withdrawn! not justified; not condemned; not retracted! And again, if Scripture, while formally admitted to be the written and authoritative word of God, yet were always in practice distinguished from the "word of God, living and powerful," as that which does not exactly teach, and which, but for the failure of the Church, would never have been needed!

If these two things should demonstrably come together, what more would be needed to show the extreme gravity of the questions to be raised?

2. WHAT IS THE VALUE OF THE WRITTEN WORD.

THINGS must have come to a pass indeed, when with Christians such as those for whom I am writing, one has to dwell upon — still more, *defend* — the value of the written Word. That which has been to us all the revelation of all the truth which we possess (and it is by the truth we are sanctified); that which alone brings into communion with the mind of God; that which, as inspired of God—"God-breathed"—furnishes the man of God to all good works;— how needless, how unutterably foolish it must appear, to tell any one who owes his all to it, the value of the written word of God!

Is this what those are thinking who, to one's utter astonishment to-day are letting pass without word of audible comment (that has had power, at least, to come across the breadth of the Atlantic) statements that would seem as if they should rouse to indignation impossible to be repressed every soul divinely taught as to what Scripture is? There is only one way besides in which this silence is comprehensible to me. Perhaps by some strange obliquity of mind words have lost for me their proper meaning, and I have failed to understand what I have had before me. If it be so, still let me state this figment of my imagination, and meet it as if it were a reality. How good it would be to get a strong knock-down reply from some one somewhere, to dispel for ever this delusion of mine, and assure me that I was dreaming! Why does not some one in pity to me, who, I think, have no evil intent, but a real longing over souls who seem drifting away from truth whither they know not, prick this bubble for me, and give relief to more than myself from as uncomfortable a nightmare of the imagination (if it be that) as for long has visited them?

The delusion which I am combating (whether mine or that of others) begins with fair speeches about Scripture (always written characteristically with a small "s") as being authoritative and the written word of God. It blurs this, however, immediately by saying, it is more the *record* of it than the thing itself. I suppose every higher critic of the decent kind would say as much. It warns us, for all that (as I have never known the decent critic do), enforcing this too by personal example, that one can study it too much, and that a Bible student is not much after all; which means, of course, that the study of the Bible does not count for much. In fact, we are told, the method of learning truth by Scripture was not God's original plan at all: if the Church of God had remained in its first estate, we would not have wanted the Scriptures. The mind of God which is in the Scriptures would have been livingly expressed in the Church without them; and that was the divine idea! A very important thought, as some one remarks, if true; and very important, of course, to know if it *be* true: for by it the whole Old Testament is practically discounted and set aside for us.

But how, then, without the Word, was the Church to become the "living expression" of the mind of God? Here a leaf is taken from an old book which is not Scripture, but which many will recognize. The truth is in the *Church*. The apostles had it and communicated it; Paul to Timothy; Timothy to faithful men, who were to teach others. Here are four generations: Paul; Timothy; faithful men; others: that is the way the truth was to be transmitted. It is the way which the church of Rome hold to-day; and the technical name for it is "Tradition."

But it failed! Yes; somehow it failed. Rome

may be excusable here in believing that God's plan could not fail; but it could and did. Have you not observed that it is in the second epistle to Timothy, not the first, that Paul speaks of the Scriptures in that well known eulogy? That was when failure had fully set in; and *then* it was that the Scriptures came to be so important!

But at any rate, one would say, the method of teaching by Scripture is that by which we come into the truth to-day; and all that one can say of it in this respect to-day is fully justified! Ah, but we must not seize that comfort yet, or all that has been said just now must go for little. No, the old method has not been given up like that. The Church is still the method as before; only supplemented by Scripture because of the failure that has come in. It is a kind of humiliation to have to send the Bible to the heathen, and it is no good sending Bibles, if there are not preachers. People do not learn exactly from Scripture, but from the Spirit of truth; and if you say, "Granted that it is always by the Spirit of truth that any true work is done in the soul at all, but do you say that God will not use the Bible to a man's soul without a preacher?" well, it is difficult to put it that way, because God is sovereign; in a day of decay and ruin, *He may speak through an ass's mouth;* but how shall they hear without a preacher? The divine way, undoubtedly, is preaching.

All as glibly said, as unquestioningly taken, even to the gross irreverence of putting the words of God alongside of the miracle of a speaking ass! Is it then a mistake of the apostle that they are "able to make wise unto salvation?" Well, that is asked and answered, if any one is wise enough to interpret the answer: that "the man of God wants to be furnished with the Scriptures because of their disciplinary value"!—the relevancy of which I confess I do not understand; nor do I think that the apostle's words need any explanation. Why should we not inscribe them in every Bible sent to the heathen as an all-sufficient justification?

But how then with regard to the truth as ministered to the believer? Well, in general, in the early days, we are told that they had to take things on trust. The Old Testament did not give the truth of Christianity; and the New Testament was not written till the Church's decline, of course; otherwise, the whole system taught here would be subverted. The safeguard people had is said to be (what again is somewhat difficult to understand) that "the spirits of the prophets are subject to the prophets;" words which are certainly found in Scripture, though scarcely in that connection. However, now that failure is come in, and Scripture as the resource in view of it, it is of the utmost importance to prove all things. Here the Bereans are commended to us as a model for imitation; somewhat in forgetfulness that this example comes to us from before the failure of the Church, and when it is supposed that another method was in order; yet it seems that they had Scriptures in their hands which they searched to some purpose. Only it is assured us that what they heard they first received; and only searched the Scriptures to get confirmation! A severe critic might say, perhaps, to see what mistakes they might have made in receiving it! Our day is an evil day; and God has given us the Scripture that we may have a standard of truth. Scripture is the limit; and though you don't exactly learn from Scripture (and indeed it is legality to want chapter and verse for doctrine) yet the more familiar people are with it the better: because a man's mind is thus continually pulled up in its tendency to go beyond the limit!

Thus for the outside world Scripture is not to be reckoned on for the conversion of souls. God may use it for that, because He is sovereign, and might be pleased to use the speech of an ass; while for the flock of Christ it is as it were a tether, to prevent their natural tendency to stray! You are right to search it for confirmation of what you hear; only you are to receive this first, and search afterwards. Even then remembering that it is legal to want chapter and verse for doctrines, and that it is possible to study the authority too much!

It would be perfectly natural to say that that must be a caricature of anybody's teaching. My comfort is that, at least, those who think so cannot have received it themselves. If they can find no one who has, or who knows of its existence, that would only show to me how few take in what they read; perhaps even while they applaud it. However, let us make it an occasion for examining what is the use and value of the written Word.

Only think of it as that!—the written word of God! a word prepared for us as the outcome of past ages which have contributed, age after age, their quota to the full result; the whole, in every line and word of it, "God-breathed,"—the quickening breath of the

Spirit in it!—from the heart of God to the heart of man! The more we look into it, the more in faith we credit it with a divine message and meaning, the more it responds and opens,—the more it draws and wins us to itself. Had *I* my life to live over again, I would study it *more*, not less, drink it in, live in it, have it my meditation all the day long. Where else shall I find the Voice of Him who seeks me for Himself? Can any one tell me where? Fancy one telling me that the use of Scripture is in its being a "limit" to *my* poor human thoughts; when it is that which, as far as may be, leads me out into the limitless,—into the "deep things of God"! Here are the things that the Spirit searches—the Spirit, wonderful to say, in me!—and which, having set before me the infinite, leads me into the measureless delight of exploring my inheritance! How many people, handing down to me with flawless accuracy, the traditional truth, could replace for me the scriptures of prophets and apostles which God has put into my hands, with their tale which they are never weary of telling,— which I can read and re-read, carry into my room, set down before me, pray over and look again,— listen to in the quiet of His Presence who is in them and with them, till the music of their chime begins in my soul, soothing, quickening, harmonizing, subduing all my nature to them! If I owe my possession of them to the failure of the Church, then blessed is that failure which, under God, has secured me so priceless a result. I speak soberly and deliberately while I say, that not the presence of the whole of the apostles with the Church to-day could replace for us the loss of Scripture. Could they all together give us one truth more than God has seen good to give us in it? *Did* they communicate, in fact, one truth besides, which we have lost? More than that, is it certain that they even *knew* all that was in their own communications? still more, can we believe that they knew all that all other inspired writers had communicated from the beginning? Have we one shred of truth, or of interpretation of Scripture even, which has come down to us by this so much lauded tradition, that any one can show us, much less show us value in to-day? What can we glean from apostolic "fathers"? Has not God been pleased to make a clean, broad mark of absolute limitation between Scripture and all else that went before or followed it, so that it should shine out to us in its own peerless character to-day? What has God given us through all the centuries since, which is more than a development from it,—a bit of the treasure from this exhaustless treasure-house?

I do not expect, then, with whatever amount of prayer or meditation, to obtain from my poor thoughts, which have indeed to be kept in order so, one thing which directly or indirectly has not come to me from the Word. Nor can I think of anything higher for myself or any other, than to be an expositor of this glorious Word. Tell me, then how I can study it too much? You need not tell me that I can pray too little: Alas, I know that well.

I suppose, we have nothing to assure us how early in Christian times the Gospel of Matthew may have been written. It is pre-eminently, as all are aware, the Jewish Gospel; as the church in Jerusalem was for some time a Jewish remnant, and little more.

Luke shows us at the end of his Gospel what special pains the Risen Saviour took to ground His disciples from the beginning in the Old Testament, and its relation to the New. Here their feet always stood firm; and the example of the Bereans a good while afterwards makes plain to what good use it could be put by those who had not had the advantage of such instruction. When they had thus assured conviction as to the trustworthiness of those through whom they had received the knowledge of the Saviour, and the pledge and witness of the Holy Spirit, there was of course abundant warrant for their reception through a channel so certified, of those additional communications which God was pleased to give. But notice here that the very slowness with which we know such communications came, gave the fullest opportunity to incorporate them one by one with all that they had known before; the scattering of the truth abroad being itself gradual, so as to carry better together the whole body of disciples. The more we reflect upon all this, the more we shall realize how fully from the beginning of Christianity the Lord grounded His people upon the written Word; and that this was no after-plan when the Church had fallen. Such thoughts may catch those who do not study Scripture too much; and alas, there are plenty of them. They are the mere vagaries of a dreaming mind, to which the word of God is not even a "limit."

We have no need to undervalue the preacher, because of the efficacy of the Word. I would emphasize it more, indeed, than all this system does. Instead of saying for instance, that God does not use us instrumentally as effecting *anything*, Scripture assures us that men can "*so* speak" that others shall believe (Acts xiv. 1). It makes the character of the speaking effective in the production of the result. But there is another reason for "how shall they hear without a preacher?" without dishonoring Scripture to furnish one; and that is serious and sad enough. It is that men, alas, have to be pursued by the grace that seeks them and the living voice of the preacher is the most effectual means in this way. Wisdom has to cry aloud, and utter her voice in the corners of the streets. "Go out into the highways and the hedges, and compel them to come in!" Scripture had always been, while necessarily safeguarded by the barrier-wall thrown around Israel, yet placed in the very centre of the chief civilizations of the old world, and on the highways of commerce. Had men desired the treasures of it, they were readily accessible, and there was no prohibition of their acquirement; but they manifested no desire. And in the midst of Christendom to-day, with the completed Word in our hands, what would we do without that publication of it in various ways, by which it is forced upon the notice of the unwilling-hearted? That does not in the least affect the power existing in the Scriptures to make men wise unto salvation which they assuredly have—a power which is being proved continually.

We have spoken, perhaps, enough of the Bereans, and their readiness to receive the word preached to them. No doubt that there is in the truth always an inherent acceptability to an earnest mind. But the belief of it is distinctly put here *after* that searching of the Scriptures which they are praised for, *not* before it. Think of the consequences of a principle such as is advocated, of receiving first, before proving! when the proving will surely follow with a laggard and indifferent step; and during the delay how many falsehoods may spring out of one error received, which may not be destroyed, even when they have lost their attachment to the root from which they sprang! How would such a principle account for the rapid and wide spread of a movement like that which we are now contemplating, in which the captivating brilliancy of many new ideas may with the ready aid of the emotions sweep the traveller off his feet too far away for any present recovery. A voyage of exploration always has its charm; and to be told that you need not know whither you are going, but may give yourself up to the guidance of one who seems so impressively confident of his ability to carry you safely, is a luxury in itself. Certainly you make progress: everything moves. By and by you can take your bearings and see where you have arrived. You can return by the way you have come, if in the end you are not satisfied. But have you guaged then the strength of the stream that is bearing you on it?

3. LETTER AND SPIRIT.

We have not yet done, however, with doctrines which affect Scripture; and I place these first, because the character of all the teaching may be rightly judged by them. If that which is the standard of truth be taken from us,—if it be obscured even, or made less available to the common mass of Christians,—it is plain that this will have disastrous effect upon every truth drawn from it, or to be compared with it. Rome herself makes great parade of late of her reverence for the word of God. She will exalt it as much as you please,—and the more she does the more gain will it be to her,— if only you will let her interpret it for you. It is the interpretation that is the great point; and if a system of interpretation is adopted which takes this out of the reach of the simple man, then you have set up an esoteric teaching which is not subject to Scripture, however much you may accredit those who receive it (as it is quite easy to do) with a higher spirituality which enables them to do so. No doubt spirituality is of all importance in the things of God; but it is not this which will refuse to submit to the plain word of Scripture: "If they speak not according to this word, it is because there is no light in them" (Isa. viii. 20).

Now the system before us, as represented in its chief exponent, avowedly sets aside the letter of Scripture, in the interests of what it is pleased to consider the "spirit" of it. Scripture, has been put alongside of a supposed faulty hymn, to say—"I do not read those hymns in the letter; *I do not read Scripture in the letter*: I try to get the spirit of the hymn, and I do." The self-complacence of the last two words is characteristic. Are we not left to infer that as with the hymns, so with Scripture, he not only seeks to get the spirit of Scripture, but he *does?* Most people would have left others to say that of them. Whatever conviction they might have as to their success in such a matter, they would not expect to move others by their own conviction—at least those of the class that it would be worth while to convince: "let another man praise thee, and not thine own mouth" (Pro. xxvii. 2) is a rule which has long been commended to us as a maxim of wisdom.

But the important point is, that we are not, as it seems, to read Scripture in the letter. It would be gratifying to know whether this is what the Book itself teaches, and how it teaches it. The thought is not altogether a new one; others have equally proclaimed their belief in Scripture as "read by the illumination of that Spirit of Christ which dwelleth in us," as contrasted with "the letter that killeth."[*] But one can hardly think of the one from whom I before quoted as meaning to refer us to a text which gives the contrast between the old covenant and the new, and this last even as ministered by grace to us in the present gospel. It could not be said indeed rightly of the new covenant in any wise that the letter killed, although as Gentiles we should not come under it. Those who do come under it will certainly not be killed, even by the letter of it. The spirit is the spirit of the letter and that is the sweetest grace.

In Romans again (vii. 6), "the oldness of the letter," in which as Christians we are not to serve, is that legal bondage which the old covenant implies, and has nothing to do with Scripture as such. For the Christian in the liberty to which God has called him, the very letter of the law as such remains, not only without injury, but with plenty of profit in it. There is absolutely no scripture which so much as suggests

---

[*] Canon Farrar.

that the letter of God's blessed word is something to be put aside, even in favor of the spirit which resides in it. If I want to be in communion with the spirit of a man, I do not kill his body for that purpose; and grotesque as such a comparison may seem to be, it is a joy to me to believe that God's word is as it were a living organism, in which even far beyond what we find in man (as man is now) the spirit residing is expressed in every part; so that every jot and tittle has importance from it, and must be preserved, for the spirit to be in any proper manner realized.

I own, therefore, with gladness and thankfulness of heart, that I *do* read Scripture in the letter—that is, in the very form and expression which God has been pleased to give it—and that more and more. Can I give it a form more suited? To convey to another what I find in it I may use other terms, and find them useful, to break through that crust with which a mere external familiarity often encrusts them:—all well; yet shall I find that not only will the same crust form over these new inventions, so that to those familiar with them in the same external way they shall become still a lifeless verbiage, but also that, after all, the words by which I have expressed what I have found will in the end be proved too narrow to contain the fulness of the divine meaning, if happily they may not be proved in some way inaccurate and really misleading. I do not deny at all the very great usefulness, therefore, of other phraseology than that of Scripture, for the explanation of Scripture; while yet I am sure that for the rectification of all our phrases, and also that Scripture may not be narrowed into the littleness of human conceptions, we must go back, and ever back, to refresh and purify and enlarge our thoughts by the very words—the only adequate, the *divine* words of the peerless Book which infinite grace has given us.

Distil the blessed words in your alembic and give me the result: to justify it, you must show both the material and the method. But to show me that what you have got is the full equivalent of all the material is still another matter; when your material is scripture, a very difficult thing indeed. But at least you must justify all that you speak of as the spirit by the letter, which is the only thing to begin with which we have. The Spirit within us does not give any new revelation, but "searches the deep things of God" which are contained in what has been already given. The spirit of Scripture is that contained in the letter: it is the spirit of the letter; I read it in the letter to get the spirit of it. The letter has the spirit in it, and more than all that we may please to call the spirit. How important to remember, when you contrast, as in this case, the letter and the spirit, that the letter is of God, the *spirit* is that in which you have to fear the instrusion of an element which is not of Him!

The principle which we have had asserted is, undoubtedly, one of contrast: "I do not read Scripture in the letter;" but, if that which has been stated is the truth, then there is as to practical apprehension, in this case, no such contrast. The letter is but the wisest possible expression of that which you may express otherwise sometimes with benefit, no doubt, but yet in a way which is still in reality something *less* wise than the old one. How unsafe then would it be to say, "I do not read Scripture in the way it is written, but according to what I take to be the meaning of it"! Would it not assume, in fact, that wisdom was in my poor words, beyond that of those who wrote, "not in the words which man's wisdom teacheth, but which the Holy Spirit teacheth?" (1 Cor. ii. 13). Where can you show me the spirit of Scripture in words which have the sanction that such words have? After all, will it not be *your* letter in contrast with the actual letter, neither more nor less?

The whole statement is such arrogant assumption that it is hard to believe that a spiritually sane man could make it. The effect of it, if carried out, would be to give us a Bible, or rather, Bibles many, which would be anything rather than the endeared, familiar, well-proved friend of all our hearts. The adoption of such a principle would be at once to blur all lines and bring in everywhere confusion and uncertainty. This is not the Voice of the Spirit that would enfeeble and degrade what the Spirit Himself has given, as this system does; putting it at one time in company with a faulty hymn, at another time with the speech (miraculous though it were) of Balaam's ass! I do not envy the quietness of those who can take all this (go with it or not, as they may) without a protest.

"I do not read Scripture in the letter"! Why, it is just the most literal part of it that of necessity must be used to interpret all the rest. That there are figures, types, parables in it, who is not aware? But who would like to build his soul upon things such as these, without the plain letter of doctrine which alone can interpret them definitely and surely? Is it not "letter" that "God so loved the world that He gave His only-begotten Son, that whosoever believeth in Him should not perish, but have everlasting life"? Am I to read that in the spirit, and not in the letter? Who will stand forth then and tell me, in contrast with the letter, what the spirit of it is?

See now how it all works together: I am justified in accepting this guidance that is offered me, of one so spiritually wise and competent that he can give me the spirit of that which I, poor dullard, have been reading in the letter. What can I do but submit myself to this, and let the proof abide a more convenient season? I may be bewildered at first to find how things immediately begin to change, and how little remains absolutely what it was before. But then, if I am humble, this is all proof of how I needed a teacher,—how without a teacher (and indeed, with all the teachers I have had hitherto) I have been going astray. I learn to distrust myself the more, and cling to my guide. By and by indeed, I must come to a halt, and begin to see where I am,—to see if perchance anything may have gone wrong with me. I have heard that "in a day of evil it is of the utmost importance to prove all things, and not accept the dictum of anybody." That is all right, I suppose: it is the same guide says it; I am yet to prove all by Scripture! But Scripture, what Scripture? *He* does not read it in the letter; no more must I then, if I am to reach the same results! God has somehow provided me with a Bible in the letter; and this Bible in the spirit I have got to form for myself out of it, and by its help; or, at least, I have got to prove the new Bible in the spirit which has been put into my hand by that old Bible which is so different, and which it will be my wisdom in due time to give up! Think of the perplexity to a simple soul, of using in this way a standard which has to be renounced, and for the very purpose of being able to renounce it; while at the same time, it is capable in some way of putting me on a platform higher than itself! Must not all this end in inextricable confusion? Is it not, in fact, confusion all the way through?

4. NEW BIRTH: WHAT IS IT?

There has doubtless been so much said of late with regard to new birth and eternal life that many will wish that controversy as to these could stop; and many will think that all has been said that can be said about them. One can surely sympathize with those who think so, and what is said may be the briefer on that account: still these subjects are so central in their importance in relation to Christian truth, and the novel doctrines concerning them have so central a place also in connection with the system which we are reviewing, that it would be impossible to treat this in any satisfactory way without looking at what is in question here. So far also as we are individually concerned, whatever might be the purpose of God with regard to us, and whatever the blessed work upon the basis of which that purpose can alone be justified and take effect, yet where it begins to take effect is in new birth. Thus our review may well begin here, although as to the system before us it is rather in this case a blank than a doctrine—a denial than an affirmation. Yet a denial may have all the importance of an affirmation, and the meeting it be absolutely necessary in order to laying securely the foundations of truth. If we do not know what new birth is, we cannot rightly know what eternal life is either, and much else will become uncertain as the result of this. Amid this uncertainty many suppositions may assume the character of truth and be accepted for it which will for ever prevent the truth being received. If Scripture can clear up this cloud-land for us, it will not only be in itself a gain, but it may prove a way made clear to further progress. Let us inquire at least.

Not merely has the confession been made, "I cannot tell you what new birth is," but it has been openly challenged that no one has any better ability. This is the ignorance of the agnostic, which requires more knowledge than anything that knowledge would pretend to. For in this case one has to be sure that the level of one's own capacity is at least as high as any other whatever can possibly be; and with such knowledge as this, every humble mind would readily concede the palm of superiority to its happy possessor.

Such an one will naturally teach, or at least tell his thoughts; and safely, where no one has better knowledge. Thus it is not thought that there is in new birth a communication of anything, but simply an effect produced. It is the *man* that is born again: whatever may be the extent of it; it is I myself, the individuality. That is how Scripture speaks of new birth. It is a human idea that something is imparted, but Scripture says, *I* am born again. Then the Lord puts it more abstractly—"That which is born of the flesh is flesh," for it would go too far to say, "he who is born of the Spirit is spirit": it would make *me* spirit and nothing else. Yet if the wick of a lamp may represent the individual, it is as though a thread of another description were introduced into the texture of the wick! The result is a collapse of the man,—of all that makes him a man of the world, of all his self-importance. Then there is a cry, a very feeble cry! the first sign of life in a babe is a cry of want or pain; yet Scripture does not apply the term "life" to such a state!

One feels so often as if one needed to make apology for such statements, and as if it must certainly be thought that there is some misrepresentation here; but while the putting together is indeed my own, every statement made is an actual quotation. New birth makes a man appear alive, but he is not alive. In it there is no communication of anything at all, but only an *introduction* of something; with very important consequences, no doubt; but still there is as yet no link in the soul with God.

I am not responsible for the contradiction that appears in these things, either among themselves or with scripture. Scripture says,—yea, the Lord Jesus Himself,—that that which is born of the Spirit is spirit; and to say that here nevertheless there is no link with God, seems as near a direct denial of the divine word as could be uttered, if we are not to assert that it is that. And again there is a similar thing when the Lord speaks of the man as being born again, and we are assured notwithstanding that he is not alive! What kind of birth are we to call it, when although the "renewing of the mind is the outcome" of it, yet there is no life! one is born of God and yet not His; yea, has no link with Him as yet at all!

Is it necessary to go further in the examination of these statements! There should be no need. But let us look at the Lord's words themselves, and see if they leave us so much in the dark as is supposed, as to what new birth is. There is nothing imparted, says this teaching; because it is *I* who am born again. Scripture says, we are born again, not of "corruptible seed, but of incorruptible, by the word of God which liveth and abideth" (1 Pet. i. 23); and it adds, "and this is the word which in the gospel is preached unto you." The word of the gospel then, brought home by the power of the Spirit of God, is that by which the man is born again.

But here again the truth as Scripture gives it to us comes right up against the theories; which as usual also clash with each other. For we have already seen that it is denied the Scripture is of any use to souls away from God, without the voice of the living preacher. It is conceded indeed that God is sovereign, and may be pleased to use it, in the same way that He could by an exceptional miracle make use of the speech of Balaam's ass. It is useless to send Bibles to the heathen, because this is so very exceptional. God's way is undoubtedly by preaching! And yet, strangely enough (if anything is strange here) in connection with this theme of new birth we are informed that the work of the evangelist is to *enlighten the new born soul.* *When* by the power of God's Spirit a man *has* been born again, the next thing is that the soul has to be enlightened.

Thus here again we seem to be in a dilemma. It is of no use to send Bibles to the heathen: God's way is undoubtedly by preaching. And yet the preachers' work is only to enlighten those already new born! Scripture however declares that men are born again by the incorruptible seed of the word of God in the gospel, and that the Scriptures are able to make one wise unto salvation; while the preacher is God's great instrumentality for getting the saving truth before unwilling men. There is here no semblance of contradiction, the word of God being in all cases that by which new birth is effected in the soul,—whether it be in the page of the inspired Word or by the mouth of the evangelist. In either case the Spirit of God must act: as the Lord puts it in His pregnant figure, "water" and "Spirit" must go together.

The incorruptible seed is thus imparted. The seed is not the mere word, but as nature itself teaches, *the word with the life in it*. Every fruitful seed carries in it that mystery of life, which we may be little able to analyze, but which we cannot reason away: it is *there*, reason as we will; and without it there would be no growth or good whatever.

Thus there is that which is born of the Spirit, and what is born is "spirit." Will any one say that that does not convey the thought of a new nature, akin to that from which it has originated? And "the Spirit is life" (Rom. viii. 10); everything here speaks of the communication of life; look through Scripture as you will, there is no dead spirit anywhere. "The

Spirit quickeneth" (2 Cor. iii. 6): "the spirit is life;" dead spirit, dead spiritual birth, dead child of God, or new born child with yet no link with Him,—these are all thoughts so foreign to Scripture, so contrary to it, that nothing but the exigency of an untenable theory could ever suggest them to one even tolerably acquainted with it.

As for the argument that the *man* being born again is in contradiction to the idea of something being imparted in this, the answer has been given by the one who uses it. "The Scripture teaches that *I* am born again, *whatever may be the extent of it.*" There is the whole difficulty, such as it is; and it is no very great one. The man is born again, and yet he is not new in all that he is. His body does not partake in this transformation; and he has yet the old nature— the flesh in that sense. The moment you say, The man is born again, whatever may be the extent of it, you state the difficulty, and admit it to be one that you must recognize, as well as the person you are arguing with. But it is no more a difficulty than abundance of fully admitted things. The man is born again; and yet, when you come to define more closely, you speak of "*that* which is born again," and could not say of the man what you say of this. You can say, "That which is born of the Spirit is spirit," while you cannot say, "The man who is born of the Spirit is spirit." It argues nothing whatever in the way desired. Let us only change the figure, as Scripture itself enables us, so as now to take into consideration what was before omitted, that this is a yet incomplete change in a moral being, the figure of grafting furnishes you with the needed means of taking in, as before you could not, all the facts. The tree which is grafted yet retains enough of its old nature to need care lest, by allowing shoots from below the graft, it should become practically wild again. Yet we speak of it rightly enough as a grafted *tree*. In a figure taken from the human sphere, which alone fits with the Lord's application for Nicodemus, one cannot find what will fit all round; no unusual thing in figures constantly made use of. The Lord's purpose does not contemplate the old nature,—that is all; and therefore the figure of birth, in other respects so perfect, is thoroughly suited.

But the man is born again; and the thought of a new life imparted is inherent in this. This life, moreover, is all that counts for life before God. The man was dead previously; now he lives; there is but one death in this sense, and but one coming to life; and if a man is no longer dead, he is alive: there is no intermediate state between the two, and therefore no interval. The one born of God is a child of God, and He has no dead children. Spirit from the Spirit is the nature of that which is born; the child partakes of the father's nature. If life is communicated, as despite all protests it most surely is, then the life so derived is necessarily eternal life. Whether or not you allow that it is what Scripture designates under that term, (and as to this we shall have to inquire directly,) yet it is impossible to deny that life attaching to a spiritual nature originating in a new birth of the Spirit must be in the fullest sense eternal life.

How important then, in connection with questions that lie before us, is this doctrine of new birth! and how significant that the system which is sought to be imposed upon us as the truth of God has to begin with a confession of blank ignorance, which is really a denial of Scripture testimony upon so important a matter! According to the system, to be born of God is somewhat that involves neither life, nature, nor relationship,—no link in the soul with God at all! It is no wonder, but a necessity of this, that those born of Him should be denied to be His children. Thus it is asked, "Is it so that 'children' speaks of *descent?*" And the answer is,—"I do not think that is quite just. It is not the scriptural thought of children. The Spirit bears witness with our spirit: it is by the Spirit we understand that we are children. . . . You ought not to take that place, except as born of God; but the place is given you of the Father"!—an argument quite as inconsequent as anything we have listened to on the same side. Naturally, eternal life is something far beyond, and although you are born of God, if that is all, you have yet to pass from death unto life!

Thus I repeat it, the doctrine is that one that is simply born of God is not a child of God, has not life, nature, nor relationship. To put it in the dreariest form of the negation made, he has no link in his soul with God at all!

5. LIFE AND ETERNAL LIFE.

IN considering the subject which is now before us, there are two questions which lie at the foundation: first, is there any spiritual life which is not eternal life? And then what is eternal life? I shall as usual state the view from which I dissent, and then give as clearly as possible the reason for my dissent.

1. Is there any life for the Christian which is not eternal life?

As to this we are told: In Romans you see life, but not eternal life. The two and a half tribes typically had life; they stopped this side of Jordan, but they had life. Everybody who has the Spirit has life, because the Spirit is life. In Rom. viii. life is the consequence of the presence of the Spirit in a believer; that is, "The body is dead on account of sin, but the Spirit is life on account of righteousness." But that is connected with the wilderness and practice, and is connected with your pathway, which will come to an end. You can very well understand that the experience of Romans viii. comes to an end. It is not eternal life, and yet life is there; life comes out morally, in view of righteousness; the evidence of life in the Christian is that he does righteousness; he proves that he is born of God. The Spirit takes that place in the Christian till he is quickened. You are not said to be quickened in Romans; but in our state down here the Spirit displaces the flesh, and takes the place of life in the Christian, in order that practical righteousness should be accomplished. In Colossians and Ephesians we get a step further, and that is, "you hath He quickened," but you must understand that in a limited, not in an absolute way. It is at the coming of Christ we are quickened; only it is anticipated in Colossians and Ephesians in a limited way as the work of God fitting us for the assembly. At the coming of the Lord we shall be quickened and raised up together, and made to sit together in heavenly places in Christ Jesus. [?!] In that chapter it is viewed as anticipated.

2. What then is eternal life?

The answer given is: It involves a state of blessing consequent on the setting aside of death. "Life for evermore" (Ps. cxxxiii.), in regard to Israel is in the public setting aside of death. We come to that on resurrection ground, that makes the difference between us and Israel: they don't come into resurrection, we do. A person cannot say that he has actually eternal life, unless he is clear of death. If he is going to die, how can he say he has actually got eternal life? For us, eternal life is the heavenly condition and blessedness in which in the Son man is now placed, and lives before the Father. It is a sphere and order of blessing. It is to live in the blessed consciousness of the love of God, in the out-of-the-world, heavenly condition in which Christ lives.

I believe persons have made great mistakes with regard to eternal life in viewing it as a something substantive which is communicated to us. I can understand life in God, because God is eternal; He lives, He is. But I live, and so does every saint, simply by the quickening power of God. I am made alive now in my soul together with Christ, after His order, and eventually I shall be made alive in body after His order. People have looked at it as if it were a kind of material thing given to a person. People think they have life in themselves instead of in Christ. It is life in Christ Jesus, yet the Spirit being in me, it is practically my life.

It used to be commonly said, I know that I have got eternal life. Why? Because the scripture says, "he that believeth hath everlasting life." I say that you have thus the faith of eternal life, but that does not prove that you have the thing itself. Many a person has had a promise, but not the thing promised; that was the case largely with the Old Testament saints. It is the mind of God for every Christian, and God has put it there in His Son, and the whole question is as to reaching the Son. In the last chapter of John's epistle it says, "that ye may know that ye have eternal life"; because you are come to it; you are conscious of it, but not as a possession. If I talk about having the Son, the Son is not a possession, and yet I am said to have the Son, I have appropriated Him; affection has really reached Him: you cannot make the word "have" always mean possession. In scripture eternal life is not a subjective thought as a possession, but it is placed in the Son, and the whole point is reaching the Son.

This will probably be sufficient for quotation, at least for the present; we can see that there is an apparently careful grading and measurement of the spiritual life, supported by a few texts which, if we can overlook others, and accept the positiveness of an assertion as proof of its reliability, may be held for a success. Let us examine it, however, and see what may be the effect of introducing some omitted texts.

Is there a spiritual life which is not eternal life? Scripture emphatically denies this. The passages have been so often quoted, that one may fairly ask why they are not considered; especially as they used to be quite familiar texts, and face us in very familiar parts of Scripture. Here is one that will bear every effort that can be made to induce it to speak the doctrine that is being commended to us as truth, and will not do it,—one that is sufficient in itself to destroy the whole system down to the roots:—"Except ye eat the flesh of the Son of man, and drink His blood, ye have *no life* in you; whoso eateth My flesh and drinketh My blood hath *eternal* life" (Jno. vi. 53, 54).

Notice how many things fundamental to the views we have been listening to are swept away for ever by words so plain as these. First, we have either *no* life or eternal life; if you eat not you have no life; if you eat, you have eternal life. Is there any possible middle ground between these alternatives? If there be, why not let us know it; if there be not, why not be candid enough to own that there is not.

But again, look at the alternatives: "ye have no life *in you*"; "hath eternal life." If eternal life is not really *in* you, then you may eat His flesh and drink His blood, and have no life *in* you still! Otherwise there is no antithesis, as is most plainly intended: whether you eat or do not eat, it is one and the same thing! Who can accredit the words with such absolute want of meaning?

Still again, it is the flesh and blood of the Son of *man*, of which the Lord speaks: if you eat the flesh of the Son of *man*, you have eternal life; but in what we have been looking at a distinction is made between apprehension of the Son of man, and reaching the Son (of *God*); and it is only this last that gives eternal life. The Lord speaks quite differently here.

What remains of these subtle theories, if the words of the Lord are allowed any real force?

John supplements them with the remark, simple as it is, that "ye know that no murderer hath eternal life abiding in him" (1 John iii. 15); a strange sentence, according to this system, with all its self-evidence! For why speak of eternal life in this connection, when "many a good Christian" even has not eternal life? Would you not expect the apostle rather to say simply that he has not life? or, still better, that he is not born again? How strange a thing to associate a murderer, even by a negative, with the thought of eternal life, if this be an advanced condition, even for a Christian! What would you think if I asserted of a murderer, that he was not completely sanctified?

But again, he "hath not eternal life abiding in him!" Did not John know that there is not so much as a single Christian who has eternal life abiding in him? Did he not know that eternal life is a "sphere," of which you could not speak in such a way? If he did, how could he pen such an unmeaning sentence?

Once more:—it is the Lord who says, and in His strongest style of affirmation, "Verily, verily, I say unto you, he that heareth My words, and believeth on Him that sent Me, hath everlasting life, and shall not come into judgment, but is passed from death unto life" (John v. 24). These words are actually used in the interests of the system we are reviewing, to show that it is the *Christian* that has to pass from death unto life, which here as elsewhere is not distinguished from eternal life! The Lord, we are told, is here speaking as the Son of God, and it is an advanced attainment to hear the words of the Son of God, and to believe on the Father as having sent

His Son! Consequently a large number of Christians are dead and not alive. They may be born again, have the Spirit, have learned deliverance, and yet not have passed from death unto life. And this too although in having the Spirit, you have life "practically," because the Spirit is life! Yet this life is in Christ, and not in you, things which even seem to be considered in opposition to one another. But this we must look at elsewhere.

Now Scripture does indeed say that, "if Christ be in you, the body is dead because of sin;" and it never speaks of the *body* being quickened before the Lord comes. It speaks also of the believer being dead with Christ *to* sin: a very different thing, of course, from that of which we are now speaking; but I am not aware that it ever speaks of the Christian being "dead" in any other sense. Most certainly, it never puts forward such a contradiction as that a man can be "practically" alive without being really so, nor makes in this way the blessed influence of the Spirit of God in such to be an effect produced upon a dead man—a life which does not make alive! Here it is no wonder if the things said should be in apparent conflict with one another, when practical life is yet taught not to be life, and he who is working righteousness in the power of the Spirit of God may yet, as we are assured, be waiting to be quickened!

Here is an argument we must not pass over: "It used to be commonly said, I know that I have got eternal life. Why? Because the scripture says, He that believeth hath everlasting life." Well; is not that a straightforward conclusion, for one who knows himself to be a true believer? It seems not: we are to be taught a new logic, as all else. "I say that you have thus the *faith* of eternal life; but that does not prove that you have the thing itself. Many a person has had a promise, but not the thing promised." Truly! I suppose we shall all at once acquiesce in that; the misfortune is that it does not apply. The Lord's statement here is not a promise, but a direct assurance of the simplest kind. The believer has eternal life; I am a believer; I therefore have eternal life. If the premises are sure, how can the conclusion fail? If that may be doubted, how can any assurance be given, which cannot?

The argument fails so badly, that it is no wonder if another has to reinforce it. So we are told "have" does not always mean possession; "if I talk about having the Son, the Son is not a possession"(!) That is not argued, it is supposed not to need it; but is it the truth? Is not the Son ours *in any sense* now? Who will say so? Is having the Son a promise that we shall have Him? Clearly not. But it says, "He that hath the Son hath life;" does that mean, "He that hath the Son is going to have life?" True, the Son is not ours now in all the fulness of what eternity will give to this; and life too is not ours in such fulness either; for the body is still a mortal body, and will be quickened then. But there is a present "having" in both cases.

A false definition of eternal life is at the bottom of much of the confusion. Rightly enough connected with the Old Testament "life for evermore," it is forgotten that life and incorruption are brought to light through the gospel (2 Tim. i. 10), and that therefore we must not expect their definition to be gained from the Old Testament scriptures. New birth is not found in doctrinal statement in the Old Testament; and it is in new birth that we shall find what underlies the New Testament doctrine. One born of God is a child of God; the child derives its life from its father, and partakes of its father's nature. "That which is born of the Spirit is spirit;" and the life given is eternal life. Here is the fulness found of this expression: it is a life which not only has no end, but had no beginning either, being divine life. It is eternal in the full meaning of eternal, though in us, of course, beginning. This has been dismissed with the strange, curt remark, that "the life of divine Persons is *themselves;*" they cannot, therefore, it is meant, communicate themselves! But the statement and the reasoning are as crude as elsewhere, and are confuted at once by those facts of nature which God has given us as parables of spiritual things. The parents' life and nature in the child are not the *parents;* they *have* a power of communicating life which, mystery as it is, is undeniable; and God has adopted our human language, based upon the facts of creation which He Himself has created, to give us at least such thoughts as we are capable of in regard to all these things, which the strange system before us rudely cuts across. It gives us birth without life, children who are not such by descent, a practical life in those that are still dead, and similar absurdities, against which nature protests absolutely, and Scripture no less.

In life, we are assured, nothing substantive is communicated; that there is nothing *material*, will not be disputed; nor that when we speak of life, we may be unable to define it. Infidel scientists have mocked at a vital principle on this account, and told us that we might as well talk of "aquosity" as the principle of water. Yet we believe in a vital force, as well as in vital phenomena. Spiritual life will be naturally still more difficult to define, but that is no reason for denying it to be more than phenomenal, and certainly not for defining it as a sphere, etc. Personality it is not; it is not a "self"; yet there is that which is born of the Spirit, which is spirit, and which gives character to the new-born soul. There is that which is communicated to us, and abides in us, an incorruptible seed that abides in us, and because of this, "whosoever is born of God doth not commit," or better, "practise," "sin" (1 Jno. iii. 9). The phenomenal life is just the display of this in its activities; in other words, there is a life by which we live, as well as a life we live: without the former there cannot be the latter. So Scripture, in harmony with nature, speaks; and in both ways of eternal life.

That in eternal life, according to its very nature, there is the setting aside of death, is too plain to be denied: yet here also, strange mistakes are possible; though to any one who has grasp of the doctrine they should not be possible. First, we are told, and rightly,—"I am made alive now in my soul together with Christ, after His order, and eventually I shall be made alive in body after His order." And yet with the most entire forgetfulness of this limitation, we are told elsewhere: "A person cannot say that he has actually eternal life, unless he is clear of death. If he is going to die, how can he say that he has actually got eternal life?" And this is made the ground for saying that while in Rom. viii. life is the consequence of the Spirit in the believer, yet the experience of Rom. viii. comes to an end. "*It is not eternal life, and yet life is there!*" and much doctrine is built upon this;—a mere and extraordinary piece of forgetfulness: for the experience is not the life, but the result of the life in the present circumstances. The death of the body brings this to an end, and the life is transferred to another sphere; but how does this prove that the life so transferred is not eternal life? Yet he must not say, it seems, that he has actually got eternal life (in his soul), because he has not yet got it in his body! A pebble indeed, to turn one from the path of truth!

Let us remember the words of Him who said, in the consciousness of what He is for men as the Resurrection and the Life, "He that believeth in Me, though he were dead, yet shall he live; and he that liveth and believeth in Me, shall never die" (Jno. xi. 25, 26). Against the life, then, that He gives, which is eternal life, death has no claim,—over it no sovereignty. The body still awaits its change and its redemption; none the less is it true for the present partaker of His resurrection life, that death is behind, and not before him. For him, Christ has abolished death, and brought life and incorruption to light through the gospel.

6. STANDING AND ACCEPTANCE IN CHRIST.

WE have been occupied so far with the work in us—with new birth and eternal life: things which are in nearer relation to one another than the views we are examining would at all allow. Yet it is surely true, as has been stated, and as Scripture fully recognizes, that there is a life we live, as well as a life by which we live. The life we live is pressed in the new system, not merely to forgetfulness of the life by which we live, but actually to the denial of it. The consequence is that the whole thought of eternal life is lowered. It becomes merely a kind of triumph over death, which when we enter heaven ceases to be even of much significance! Here is a conversation which will enlighten us in this respect:—

"Is the expression 'heavenly' included in the idea of eternal life?

"No, I don't think so. I think eternal life refers to earth. I don't think we should talk about eternal life in heaven.

"Only we have it there.

"I don't think the term will have much force there.

"The thing will surely be there.

"WE shall be there.

"I will have to get this clear, for I don't understand it. How do you explain as to eternal life? I have understood that a sphere is included.

"I think it implies a sphere of relationship and blessing, but that is not necessarily heaven. I don't see much sense in connecting the idea of eternal life with heaven.

"Well, I don't, but still I have understood that it is connected with heaven also.

"I don't know the connection. The point of eternal life is that it comes in where death was. I think it stands in Scripture in contrast to death."

In another place an objector questions, and is answered thus:—

"I don't understand; do you mean that when we go from this earth eternal life will cease?

"I don't think the term has any longer force.

"Is it only the term then?

"What the term expresses has not any more force." (!!)

So man's "thoughts" (of which there are plenty here) belittle and degrade everything they intrude into. In new birth we are taught that no life is communicated. Life itself is not to be understood as anything "substantive" that *can* be communicated. "Nature" disappears in this way along with life, as we find in the following:—

"Have we not had a wrong idea as to what 'nature' means?

"It is the looking upon nature or life as something substantive: any *substance* is characterized by its nature; but you cannot talk of the nature of a thing till the thing is there." (!).

So as we (like the "murderer") have no "eternal life abiding in" us, we cannot, of course, talk of a nature as attaching to what does not exist. The argument is demonstrative if the basis is sound; but it shows how far a false step may carry one. Let us listen again:—

"I have sometimes said that Scripture does not recognize two natures in the Christian: the *flesh* is the nature in an undelivered man; when he receives the Spirit he is not in the flesh but in the Spirit, and the Spirit is not a nature but a Person." (!)

Poor Christian! when undelivered he has nothing

but the flesh; when he receives the Spirit, it would seem he must have no nature at all; for the flesh is no longer that to him, and the Spirit is not a nature, but a Person! No doubt there is some way of filling up the void eventually; but with that we are not here concerned.

But this leads us on to what is before us now, the question of our standing in Christ, which according to Scripture is connected with the life we have in Him. Our natural life in Adam has involved us in the fall of the old creation; our spiritual new life in Christ has given us what we have been accustomed to call our standing in Him. The very term (although they use it) seems offensive to those who accept the views we are considering: "ecclesiasticism, *standing*, ground, and such ideas," we are told, "have almost ruined us." Yet, as I have said, the term is retained; perhaps it is only in accommodation to the weakness that has been induced by it: "If you talk about standing, I am a justified man, who have received the Holy Ghost." When it is asked, however, "But what about being in Christ?" the answer is, "The moment you bring in 'in Christ" it is new creation." And again:—"The moment you come to 'in Christ,' you get the revelation of God's purpose in Christ, and the work of the Spirit in the believer according to that purpose; that is new creation, it is not a question of standing."

Yet it is allowed that "the presentation of my justification is in Christ: He is my righteousness." One would think that to be in contradiction to what has just been stated; however that may be, it is only what is needed for the earth: "in heaven he will not be a forgiven or a justified man. He will not need that in heaven: nothing enters heaven but new creation."

Of necessity then the being in Christ has nothing to do with any thought of His being our Representative. Our Substitute in death, it is allowed, He was, and His resurrection therefore for our justification; but this does not involve any thought of representation in glory. "In Christ" is my state, as we have been told, a state which God has wrought by His Spirit, true, but still my state, and nothing else. So thoroughly is this maintained, that a Christian is said to be "in Christ as he is formed in Christ;" and "in Christ is the measure of our spiritual state."

The complete denial of all the positive side of representation in glory is made plainer perhaps by a quotation I have elsewhere given, which for its importance I shall give again here. It relates to the meaning and value of the burnt-offering, and I quote it fully that there may be no possibility of mistake:—

"*The blood of the burnt-offering never went inside;* but that of the sin-offering did. I have thought this remarkable. The blood of the burnt-offering is connected with acceptance *down here*, but the blood of the sin-offering goes in to meet and vindicate God's glory—all His claims met and vindicated, and on the ground of this we can enter. We go in *in the life of Christ*. It was on the day of atonement that the blood of the sin-offering was carried in: we go in in a life which needs no acceptance, but the burnt-offering being all burnt on the altar is the ground of acceptance for man here on earth, and that will be equally true in the millennium. We get it set forth

STANDING AND ACCEPTANCE IN CHRIST. 53

in figure in Noah's offering. There is *no ground of acceptance for man down here* save the death of Christ."

Let us look now at what is here presented to us as the scriptural and beneficial truth, in opposition to the well-nigh ruinous idea of "standing." Since it is allowed, however, that we may use the term as applying to our justification, and that Christ is our righteousness, the idea so far cannot be ruinous. Acceptance as symbolized in the burnt-offering is allowed also, and that "Christ has gone into heaven itself to appear in the presence of God for us representatively, *that we may reach there*." How far acceptance differs from justification is not apparent in this scheme, and the representation which brings us to heaven must have to do with the sin-offering aspect of Christ's work simply, as is plain: for the blood of the burnt-offering, we are told, never went inside the sanctuary, and avails only for man down here.

Now at the outset, whatever may be conveyed to us by the burnt-offering becomes, in this way, of comparatively small account. The sin-offering is competent for the removal of sin, and to bring us to heaven. When we are once there, we need it no more. If a man were taken to heaven immediately upon believing, he would not, so far as appears, need it at all. Israel as an earthly people will somehow need it till the close of the millennium; the heavenly people (*as* that) never need it, though as in the meantime upon earth, they do.

What does it symbolize? It seems to be answered in the quotation given, "the death of Christ." But the death of Christ is shown forth in all the sacrifices, and the sin-offering is as competent to express that as the burnt-offering. The evident point of contrast between the two is not found in this, but that in the one the necessary judgment of sin is set before us, in the other the peerless obedience of the Sufferer. For this reason it is that, in complete contradiction to the place assigned it in what we are examining, while the sin-offering is offered in the outside place, and upon the ground without an altar, the burnt-offering gives its very name to the altar upon which it is offered, and upon which it all goes up as a sweet savor to God! The one is for the removal of sin; the other is for positive acceptance of the offerer. Thus while the one had indeed its absolute necessity with a holy God, the other was His delight, and was continually to be burning upon the altar, never to go out. The work which Christ had to do to put away sin was seen in the one case; in the other the glory of Him who knowing all that was to come upon Him, could say, "Lo, I come; in the volume of the book it is written of Me, I delight to do Thy will, O my God."

Did this avail merely for the putting away of sin or sinner from before God? and was there no overplus of value to give corresponding blessedness to our acceptance in the Beloved? Is this to be lost when we enter heaven? left as an old garment no longer needed, to be inherited by the millennial saints? "We go in in a life which needs no acceptance," is to be our comforting assurance; and in consistency with this we are informed that the "best robe" which is put upon returning prodigals is "really new creation, Christ formed in the Christian!"

After the millennium, therefore, it is to be supposed that the sweet savor of an infinite sacrifice will go up no more. With the saints' state perfected, they need no more that which covered them for a time until they could shine out in their own beauty! Is this your thought also, reader? and does this song please you better than that we used so lately to sing:—

> "Jesus the Lord, our righteousness!
> Our beauty Thou, our glorious dress!
> Before the throne, in this arrayed,
> With joy shall we lift up the head.
>
> "This spotless robe the same appears
> In new creation's endless years,
> No age can change its glorious hue,
> The robe of Christ is ever new."

There are some, we trust, who if they are offered this so called advanced and heavenly truth as the new wine, will say with their whole hearts' approval still, "The old is better."

"If any man be in Christ, it is new creation:" for that we have the full authority of Scripture; for it is by a new creation alone that we come into relationship with Him who is its Head. Adam, says the apostle, "is the figure of Him who was to come" (Rom. v. 14). Our connection with the fallen head is by our part in the old creation, and so by the life communicated to us. According to the type the communication of spiritual life from the Last Adam who is a quickening Spirit (1 Cor. xv. 45) brings with it consequences in blessing more than commensurate with the inheritance of sorrow entailed by our relation to the first. "As in Adam all die, so in Christ shall all be made alive" (ver. 22). In Rom. v. the apostle carefully develops the heritage on each side of the many from the one, before he goes on to enlarge upon the results to us of that death with Christ which frees us judicially from our place in Adam. The sixth and seventh chapters cannot be understood aright until we have made our own the teaching of the latter half of the fifth. The study of it ought to assure any one of what is a riddle yet to the leader in this new departure, "where the idea of standing comes from." As in our former head we fell, so in our present One we "stand;" and "in Christ" means identification with our new creation Head. Thus the apostle can say, "If any man be in Christ, old things have passed away," as he could not if merely the inward change were contemplated: for the new life does not accomplish in itself this passing of the old things; but looking at the new place which accompanies the new life, it is absolutely simple. Identified with Christ before God, the flesh is gone: we have our part in His perfection. "In Christ," in its natural force, neither speaks of Christ in us, nor of association with Him, with both of which these teachings confound it; and this is seen in the very text which is claimed by those who hold them as conclusive in their behalf.

The simple fact that there are two opposite modes of expression for these two opposite ideas, we in Him and He in us, ought to be convincing: they surely do not mean, as they are made to mean, only the same thing! The Lord puts them together for us in His parable of the Vine and the branches. We have only to remember in the application of it, that no one is naturally in Christ, and that the scriptural figure which takes in this fact is that of grafting. This prepares us for what has stumbled some, that in a parable of vital relationships there should be branches that are taken away because they bear no fruit. It is simple enough if we only realize that they are grafts which have not *struck*. The Lord does not speak of grafting, because He is not showing how the connection of His branches with Himself is begun, but only the necessity of fruitfulness, and how it is realized: but the difficulty suggested is accounted for by what we know to be the truth. That the branch should abide in the vine is needed for fruit, and the graft that does not abide has formed no vital connection. That vital connection is that by which alone, the branch being *in* the vine, the vine (in its sap) comes to be in the branch, needs no demonstration.

Living connection is that which, as we have seen, subsists between the Last Adam and those to whom He has become a quickening Spirit. The nature of the parable forbids more than a certain idea of the results in blessing of the identification of the living soul with its Head of supply; but there is the same limitation in all parables. The parable of the Vine is found in the midst of such expressions as those we are considering, and shows, if there were otherwise cause to doubt, the essential difference of the two things which are vainly sought to be made identical.

It is simple enough that the new creation "stands" in the sufficiency of its glorious Head, and that our standing individually results as part of this; while our acceptance in Christ is much more than the putting away of sins or of the "old man;" it implies the positive value of the wondrous person of the Man Christ Jesus, of which our place before God is the due recompense. And this is expressly declared in the apostle's statement, that "He was made sin for us, who knew no sin, that we might be made the *righteousness of God in Him*" (2 Cor. v. 21).

So far then as we have gone, the system we have been examining is negative and destructive wholly. New birth is robbed of life; life is nothing substantive, and can have therefore no "nature" attaching to it, for there is nothing for it to attach to; eternal life will have no particular force just when you have fully reached it; standing (if you talk of standing) is merely that you are a justified man who has the Holy Ghost; the best robe in heaven is just the change wrought in yourself; you may need to be accepted in Christ until you get to heaven, then you will be so perfected as not to need it; your being in Christ, and Christ being in you are only equivalent expressions: and so, like the blast of a simoom the work of desolation moves along.

7. RECONCILIATION, AND THE REMOVAL OF THE OLD MAN.

THE presentation of what is claimed to be the truth as to reconciliation is a very good example of the style of argument which largely prevails among teachers of the school we are reviewing; with whom boldness of assertion seems to make up for lack of demonstrative force. It is amazing in these reports of conferences from which our knowledge of their utterances have mostly to be gained, how little serious attention is given to the Scriptures which are professedly before them, and how little serious attempt there is to hold them to Scripture. Texts are cited, of course; and sometimes a feeble demurrer is made, sure to be silenced immediately, though it were only by an emphatic repetition of the statement questioned. It is easily seen, as the present leader, though with a certain wise caution, says himself, that they are not "simply!"— who are "simply?"— expositors of Scripture, but only of what Scripture has taught them; but we are right in expecting that what Scripture has taught them shall be able to stand an appeal to both text and context; and this one finds here indeed little asked or proffered. There are *remarks*, to be sure, upon texts many, the effort to connect which with the context, and so with serious exposition is sometimes remarkable enough.

For instance, in a question raised with regard to the assertion that "fellowship with the Father and the Son," as spoken of in John's first epistle, was limited to the apostles, reference is made to the sixth verse of the first chapter, "If we say that we have fellowship with Him." The answer is ready: "That is saying, if we say we have it. *It does not say we have it.*" And here is the exposition: "The pretension is, that you have fellowship with Him, and walk in darkness. The truth is that we walk in the light, and have fellowship with one another" (!!) But the pretension then is, in fact, to be apostles; and the walking in darkness (which cannot be part of the pretension, but is the mournful reality which exposes the pretension) is a strange and round-about proof in denial of so exceptional a claim. The "we," as spoken by an apostle, would in that case be as strange as all the rest. For manifestly he would not exclude himself or any one else from the searching test of such a principle; and in this is putting himself in the common rank of Christians, and not separating himself from them as one of a peculiar class. The "we," all through his various use of it, is that of Christian profession, and the light or darkness characterizes the true or the false profession—nothing else. Notice also whence the light shines: it is that of the sanctuary, where God Himself is revealed. *He* is in the light; and that light is just what creates Christian fellowship: "*we* walk in the light, as He is in the light;" and that establishes the true fellowship for us all, into which every true Christian enters. The apostle is bringing to bear upon this the great central truth of Christianity—the open holiest, and thus has already shown the fellowship to be divine, as to which he is now concerned to maintain the fact that no Christian can be found outside of it. "Our fellowship" is thus not a different one from this, but that into which (by the ministry of the apostles indeed) all believers are introduced; and in the "we" so constantly repeated here, we have the apostle putting himself thus with all the rest, instead of claiming for himself or others a peculiar and exceptional fellowship.

Fellowship is rightly said to be participation in common; but community of thought is strongly objected to: "they that eat of the sacrifices have fellowship with the altar; it is evidently not community of thought there." But if we look at this more closely, we shall surely realize that it is after all the principles which are identified with it that the altar embodies. The altar itself literally is only an inanimate structure, with regard to which the term can only be used as it is idealized. But as to all mental objects, ideas, fellowship in these may be rightly spoken of. One might quote, I suppose, every dictionary that exists, only that, as we shall see directly, the dictionary goes for nothing with those whose views we are examining. Let us take Scripture then, and the very Scripture which they cite against it, and it may be maintained without possibility of successful denial that the altar in this case, apart from the principles which it represents, would mean nothing —be utterly senseless in the connection in which it stands. And just so with the idol of which the apostle speaks in the same relation: the idol in itself is "nothing in the world." Take it in connection with all for which it stands, and for idol you may write "devil."

But there is another interest in maintaining things like these: "Is it not helpful to see that on account of the difficulties and opposition around, there must be a fellowship?" "The word (fellowship) implies to me a special bond in a scene of contrariety; that is, I believe, the force of it in Scripture. *And there will be nothing in heaven to call for fellowship.*" Thus we see how to preserve consistency, and rule fellowship out of heaven, it must be denied that any element of it exists that would entitle it to be there. Thus it is another of those terms, whose number seems continually increasing, which in the hands of these teachers lose their significance for eternity, and are lowered from heaven to earth; and thus error to be maintained requires continually fresh concessions to be made to it. Alas for him who has committed himself in anywise to it, and has not lowliness to judge his departure and draw back his foot from the ever more devious and downward way!

But to come to what is our theme at present—reconciliation; we shall, as usual, put together the statements made regarding it, and without comment, that they may speak thus for themselves, and make their own impression. Afterwards I shall examine them. It is a pity that the doctrine is only to be found in these conversational remarks which, as already said, can hardly, save by courtesy, be called "readings." Yet the sense is after all sufficiently clear, and the extracts are, save where noted, from one speaker who is entitled to be considered the foremost leader in a movement which is rapidly changing the aspect of many of the central doctrines of Scripture for those who are being carried by it.

Reconciliation, then, we are told, "is one of the terms the force of which you must find from its use in Scripture. The dictionary would not give you the scriptural use of it. In the ordinary use of the word the sense is that two persons estranged have been brought together. That is not the scripture-idea. It is not *minds* that are reconciled. There was no enmity on the part of God towards the world; and certainly the mission of Christ was not to make people more pleasant. Yet in Christ God was reconciling the world unto Himself, not imputing their trespasses unto them. If you say that 'it came out in the Lord's ministry of grace here on earth,' then you will be bound to admit this, that His ministry was ineffective." "The truth of reconciliation is plainly stated in 2 Cor. v.: God was in Christ; He ignored every other man in a sense, for the moment; there was one Man before Him, and that was Christ." "The ministry of reconciliation began with Christ Himself, and meant that in the presence of Christ here everything was under the eye of God on a wholly new footing in connection with Him. That was the effect of the presence of Christ. The new footing was grace and favor. God was in a new light towards man. He saw what was perfectly suitable to Himself in Christ.

"The ministry of reconciliation was effected in Christ in His life. God approached the world outside of it. He was favorable to the world in Christ, not hostile; but when you come to the word of reconciliation it is the testimony that reconciliation has been effected in death. It is not now simply that God has approached the world in another Man, in Christ being here, but the man hostile to God has been removed. So you have both things now, God's approach to man, and the man antagonistic to God removed in death. That is what I understand by the word of reconciliation, and we have to accept it."

"The difficulty," says another, "with many of us as to reconciliation is, that we have looked at it as reconciling us to God, instead of seeing it as the abolition of us, that all might be in a new Man."

"That is the idea."

And now in opposition to the dictionary meaning:—

"We have stopped at this, Alienated and enemies in your minds by wicked works, yet now hath He reconciled."

"*How* could that man be reconciled? you could not reconcile a man who is an enemy in mind by wicked works. He can only be so as being in another individuality."

Again:—

"You cannot reconcile *what* is alienated; it is impossible to reconcile that which is at enmity. If enmity is there, it is there; it is enmity of will; that is not to be reconciled. 'They that are in the flesh cannot please God.'"

"It is you that were alienated."

"But the point is that you are reconciled by being removed, and where the distance was complacency is, because Christ has come in. Hence it is that reconciliation involves new creation."

"That which you are morally has to go; personally you are reconciled. Is that the thought?"

"I don't object to that, but you may depend upon it, if you press that on people you will give them the idea that reconciliation is some kind of change of sentiment in them. I have no doubt that this is in the mind of the vast proportion of Christians." . . .

"That is, in new creation the saints are presented 'holy, unblameable, and unreproveable.'"

"It must be that; you could not conceive of any process which would change the man who was an enemy in mind by wicked works into holy, unblameable, and unreproveable; no such process is possible, even to God."

Elsewhere we find:—

"The reconciliation of things is remarkably simple. Everything is taken up in Christ. The reconciliation of persons refers to individuals, and has to be individually accepted. 'Through whom we have now received the reconciliation.' In Corinthians it is, 'We pray you in Christ's stead, be ye reconciled to God.' Reconciliation has to be accepted when it is a question of persons, therefore there was the ministry of reconciliation."

"Is there any thought of the enmity being brought to an end in reconciliation?"

"The enmity is only brought in to show that the one marked by it must go. You cannot improve with reference to enmity. You cannot reconcile what is at enmity. It is the purest folly to think of reconciling what is hostile."

"It says, 'When we were enemies we were reconciled.'"

"Yes; but it was by learning that what was at enmity had been removed by the death of Christ. That is the way of it. I do not think that the apostle refers to a change of feeling on the part of people, but to acceptance of the truth that what was at enmity has been removed. They had received the word of reconciliation—'When we were enemies we were reconciled to God by the death of His Son.' They had accepted that as their death. This is the truth on God's side—on the experimental side it is somewhat different."

Once more, even though it may be *ad nauseam :*—

"Do you think a man, an enemy to God by wicked works, could ever be changed into unblameable and unreproveable in His sight? It could not be. That *person* could be, but not that *man*." . . .

"How would you explain our identity remaining?"

"That is the point; the complacency is where the

distance was; that is in you. It is not that God sweeps all away and brings in an absolutely new race. He does so morally, but not actually. The old man has gone, and where he was Christ is; this has come to pass in the Church."

What then is reconciliation?—

"I think the idea of the text is a bringing into conscious complacency with the divine mind and pleasure." "What I understand by it is, that where distance was there is complacency. . . . The distance has been removed in the removal of the man. I don't see in what other way God could remove distance. The distance came in by man, and the removal of the distance means the removal of the man. But the point is that where the distance was now there is complacency."

"Would you preach the ministry of reconciliation to sinners?"

"It would not be much good to them."

"Where is the ministry of reconciliation to be exercised?"

"I think very much amongst those who believe."

"But do they need to be reconciled?"

"I think so, if they are to be for the satisfaction of God."

"When the apostle says, 'Be ye reconciled to God,' had they touched it?"

"I do not think the Corinthians had touched it. . . . I think it is practical; the Corinthians had not left Adam for Christ. They were practically very much in Adam. They had believed in Christ; I don't doubt for a moment they were Christ's, and had received the gift of the Holy Ghost. But certainly, judging by the epistle, they had very little readiness to leave Adam for Christ."

"The truth for the Christian is this, that in the acceptance of reconciliation he has put off the individuality connected with sin, but at the same time he has put on the new man which after God is new created."

We have now before us — produced, some will think perhaps, at unnecessary length—what ought to enable us to arrive at a sober and sufficient judgment of what is presented for truth with regard to the doctrine. Truth there is in it also, along with much that is new, as generally in these teachings. The misfortune is that here, as in so many cases, the true is not new, and the new is not true. Not merely so, but some of the statements seem absolutely wild and reckless, easily as they were accepted by those who heard them when first made. Only the knowledge that they have been and are being so by so many could make it worth while to repeat or challenge them now. Their currency and the gravity of much with which they connect themselves, give them an importance which in themselves they are far from having.

At the outset we are warned against the dictionary meaning of the word; though it is not and cannot be denied that it is the correct translation of that which has been chosen by the Spirit of God as fittest to convey His meaning, and it would not seem to be one of those words for which, as is well known, when Christianity came in, it had to coin a meaning of its own. Scripture also, at first sight, would certainly appear to confirm the dictionary use. Any simple person would suppose so upon reading that "when we were enemies, we were reconciled," "you that were alienated and enemies in your minds by wicked works, yet now hath He reconciled," and "to reconcile both to Himself, having slain the enmity." The general consent, one may say, of Christians for many centuries has without suspicion accepted Scripture and the dictionary as speaking in the same way.

It is startling to find, in what might seem to be the same line of things,—that is, in arguing against some kind of change of sentiment, as from enmity to friendship (which the dictionary use favors, if not involves) the strong assertion that no process of changing a man who is an enemy to God by wicked works, is possible to God! To save the speaker's character for sanity, we have to assure ourselves that he is only using the word "change," so confusing in this connection, for "whitewashing," perhaps. God cannot whitewash a man, of course, and take him for what he is not. And we are encouraged to believe that that is his meaning by what he says elsewhere, that "it is impossible to reconcile that which is at enmity; if enmity is there, it is there." Truly; we shall not dispute about this; but why so earnestly and with such extraordinary emphasis, insist upon this? was it ever in dispute? while another passage still, very similar to the one we have been trying to mend, seems to assert for it that "change" is really meant: "Do you think a man, an enemy to God by wicked works, could ever be changed into unblameable and unreproveable in His sight? It could not be. That *person* could be, but not that *man*."

So it is evident that we must walk very carefully, and define very closely, to suit these leaders of the poor perplexed sheep of Christ! How good to have a Bible that always remembers that God has chosen the poor! But we may say then that a "person," an enemy to God, may be changed in this manner; but a "man," an enemy to God, may not! Is that intelligible? Let us go on and see what is to come of this.

Some one asks, seemingly in the same perplexity with ourselves, "How would you explain our identity remaining?" Perhaps he wants to know whether he is after all still a "man," or only a "person." But happily he is assured that his identity remains: —"That is the point; the complacency is where the distance was; that is, in *you*. It is not that God sweeps all away, and brings in an absolutely new race. He does so morally, but not actually. The old man has gone, and where he was Christ is."

"The *old man* has gone!" Ah! does not a ray of light break in there? Is perhaps the *old* man the "man" about whom our guide was thinking, when he spoke of the impossibility of the *man* being changed? But then why distinguish so carefully between the man and the person? The old man is in fact the person that was, before grace had brought him under its dominion, the child of Adam in all the sad inheritance of his fallen father; and because we were all naturally alike in this pre-Christian state, Scripture speaks of "our" old man. But it is not the nature—the flesh—which still remains in us, and with which so many confound it; "our old man was crucified with Christ," and for every Christian is put off, and non-existent. Thus the question is never raised of "changing" the old man, nor could be raised by one properly acquainted with its force in Scripture. This new man does not dwell in us alongside of the old, but displaces it; yet it is the same man who was once "old" who now is "new." He has put off his former self, which the cross of Christ has ended before God in judgment, but from which it has thus liberated him, that the body of sin might be annulled, that henceforth he may no longer serve sin (Rom. vi. 6).

The old man cannot then be distinguished as man or person distinct from the one individual alone existing throughout. The assertions made are false and preposterous; and, of course, you do not find a trace of them in Scripture. They are simply the inventions of a fertile but unbalanced mind. It *is* the man who was once alienated and an enemy to God by wicked works, who in every case of conversion becomes the holy, unblameable and unreprovable child of God. There is no impossibility with God of changing the one into the other; and there is no unchangeable "man" to pronounce or speculate about. And reconciliation, instead of being so far on in Christianity that persons who are indwelt of the Spirit (as the Corinthians) may yet be strangers to it, is at the threshold of Christian life. "When we were enemies, we were reconciled;" not as Christians, but as "alienated and enemies to God by wicked works, He hath reconciled us;" "God was in Christ, reconciling the *world*"—and not believers—"to Himself." No subtle distinctions can take away from us what God has thus written with a pencil of light in His immutable Book. "If they speak not according to this word, it is because there is no light in them."

How plain, therefore, that the reconciliation does involve a change in the man from this alienation and enmity, wherever it takes effect! How plain that the answer given to the invitation, "Be reconciled to God," involves the dropping of resistance and estrangement, upon the assurance of gracious provision made by which His banished may be restored to Him. The weakness of God is stronger than man, and the foolishness of God is wiser than man; and the amazing spectacle of the Son of God dying for His enemies has power still, through the might of the Spirit to subdue enemies to the love that seeks them.

Consequently the testimony of reconciliation is not that of the removal of the old man; nor can this be found in connection with it: it is merely forced in in this way where it does not belong. One wonders at the feebleness that can either put forth or accept such triviality as the following. In answer to the objection that Scripture "says, When we were enemies we were reconciled;" it is replied—

"Yes: but it was by learning that what was at enmity was removed by the death of Christ. That is the way of it. *I do not think* that the apostle refers to a change of feeling on the part of people, but to acceptance of the truth that what was at enmity had been removed. They had received the word of reconciliation—'When we were enemies we were reconciled to God by the death of His Son.' They had accepted that as their death."

Now the whole of this is necessarily and at once

overthrown by the very sentence which it is supposed to explain. We have the testimony of the very man who says this, that [such a] ministry of reconciliation preached to sinners "would not be much good to them;" and the very words he is explaining assert that it is enemies who are reconciled! Where are we told that it was "by learning that what was at enmity had been removed"? One can only answer, "Nowhere." Instead, we have confessedly the speaker's thoughts: "*I do not think!*" And where does it say or suggest that "they had accepted that death as their death," in any such sense as the removal of the old man? Not a hint is given of this in that part of Romans from which the text is quoted. It comes afterwards in the sixth chapter, and in quite another connection from what is given to it here. Would it not be well if there were indeed an expositor to help us, instead of men whose knowledge is of fragmentary texts, threaded together with their own thoughts, and in supreme disregard of context?

Before we close we must look at what is said concerning the ministry of reconciliation on our Lord's part, as it is stated in the second of Corinthians: "God was in Christ, reconciling the world unto Himself, not imputing their trespasses unto them." Here, as it was in the ministry of Christ on earth that this was accomplished, there could, of course, be no word of the removal of the old man; but here is the comment:—

"God was in Christ: He ignored every other man in a sense, for the moment; there was one Man before Him, and that was Christ. The ministry of reconciliation began with Christ Himself, and meant that in the presence of Christ here everything was under the eye of God on a wholly new footing in connection with Him. That was the effect of the presence of Christ. The new footing was grace and favor. God was in a new light towards man. He saw what was perfectly suitable to Himself in Christ."

Now that it is the truth that in every intervention of God for man Christ was before Him, the justification of the love manifested, is fundamental truth, surely; and that when Christ was born into the world, His good pleasure in men had not only decisive expression, but its justification in the Son of man. But that does not make the interpretation of the apostle's words which has been given us the more exact. True as what is said in itself may be, it is yet assuredly *not* the truth which is stated in them. God in Christ reconciling the world to Himself is not at all the same as God having Christ before Him; and one may say, manifestly not. God in Christ as seen in His gracious ministry to men, is that identification of God with Him who represented Him on earth which showed Him in a grace which did not deal with men according to their trespasses. It does not speak of Christ as the ground of such favorable regard, but as the One who expressed this regard on God's part. The effect or otherwise of the Lord's revelation of God in this way is not in question; and His sorrowful complaint through the prophet, of laboring in vain and spending His strength for nought, should have hindered this being pleaded as an objection. Yet was His work with His God, as He declares. It could not be in vain, whatever the effect among men, to reveal God thus; and where must one be to say it? God's attitude is what is declared: "He was favorable to the world, not hostile," is the truth of it. But the whole object of the proposed interpretation of this passage is evidently to make reconciliation in it as far as possible in accord with what I can only call the theory that reconciliation means the removal of the old man. The reconciliation here, therefore, cannot be permitted to involve the invitation to a change of attitude on man's part, however much this is favored by the direct appeal of those to whom the word of reconciliation is now committed, "Be ye reconciled to God." This too is enfeebled as much as possible by being turned into "accepting the reconciliation." You must guard this from any suggestion of *minds* being reconciled, which we have been told is not in it! You are only to think of enmity being removed as this may be contained in the old man being removed.

"*Minds* are not reconciled"; and yet to be reconciled is, according to another definition, to be "brought into *conscious* complacency with the divine mind and pleasure!" How is this to be done *without* the mind? But indeed there is no putting together the various and conflicting statements. Reconciliation is, of course, on God's part towards man—*He* reconciles; man is reconciled—not reconciles: reconciliation is that "where distance was, there is complacency;" and this means divine complacency. God has removed the distance by removing the man; that is the reconciling to Himself, and no work in us comes into this.

Well, then, is the whole world reconciled? Why

no! we must accept the reconciliation. After all, then, if divine complacency is to be where the distance was, and that is in us, reconciliation there is not until *we* are reconciled: the "be ye reconciled" must take effect. Reconciliation awaits, then, the response on our part before it is accomplished; that is, before it *is* reconciliation. This is the opposite of what has been so strenuously contended for, and is proved by the very statements which are meant to be the denial of it! Scripture does not negative the dictionary after all.

But more than this; if this is true, and it is as asserted, Christians who have to be reconciled—people, it may be, as in the case of the Corinthians, who have already received the Spirit of adoption, and cry, "Abba, Father,"—then they must be doing so, and rightly doing so, while yet in them the distance is not removed, and divine complacency has yet no existence! There is no divine complacency, but distance unremoved, for those whose souls refuse the distance and draw near to God in the place of children! This is the contradiction into which men fall who "do not read Scripture in the letter," in which God has been pleased to give it, but in that which their own minds have distilled out of it, and which they call, the spirit. How plain it is, that if reconciliation means divine complacency now where distance was before, then, unless there are believers who are not in the value of Christ's work before God, reconciliation *must* be coincident with the very beginning of true faith in the soul, and not in the place in which these teachings put it; and then, as a further consequence, that the word of reconciliation is not the announcement of the removal of the old man, but the simple story, than which nothing deeper or more wonderful exists, that "while we were yet without strength Christ died for the ungodly," and that "God so loved the world, that He gave His only-begotten Son" for the salvation of the lost! By and by those who have received the message of reconciliation will still need to know about the crucifixion of the old man; but God's reconciling kiss waits not for this, but meets us in our very rags and wretchedness. When we are enemies, we are reconciled to God by the death of His Son.

8. DELIVERANCE AND DEATH TO SIN.

In taking up what is now before us, we shall be treading ground already plentifully trodden by the feet of combatants, and where we shall find ourselves under the necessity of recalling what has been elsewhere said, and in connection with the doctrines also which we are now reviewing. But the topic is one of such great importance for doctrine and for practice, and is still so little clearly understood by many who might be expected to be most clear, that it cannot be in vain to take it up once more, and in view of statements and arguments which it cannot but be for profit to appraise at their full worth, both scripturally and experimentally. The experimental test is necessarily of great value in a matter so eminently practical as this.

According to the writer whom, as in general, I shall quote here, "If I were to put the question, 'How is deliverance effected for the Christian from sin and from the world?' the natural answer would be, 'By death.' I admit it; it is effectuated in that way. *But then the Christian has to die to it*, and how is he to be brought to that? I dare say some would answer, 'We have died to it in the death of Christ.' That will not do. I say the death of Christ is your title to die to it, to die to one as to the other. 'Our old man has been crucified with Him'—that is your title to die to sin; and the world is crucified to the believer in the cross of Christ—that is your title to die to the world. I quite admit the title of the Christian to die by the death of Christ both to sin and to the world, but my present point is what it is that gives power in the soul to die to sin and to the world. I believe Scripture makes it very plain; if a Christian is going to travel that path, and to enter into the thought of God about him, he must be attracted by the grace of God and by what God presents. . . . . There are two things in Scripture to which the Christian is said to die, sin and the world. In regard to law you are become dead to it; God has released you from one bond, and formed another. Then in regard to the flesh 'You are not in the flesh, but in the Spirit, if so be that the Spirit of God dwell in you;' that is the change that takes place in the Christian, he is no longer in the flesh, but in the Spirit. You are never said to die to the flesh, that I know, but by the Spirit you mortify the deeds of the body. But you can very well understand that in that case deliverance stands on a different basis. The law is compared to a husband; and you could not be free from law if God had not dissolved the bond. On the other hand you could not be in the Spirit, if you had not received the Spirit of God. But in regard to sin and the world we have to die.

". . . I could not think of dying to sin if our old man had not been crucified with Christ. That is my title to die to sin. What I understand by it is that all that comes under the idea of our old man, what a man is as in the flesh, God has dealt with judicially in the death of Christ for Himself and for me too. If it were not so you could not die; if our old man had not been crucified in the cross of Christ, you would be on the footing of responsibility as to the old man; but our old man has been dealt with in the cross of Christ, that we might not be on that footing, but might be privileged to die with Christ."

Let us pause here, and try to get clearly hold of what is being taught us. The language is plainer than it often is, and there ought not to be much difficulty in arriving at the meaning, whatever we may think of the conclusion that we reach. The scripturalness of it will not be hard to settle either, when this is done.

Deliverance from sin, it is stated, is effected for the Christian by death—true; but not simply by Christ's death for him: this gives him *title* only to die to sin, the death which in fact delivers him. And in the same way exactly as to deliverance from the world. It is *not* the same as to deliverance from the law: here a bond existed which only God could dissolve; and therefore here he becomes dead by the body of Christ. Then as to the flesh, while you are not said to die to it, you must have received the Spirit to be in the Spirit; and that is (or shows?) your deliverance.

How far does this asserted difference exist? It is allowed that "our old man was crucified with Christ,"

—"was dealt with in the cross,"—and that that is equivalent to what we were as men in the flesh. This was "crucified," put to death, so that "we died with Christ," says the apostle; and He thus having died to sin (*our* sin) we are with Him dead to sin; our old man—we, such as we were in nature and in practice, were crucified, died, are dead, with Christ: our reckoning ourselves dead to sin is only simple acceptance in faith of a most blessed fact, which must be true before we reckon it, or we should have no right to do so.

But thus we have no need of dying. We start with being dead, through the death of Another for us, but which is in this way our death. The reasoning of the apostle with regard to it (Rom. vi. 7, 8) makes it perfectly plain in what way we are to understand this; for he argues that "he that has died is *justified* from sin"—so the Greek—and that "if we have died with Christ, we believe that we shall also live with Him." He is speaking, therefore, of atonement and its results for us, not of any work *in* us. It is evident that our having died and being dead with Christ have, all through, the same meaning and application: there are not two deaths or two modes of dying. Our dying with Christ is not something accomplished by the energy of our own wills, —even of our renewed wills; and so the full significance of the change proposed for us becomes apparent. Change it is indeed; for no one can pretend that Scripture anywhere exhorts us to die with Christ; and it may be safely trusted to give us its own meaning, and not to leave us to the tender mercies of interpreters to supply us with more competent phraseology. We die to sin (we are told elsewhere) in reckoning ourselves dead! On the contrary, as surely as we do reckon ourselves dead, we cannot think of dying. Dead men do not die, but only living men. Scripture, perfect here as always, has given us the very contrary of the thought suggested to us, and in complete consistency with what we have seen of its argument all through. It could not bid us to die with Christ, because the dying with Christ of which it speaks is on the cross and the cross is, blessed be God, not a thing in any sense in the future, but an accomplished fact. We have to accomplish nothing, but to accept thankfully what is done. We can reckon it done, just because it is done: the death which is ours is that which Christ died; and therefore not a title for us to die,—which would mean of course, some other death. The apostle in bidding us reckon ourselves dead is not exhorting us to aught else than to set to our seal in faith to that which he has been proclaiming to us. It is a living faith he wants; not a cold assent to an orthodox creed. This surely we need to press, and shall always need; but not to exhort Christians to do what they cannot, and what needs not to be done, because it is done.

After all, it may be urged, are we not contending about a mere clumsy expression, when the same thing is meant at bottom? One would certainly be wrong in making a man an offender for a word, and are bound to give all the credit that one can to those who may in their very zeal for a godly walk have used strained arguments, and misinterpreted, perhaps, some texts of Scripture. But with the motives

DELIVERANCE AND DEATH TO SIN.

or influences which incline people to the views they hold we have nothing really to do; and we may easily make great mistakes about them. Besides, the misinterpretation of Scripture may have the most serious consequences, whatever the rightness of intention on the part of those who make it. The heart may indeed be better than the head; but that affects only the question of one's own responsibility. Error is that with which the enemy continually works, and which he is constantly recommending by the respectability of its advocates.

In this case there is a recklessness about the statements which involves a treatment of the word of God most dangerous in its character. We are not to say we have died to sin in the death of Christ: "that will not do;" although Christ died to sin, our old man was crucified with Him, and we died with Him! But again,—we *are* to say that we *have* to die to sin (which Scripture never says), and that His death gives us *title* to die to sin,—which it never says. Then comes up the very important question, how we are to find power to do what Scripture has never told us to do; and to do which is indeed, as is elsewhere said with regard to parting company with the first man, "not quite so easy as it may seem!" So this gap has to be filled. And exactly the same thing with regard to dying to the world; there is "leverage" needed to enable one to accomplish it. Here it is: "I believe that the apprehension that such a circle (the heavenly circle of the church) is revealed in Scripture, and the anxiety to reach it, encourages and strengthens a person to accept the place of death to the world, for if I am going to have part in that circle, all that binds me to the world must go." *Paul* was content to say in such a reference, "God forbid that I should glory, save in the CROSS OF OUR LORD JESUS CHRIST, by whom the world is crucified to me, and I unto the world;" but the modern commentator has found that the cross is only *title* to die to the world, and not attractive power, and "believes" that he has found something more effective in the New Testament representation of the Church!

All this, alas, goes but too well with what we have heard from the same person, that if he had his life to live over again, he would study Scripture less! Evidently his study of it hardly yields satisfaction to himself. May one suggest to him that, if he *did* read it more (as he says he does not) "in the letter,"—if he attended more to its every jot or tittle, and thus showed it more the respect that the word of God should inspire, while there might be less of meteoric brilliancy in his expositions, there would yet be much more of what would command the confidence of those who require to know whence as well as what the teaching to which they bow may be.

But to return to what is (thank God) the unscriptural injunction that we die to sin; if that is to be the definition of our separation from it, who that knows the treachery of his own heart could ever satisfy himself as to his accomplishment of such a complete and absolute separation as is implied in *death?* How many of us would venture to claim being in such a condition? There is power for it, we are told, in the attraction of Christ as the Second Man! The plain answer is, that attraction is one thing, and power to fulfil what we desire is quite another. It is a strange thing to be told that what a Christian needs is to be "strengthened and encouraged to part company with sin." One can understand, alas, the conscience of a Christian being too little exercised with regard to the less manifest forms of it, and the hindrance to going on with God that is the necessary result of this; but in the man in the 7th of Romans, the specific case by which the apostle illustrates the need of deliverance, the lack of either will or exercised conscience is not what is supposed, but that when he would do good, evil was present with him: the thing which he *hated* still he did.

It may be said that it is deliverance from the law that is in question here. Of this we hope to speak at another time; yet it is evident that the "law of sin in the members," which the experience here reveals, is not produced by law, and has no essential relation to it. The inefficacy of the law to deal with it, (nay, the aggravation of the case by the would-be remedy,) is indeed insisted on, and the need of deliverance from law for any deliverance from the bondage of sin revealed by the experience is emphasized in a way which clearly the teacher before us does not understand. But the point before us is at present, that here is a man who, as is represented, needs no "encouragement to part company with sin," and yet cannot do it. Indeed the man who, without compulsion, yields himself to sin is dealt with by the apostle in another and much severer manner (Rom. vi. 16): "Know ye not that to whom ye yield yourselves servants to obey, his servants ye are to whom ye obey? whether of sin unto death, or of obedience unto righteousness?" So that the apostle evidently does not consider the Christian as needing to be encouraged to part company with sin, but supposes the readiness to this to be implied in his conversion.

Spite of this, a death to sin is "not so easy as it may seem;" and the effort to accomplish this is, in fact, the lure that, in some form of it or other, leads so many astray from God's true remedy. God must help us, of course; that is easily conceded; but God does *not* help us to produce in ourselves the state we are seeking to find satisfaction in; and, on the other hand, He has already done for us what, when in faith we lay hold of it, is effectual deliverance. "Our old man has been crucified with Christ, that the body of sin may be annulled, that henceforth we should not serve sin; for he that has died is freed (or justified) from sin." We are in Christ before God; and while we identify ourselves in faith with Him, the whole difficulty that we had drops away and is gone. His death is not our title to die in some other way, but is that in which we died, and died to sin, because He, our Substitute, died to sin once for all. "In Him is no sin;" and "he that abideth in Him sinneth not." He is the storehouse of every blessing for us, upon whom as in Him the favor of God continually rests; and as we are in Him, identified with Him, before God, so is He in us, identified with us, in the world. He is in heaven for our interests, which are thus amply, and beyond all need of anxiety, secured in Him; while we have the privilege of being here for Him. In proportion to the simplicity of our faith in receiving this will be our realization of peace, and joy, and power over circumstances, as well as over the sin in us that still remains, and remains to make self-confidence impossible to us, and Christ our continual necessity and dependence.

9. DELIVERANCE FROM THE LAW.

For deliverance from the practical dominion of sin, we must of necessity be delivered from the law; and therefore the order of truth in the sixth and seventh chapters of the epistle to the Romans. Deliverance from the law and the necessity of this are dwelt upon in the seventh chapter; where the great point is that being under law means self-occupation in a religious way, the attempt to make something of that from which God would turn us away; and in which we find ourselves confronted with an unmanageable evil rooted in our very nature as born of Adam, and from which God Himself does not, in the way we look for it, come in to deliver us. Alas! pride tends ever to come in by the natural and conscientious endeavor to be right with God carried out by legal ordinances and self-culture, with all forms of asceticism superadded. God's remedy for all is the eye off self and upon Christ, with the apprehension, as given by the Spirit, of our identification with Him, so as to make God's delight in Him the joy in which we dwell, and thus the power by which in self-forgetfulness we live and serve Him.

We have therefore only to express our cordial and entire agreement with the teaching we are now examining that the true lesson of the law is that of one's own powerlessness. It is curiously put as a supposition, though it is to be hoped that the writer does not mean that it is no more than that with him: "*I suppose* it works in this way, that law brings home to a man the truth of his own utter powerlessness. That is the lesson to be learnt; I do not care how it is learnt, in all probability by law, but it has to be learnt." It is evident, one would say, that the apostle expected it to be learnt in that way; and that law is so entirely the human method of religious accomplishment that, apart from the revelation of God in the matter, we have no reason to imagine any excogitation of another. But we need not dwell upon this: so far we are glad to agree with him that the entire "end of the law" is Christ.

When we come, however, to the necessary question as to what is the practical outcome of this for us, we find our agreement soon reaching its end, and a doctrine laid down which we have already sketched, but which is being pressed with continual earnestness, and (one must say) audacity. It is undoubtedly the root of the whole system presented to us. We have, of course, things inconsistent with it presented to us too; if it were given clean cut and with entire consistency, it is hardly to be thought that Christians could go on with it as they manage to do now; but this evasive character belongs naturally to the devious ways of error wherever found, a kind of Jesuitism which may be perhaps unconscious, but which all the more does its work. One may boldly assert that it passes the power of man to reconcile the different statements made. When for instance we have the question directly asked,— a question apt enough if we consider the many depreciatory remarks about it,—"*What is the use of Scripture to us?*" we are comforted and quieted by the assurance: "It is for doctrine, and is a guard to us, and it is a very important point in regard to it that our minds are thus kept from getting out of bounds." Yet none the less confidently is it declared that if you *go to it* for doctrine, it only shows you are not yet delivered from the law! Here are the words:—

"This question of law is a very great hindrance to many of us, and I think it takes us a long time to get free of law. I will tell you how it works—people go to the Scriptures to find exhortations and rules; *they want chapter and verse*, as they say commonly, *for their doctrine*, and they want precepts for their conduct. *That is all legality*, it is the letter, and I think people are uncommonly fond of the letter; they go to Scripture in that sense to a large extent."

So, though Scripture is "for doctrine," to go to it for doctrine is legality! and although it is a very important point that by it our minds are kept from getting out of bounds, yet where the bounds are in this case is a mystery which must remain a mystery. When it is suggested that "the unsearchable riches of Christ are accorded to us by the Scriptures," that supposition is promptly repelled with a "No; you cannot get them except by the Spirit"! Who ever thought you could? But are they communicated to us apart from those inspired Scriptures the possession of which has been thought of as furnishing us with all the mind of God for His people here? But let us go on:—

"The idea of the word of God is, that God puts Himself into direct communication with man. . . . A man preaches effectually only what he has learned from God, *not* from what he has found in Scripture."

These things are put in fullest opposition; and yet what a man supposes he has learned from God is to be kept from getting out of bounds by what he has learned, not from God, but from Scripture! "I do not think people learn exactly from Scripture, but from the Spirit of truth, but the more familiar people are with the Scripture the better; because a man's mind is thus continually pulled up in its tendency to go beyond the limit"! To make the contradiction more complete and absolute, it is the same person who says, "I claim only the light of Scripture." Thus, though of course, he did not find it in Scripture, the light of Scripture is all he has! He was taught it, perhaps, independently; and then taught that it was all the while in Scripture, although he himself did not find it there, and "effectually" no one could. There is thus a continually fresh revelation being made to souls, not derived from Scripture, and which yet Scripture gives them authority to press on others, although it cannot, of course, teach others what it did not teach them, and people are legal and wrong if they go to Scripture for doctrine at all! Surely, as the wise man says, "The legs of the lame are not equal."

And after all it may be doubted whether any of us know what deliverance from law is, even the one who is teaching it to others. He has been himself studying Scripture, (only too much, he thinks,) and all his teaching he finds in Scripture, and only thus can press it with authority on others. How can he himself know for how much he is really indebted to this, which has thus been floating in his mind, and which he recommends us all to be familiar with? Really it seems as if the only thing that we could be quite sure he did *not* learn from Scripture is just this doctrine of his not learning from it. A good deal more, however, will be found to be involved in this.

It is legality also, we are told, to go to Scripture for precepts as much as doctrine. Precepts there surely are, in the New just as well as in the Old Testament: is it meant that we are not to listen to them? Well, at any rate, we are not to go to it for them. Are we to be taught them outside of Scripture? But then we must go to Scripture, to find out if our minds are betraying their natural tendency to get out of bounds! Nay, it would seem that we must be taught even more decisively by Scripture thus, than we have been already taught without it. Yet this primary teaching is supposedly by the Spirit of God, which after all we cannot rightly accept save under the "guard" of Scripture! What a wilderness of perplexity and unreality it is, which nevertheless cannot escape from the control of what the Spirit of God has provided for us all, except as, alas, this loose and careless slighting of the Spirit's instrumentality may enable us to leap the "bound," and follow our own thoughts with little check from aught beyond them.

And this is sure to be the result where (although it is confessedly good to be familiar with it) the *study* of Scripture is treated lightly: "a Bible student is not much after all." Aye, but "if thou criest after knowledge, and liftest up thy voice for understanding, if thou seekest her as silver, and searchest for her as for hid treasures, then shalt thou understand the fear of the Lord, and find the knowledge of God" (Prov. ii. 3–5). Where but in Scripture shall we search, where find, after this fashion? Let us set then these human thoughts within the so necessary bounds which befit them.

Notice once more, that the precepts of the epistles were never anything else than part of Scripture. They address themselves directly to the heart and conscience of those to whom they were addressed. Precepts as they were, they were not legal; or else the great apostle who gave us the lesson of deliverance from the law made a terrible mistake. We at least will not charge him with it. He knew surely also, that the Spirit must act through the written Word in order that it may be effectual, whether for sinner or saint; yet that did not hinder him from claiming the most absolute obedience to what he wrote; and that obedience is no less due from us than from them. It is not merely that we are in a loose way to have it before us, but to learn from it, and to give heed as to the voice of the Lord Himself: "If any man think himself to be a prophet or spiritual, let him acknowledge that the things that I write unto you are the commandments of the Lord" (1 Cor. xiv. 37). The Spirit of God does not come in between, to make this a degree less direct or decisive, but to give it all its power for the subject soul.

10. THE SUPPER, THE ASSEMBLY, AND THE SANCTUARY.

It is not my purpose to pursue the doctrines which we have been considering much further. The fundamental point as to the Person of the Lord has been already and by others sufficiently gone into. We are told that the Lord was not personally man, but man only in condition. His Spirit seems to be spoken of always as His deity which tabernacled in a human body. Thus He was not Man in the truth of His nature, as we understand man, or as He, in the way in which Scripture constantly speaks, is represented as able to enter into the full realization of manhood apart from sin. The Christ presented to us, if a man at all, is truly another man, far other than the One "touched with the feeling of our infirmities," the One "crucified through weakness," now "living by the power of God." But I do not intend to enter upon this further now.

There is yet one thing which should be considered before we close,—a doctrine which is indeed, as it would seem, rather shaping itself than already having received its final shape, but which, nevertheless, presents certain features that can be distinctly enough set forth. It is, in fact, a new ritualism, a sacramental doctrine which, however, in contrast with most doctrines of this character, lowers instead of exalting this so necessary sacrament itself. The doctrine is, in other words, that the sanctuary in which we approach God is the assembly, come together, with the Lord in His place; and the Lord's supper is the way into it, it is the introductory act into the assembly. Once in the assembly your worship becomes of another and distinctly higher character. It is a distress to have hymns and praises expressing the worship of the sanctuary in connection with the remembrance of the Lord in the supper or before this. The supper is the way in which He makes His presence good to and felt by us. When He instituted it, He was about to leave His own after the flesh, and shows them how He would make good His presence to them after He left them. It is a question whether the remembrance of Him connects itself with the sufferings at all. It is calling Him to mind. The instant you call Him to mind, you call Him to mind as the living One. It is the Person. The bread and the wine set before us death accomplished, not accomplishing. One would be slow to make limitations, to prevent the heart traveling over all His sorrows, but we must have it set in the right direction.

In some expressions of this doctrine there is, in fact, a perfect confusion between the remembrance of Him and His presence in the assembly; but it is agreed that as soon as the supper is ended you are in the assembly proper. The praises assume a new character, a character of worship in a higher sense than you were capable of before. In fact, now the sanctuary is open to you, although this must be a practical realization for each one; as to the mass of those gathered, a realization little found, but it is what we are now invited to. Outside of the gathering of the assembly you may have a sense of boldness, but you cannot really enter into the sanctuary except when gathered together, because all is dependent upon Christ, upon the place which He has taken, and it is in the midst of the church that He gives praise unto God; that is, He does not sing with you individually. You sink your individuality in the assembly. His presence makes it the holiest.

This will suffice at present for the doctrine. In taking it up, let us first of all consider how Scripture puts these various subjects before us, the manner of its doing this having great importance, as we shall see. The doctrine we are considering is evidently based largely indeed upon a supposed order of Scripture,—the order in the first of Corinthians. You find there the supper first, then you go on to the assembly and the various gifts exercised according to God. It is admitted, however, that Corinthians omits this very important view of the "sanctuary." The sanctuary constituted by the gathering of the saints is, in fact, nowhere in it, nor the worship of this highest sort, of which we are told. This is noted, indeed, by the advocates of this view. It is explained very simply by the fact that the Corinthians were too unspiritual for the apostle to enter into it with them, so that the omission of what is essential to the doctrine is quite easy to be understood !

To find the doctrine you must go on to Hebrews; only in Hebrews, in fact, you don't find it either. In Hebrews you have, as is evident, no gathering of the assembly as such at all, no constitution of the gathered saints into the sanctuary, no supper of the Lord as introducing you in. All these things, Scripture in the most distinct way, and surely with divine wisdom, has separated widely from one another, in order that there may be no possibility of founding a ritualistic doctrine upon anything for which it can be really quoted. The simplicity of Scripture as to all this is indeed of the most striking sort. No doubt you have in Corinthians the assembly as the temple of God, but it is not connected with worship in any way whatever. Both in the first and second epistles, the doctrine is given to show you the holiness that attaches to the assembly and to warn against any thing that would be a profanation of this. When we come to the supper, you have what is simplicity itself. It is the remembrance, not of a living, but of a dead Lord. We show the Lord's death. Living He is, surely; if He were not, all this would be in vain, but it is not as living we remember Him. This is the confusion which, as we know, Romanism has made, but which it is strange to find continued by those who are almost at the other extreme from it. Nothing is plainer than that the bread and the wine signify for us the body and blood of Christ, the body and blood separate, a dead Christ and not a living One. You remember Him, you don't realize His presence with you; that is not the way it is put, but the very opposite.

You remember the past in the present. It is a past indeed, which presents the One who is a living Person in the most blessed way to the soul. His death is that which surely expresses His love in its fullest, in His gift of Himself for us. Nevertheless, we are looking back, not forward. We are looking down, if you please, not up. Our fellowship is the fellowship of His body and of His blood. The blood presented to us in memorial is, nevertheless, that which was most distinctly shed in the past. He is not entered as flesh and blood into heaven. He is not with us now in that character upon the earth. Yet we know Him by what He was upon the earth, and in no way more deeply than in all this story of His love-death for us to which the supper recalls us. Think of being told that the highest character of worship cannot be rightly found in connection with that in which the Lord's heart is told out as in nothing else! Yet this is only the threshold. It is only the way in. We must leave it behind and get beyond it, although in the Acts the disciples were gathered together to break bread,—not by means of the breaking of bread to do something else. The breaking of bread was the object of the gathering, and how simple is the language used ever!—"the breaking of bread." With all the wonderful implications there are in it for us, yet how sedulously does Scripture keep us to the most perfect simplicity about it! We are not even told that we gather together to worship God. It is sufficient, it expresses all that need be said, to say that we are gathered together to remember Christ,—on the resurrection day indeed, but to look back upon His death. Resurrection is surely needed in order to put the remembrance in its right place, but to say that we must get past the remembrance in order to enter into the worship aright, is the most presumptuous violation of Scripture and of all propriety for the Christian soul that one could think of, as committed by those who own, nevertheless, what Christ's death is for them.

When we come to the assembly afterwards in the fourteenth chapter of 1 Corinthians, we have the regulation of gift in its exercise for the edification of the assembly. We have no doctrine of the assembly as the sanctuary at all. It is not even worship that is spoken of. It is *ministry;* and that so clearly that there cannot be a possibility of question as to it. If, therefore, the way in which these truths are put together has any meaning for us, the ritualism which is now intruding amongst those who might be thought the freest from it, can have no place.

When we go on to Hebrews, as already said, there is no gathering of the assembly as such, that is contemplated at all. The approach to God in the holiest is entirely separated from every question of circumstances. It is as open, so far as Hebrews leads us, to the individual saint anywhere, as it is to the assembly; and how important it is to realize this; for the rent veil, (which indeed is denied to be in Hebrews at all,) is that which is the very characteristic of Christianity itself. It is that in which the true light already shines for us and which is the sign of the full liberty of worship that belongs to us now, as those no more at a distance, but brought near to God. Our drawing near does not depend upon a meeting, but it depends upon power in the Spirit alone. We have access through Christ, by one Spirit, unto the Father.

It is surely true that Christ, in the midst of the Church, gives praise unto God. No doubt it is true that we are able by grace to be in fellowship with Him in these praises of His,—nay, in our measure to express them as gathered together. Nevertheless, that is an inference, and not a direct scripture doctrine. The doctrine is that it is He who in the midst of the assembly,—not by means of the assembly,—

—gives praise to God. As we find it in the twenty-second psalm it refers indeed to the gathering of the disciples after His resurrection when they are put into the place in which His work has set them. The praises at that time were surely His alone. Let us make whatever inferences are legitimate from it. No Christian will make any objection to that, but every right minded Christian will make an objection to having an inference forced upon him as a doctrine of such weighty import as is supposed, and which is used, in fact, to divert him from the very object for which the assembly comes together, which is to remember Him.

In Hebrews there is no supper and no assembly. We have a blessed way of access to God. There is a new and living way which He has opened for us through the veil, that is to say, His flesh, and we have boldness to enter into the holiest by the blood of Jesus. It is remarkable that where, in the doctrine before us, we have the gathering of the saints, as in Corinthians, there is no sanctuary worship, and that where we have the sanctuary worship, as in Hebrews, it is denied that there is a rent veil, and therefore a way of access in that way at all. The fact is we are told that the object of Hebrews is to give us boldness to enter, but there we stop. There is no entrance actually spoken of; yet we are of course to enter, but the very idea of entering *through* the veil, it seems, shows that the veil is not rent. How it shows it will be a mystery to most, probably, to understand. It is quite true the veil is not looked at as put away, but that we do enter through it. The veil is the flesh of Jesus, and the entrance is made for us by His death. We enter by the veil, but by a way of access opened for us through it. Where is the contradiction between the *rent* veil being there, and our entering through?

But this unrent veil in Hebrews has another purpose in the view that is held. It cuts off still the holy place from the holiest, only with this effect, that the holy place, the place of the table, the candlestick and the shew-bread, has dropped out now. It is Jewish and we have nothing to do with it. All that you have in the present time is the holiest. You have no holy place. That has no present standing; and if it is still said that Christ is the the Minister of the sanctuary,—or, as we are reminded we ought to take it, as the Minister of the holy places, that has a sort of general reference, wider of course than Christianity, in order expressly to guard against the thought of the holy place having any reference to the Christian. It has been asked, why does it say, then, that Christ entered into the *holy place* with His own blood? but that is very simply settled. It is supposed that that *means* the holiest. There is no other word for holiest and you must take it in its connection; and if it be asked, did not the rending of the veil bring the holy place and the holiest together? it is answered, the ground taken is that the first tabernacle has no standing. Therefore you have nothing left except the holiest.

Now the doctrine of Hebrews is, in fact, quite otherwise. "The first tabernacle," as the apostle says, was practically the holy place for Israel. They could not (except the high-priest, on one day in the year) enter into the holiest at all. There was a first tabernacle that they could enter, and a second tabernacle that they could not enter. This first tabernacle, as such, has necessarily come to an end by the rending of the veil. The moment the veil is rent you have a holy place which is formed of the two holy places contemplated before. The first, *as first*, has come to an end. There is for us no *first* tabernacle; that is true; but as the word really is, we have "boldness to enter into the holy *places* by the blood of Jesus." That is the express doctrine as taught in Hebrews itself, that the holy place exists still,—nay, the holy places; while indeed they are one for us. Thus it is that Christ entered by His own blood into the holy *place*. It is sufficient to say that, while this holy place is by that very fact holy and holiest all in one, thus we have liberty to draw nigh indeed, and we enter not by some new experience of our own about it, but simply "by the blood of Jesus." This in its essence abides for us as Christians wherever we may be,—alone, together, in the assembly, or in our daily walk. It is the character of Christianity; and we are not Christians at certain times or occasions, but we are Christians all the time. A "better hope" has come in for us than the law could give men, for the law made nothing perfect, but we now, by Him who has entered into God's presence for us, draw nigh to God.

In a word, all this ritualism is a plain invention. Neither Corinthians nor Hebrews knows anything of it. Let anyone take simply the passages in which the Lord's supper is spoken of, and let them realize the impression that is made upon them by the deepest consideration that they can give such things.

The simplicity of Scripture appeals to us all and would put the simplest believer into his place with God, privileged to be a worshiper, not through any attainment of his own, but through the work of Another. The constant aim of all that view of things that we have been considering is aristocratic. It is to make a distinct class amongst Christians, to comfort some perhaps with the thought of how much they have attained, to occupy others with themselves after another fashion, and put them practically at a distance.

It is not Christ Himself that in all this is rightly set before the soul, but our experiences with regard to Him; which indeed the Spirit of God works in us as our eyes are upon Christ and our hearts realize His love, but which are put in the wrong place, so that, in fact, we lose very much that which it is the apparent effort to make us gain. Let us keep Scripture as God has given it to us, surely best so, and let us not supplement it with thoughts to which Scripture may perhaps be supposed to give the limit, lest we should go astray, but which Scripture itself has not inspired.

F. W. G.

REASONS FOR MY FAITH AS TO
BAPTISM.

THE scripture that bids me be ready to give an answer to every man that asks a reason of the hope that is in me (1 Pet. iii. 15), may, in the spirit of it, if not the letter, be the justification of the present paper. Among many of those with whom I have the fullest sympathy and fellowship in spiritual things it is plain that there is more and more question of such views as I must acknowledge mine,—branded even as heresy by some; by others, considered at least to be the result of laborious reasonings—the fruit of intellectualism intruding upon what is the province of faith (—of "leprosy in the head," as some claim). On the other hand, of all that to my knowledge has been written upon the subject,—and this will be thought, perhaps, a sufficiently damaging admission,—I am aware of nothing that exactly expresses the doctrine for which I am willing to be held responsible, and which I believe to be the doctrine of Scripture upon the subject. If, then, "*all* Scripture be profitable," it would not be of faith to hold back what in my apprehension it teaches upon such a matter as baptism. Even for those who after all may never agree with me, it may do what is of more importance even than this,— it may show how little the faith as a whole is affected by different views about it, and how those who so differ may preserve unhindered the unity of the Spirit, and walk in love and peace together.

It is our common shame, indeed, that, with regard to a simple external rite such as this is, Christians orthodox and evangelical, and professing adherence to the Bible only, should yet be unable to agree upon almost any point in connection with it,—form, subjects, meaning. Amid this wide-spread confusion, there is little ground indeed for self-satisfaction, much that should keep us humble and distrustful of ourselves. What a reproach, if after all the long patience of God with all of us, we are unable still to have patience with one another, even perhaps enough to understand one another's speech!

On the other hand, it must be confessed that in the traditional creed upon the subject errors so gross and corrupting have been maintained—preserved in measure even in the creeds of the Reformation, that it is scarcely to be wondered at if that should seem the only true view which was in every way farthest from the "Babylonian" one, and which, in its adoption, would remove at once all danger of contamination with it. Nevertheless it has to be asked whether the truth does not most naturally lie between the extremes,—whether it is not rather, in general, by the perversion of some truth that Satan prevails among Christians, rather than by the introduction of a whole lie in absolute contradiction to it. If it be so in this case, the extreme recoil from traditionalism will not be found the point of rest, but, in fact, will favor oscillation toward the traditional.

Our business is with Scripture, which the writer desires to have brought in the fullest way to bear upon all that is here put forth. He dreads not the keenest criticism, but invites it. Every untruth exposed is an advancement of the truth itself; where the truth is known, it is yet a buttress for it.

1. THE CHURCH OF GOD.

WE need, first of all, to see with what we must *not* connect—or entangle—the doctrine of Baptism: the idea of baptism into the *Church*,—that is, of water-baptism introducing into it,—must be named in order to be refused, in whatever form it may be presented.

What *is* the Church as we find it in the New Testament? On the one hand, it is a body—the body of Christ. Its members are of Christ—*living* members of Christ, for there are no others.

What *forms* this body? No human power, clearly; none is competent: it is the baptism of the Spirit only. (1 Cor. xii. 13.) Nor do I take up now the confusion of this with water-baptism, which is habitual in traditional teaching, except to say that when the apostles were baptized of the Spirit on the day of Pentecost, (comp. Acts i. 5,) there was plainly no water-baptism at all. As plainly, it was not new birth that the apostles then experienced, but the gift of the Holy Ghost that they received. (Acts ii. 33, 38.) This gift, as something additional to new birth, is that which distinguishes the Church as united to Christ on high: "He that is joined to the Lord is one Spirit." (1 Cor. vi. 17.)

But the Church, as indwelt of the Spirit, is also spoken of as the "house of God,"—a building which Christ builds, and which is composed of "living stones," just as the body is of living members. (Matt. xvi. 18; 1 Pet. ii. 5.) In this way, the body and the house are plainly but different aspects of the same thing: in extent, they are exactly the same.

But there is another aspect of the house also, which we find both in Ephesians and Corinthians. In Ephesians (chap. ii. 20–22), there is the double thought of the Church—as being built on the foundation of apostles and prophets, *growing* to a holy temple in the Lord, and of a *present* "habitation of God in spirit." Here, human instrumentality is seen; and in Corinthians (1 Cor. iii. 10), the apostle Paul claims himself to to be a "master-builder," and to have laid the foundation, warning those who follow him how they build upon it. The foundation, as he says, is Christ,—the truth as to Him which the first inspired teacher communicated. All after-building is by teaching,—teaching by which are influenced and fashioned those who accept it. Building and edifying are thus the same thing—in the original, the same word. The care was to be as to the material used: "gold, silver, precious stones, wood, hay, stubble" (*v.* 12); and these materials therefore refer primarily to *doctrines*. The day is coming, says the apostle, which will try all,—a day in which the fire will try (and "our God is a consuming fire") every man's work of what sort it is. "If any man's work abide which he hath built thereupon, he shall receive a reward. If any man's work shall be burned, he shall suffer loss; yet he himself shall be saved, yet so as through the fire."

So, in responsibility for the present time, the house of God is being built. But, alas! what responsibility did man ever come under in which he did not fail? So have the builders failed in this case; and thus while in the first epistle to Timothy the apostle writes that he may know how to behave himself in the house of God, which is the Church of the living God, in the second he makes only mention of a "great house,"

in which are vessels of gold and silver, of wood
and earth, and some to honor, some to dishonor. And
now the word is, that "if a man purge himself from
these, he shall be a vessel unto honor, sanctified, and
meet for the Master's use."

I do not here go further into the doctrine of the
house, because it is clear that whatever builders might
in fact build, and with whatever far-reaching results,
nothing can affect the fact that *Christ's* building is
only of living stones, and that the Church, in either
aspect, is thus one thing essentially: none but the living
form any part of it. Also as to introduction into
it, the two things by which alone any are introduced
into it—new birth and the gift of the Holy Ghost—
neither is in man's hand to bestow.* Man cannot
form or introduce into the Church; he can but recognize
what God has done.

But here we are brought at once face to face with
the view that many have with regard to baptism. They
would say at once, That is just what we believe baptism
to be—the recognition of the work which God has
done, and which He alone could do, in souls. Just as
Peter, when the descent of the Spirit upon Cornelius
and his house had taken place, asks, "Who shall forbid
water, that these should not be baptized who have received
the Holy Ghost as well as we?"

But this is too partial an induction; for if we infer
from this that baptism is therefore that in which we
recognize that the gift of the Spirit has been received,
how entirely out of its place must the same apostle
have used it on the day of Pentecost, when he bids the
listening Jews "repent, and be baptized, every one of

---

* The laying on of apostles' hands in certain cases, as at Samaria and at
Ephesus, will be considered in another place.

you, for the remission of sins, and ye *shall* receive the gift of the Holy Ghost" (Acts ii. 38)! How wrongly must it have been administered in Samaria, where it is stated that "as yet He was fallen upon none of them, only they were baptized in the name of the Lord Jesus." (viii. 16.) And again at Ephesus, where we read of certain disciples of John, that "they were baptized in the name of the Lord Jesus; and when Paul had laid his hands on them, the Holy Ghost came upon them." (xix. 5, 6.) Here it is plain that if baptism with water be the recognition of the reception of the Spirit having taken place, Paul, Philip, and Peter himself must have been mistaken. It is simpler to believe that the inference from the case of Cornelius is the real mistake.

And the more we think of it, the more we may thank God that He has not appointed any ordinance as introduction into His Church on earth. The contention about baptism to-day perfectly illustrates the confusion which would have arisen. Have you been sprinkled or immersed? as a child, or an adult believer? What was the formula used? Into what faith? By whose hands? How many questions with which to torture my own soul or the souls of others! How beautifully the very case of Cornelius rebukes it all, where the Holy Ghost falls upon those uncircumcised and unbaptized; and to Peter, hesitating with his Jewish scruples about ordinances, the voice from heaven replies, "What *God* hath cleansed, that call not thou common"!

If, then, the Church is formed by the baptism of the Holy Ghost, and we find in the inspired history of Christianity at the beginning that the Holy Ghost is bestowed *both after and before* the baptism of water, we may see clearly that God has guarded His Church from any such usurpation of ordinances over it. Christ has "blotted out the obligation to ordinances, which was against us, which was contrary to us, and taken it out of the way, nailing it to His cross" (Col. ii. 14, *Gk.*), *not* to replace them with Christian forms for Jewish : baptism and the supper of the Lord stand upon other ground than this.

2. THE POSITIVENESS OF THE GRACE WHICH THE CHURCH EXPRESSES.

Now, if we will consider but a moment what is implied in being a member of Christ, we shall see that there is in it a positiveness of grace such as was never expressed before, such as we can find nowhere else. In Judaism, the house of God was the temple or the tabernacle, not the people of Israel. The body of Christ was a thing unknown. A Jew might look forward to being under Christ, a happy subject of His righteous rule; but of being a member of Christ he could know nothing. Christ had not come, still less taken His place as the human Head of the Church in heaven. The Spirit of God had not come : there was yet no baptism into a body of which there was no head.

The Christian is a child of God, and there were children of God from the earliest ages of the world; but he has, as none had before, the Spirit of adoption, by which he is able to cry, Abba, Father, and to take his place thus *as* a child of God. He has received an everlasting salvation. He is in *known*, near, and eternal relationship, possessor of eternal life, though in the world, no more of it, but dead with Christ, quickened and risen with Him, seated in heavenly places in Christ Jesus.

This is not the place to enter into or discuss the

nature of these blessings: for my present purpose, I must assume them to be known, as they are indeed the common blessings of Christianity, though unbelief and bad teaching may obscure them more or less for even the mass of Christians. But all these things imply a security of blessing which Scripture proclaims to us as to be held in full assurance of faith, never would cast a doubt upon, even for a moment.

The conditional texts, (and there are many in the Word of God,) are all, as it is easy to see if one will examine them with this in view, *tests of profession:* they never imply doubt as to the real child of God. They may say, "Lest, having *preached to others*, I myself should be a cast-away;" never "Lest, after being born again," or "justified," or "having eternal life, I should be a cast-away." That could not be supposed without upsetting the gospel. On the contrary, "he that *saith* he is in the light, and hateth his brother, is in darkness"—now! But may be not once have been in the light? no: he is "in darkness *even until* now." (1 Jno. ii. 9.) And if some have gone out from the Christian body, the apostle is assured by that fact that they were not of it: "They went out," he says, "that it might be made manifest that they all are not of us." (*v.* 19, *R.V.*) So, if justified by the blood of Christ, "much more shall we be saved from wrath through Him." (Rom. v. 9.)

All this is peculiar to Christianity. In Israel under the law such blessed assurance was not attainable, however God might and did minister strength by the way. There was no "Abba, Father," from the Spirit of adoption. God was a Father to *Israel*, a family of the earth brought nigh to Himself, but such relationship involved no necessary salvation, as it implied no new birth. The best saints had to cry, "Cast me not away from Thy presence, and take not Thy Holy Spirit from me." (Ps. li. 11.)

Together under the law, and in the final uncertainty which sprang from that, servants but not sons, the congregation of Israel was a mixed gathering of saints and sinners,—what indeed men have made of the Christian "assembly," but as far as possible from what it was designed to be; the result, too, largely of that Judaizing process going on, which we see at work from the beginning of Christianity, and so steadily resisted everywhere by the apostle of the Gentiles.

3. THE KINGDOM OF GOD.

THE relationship of God to His people Israel was that of King. The temple was His palace, the ark His throne, the human king but His representative, as it is said of Solomon, they "sat upon the throne of the kingdom of the Lord over Israel." (1 Chron. xxviii. 5.) The law of Moses was the rule of this kingdom, the terms of the covenant between God and the people. (Ex. xxxiv. 28.) Of the covenant itself circumcision was the sign, although, as we know, dating from Abraham: the circumcised man was a debtor to do the whole law. (Gal. v. 3.) Every male in the household had to be circumcised, whether Israelite-born or slaves, and only in houses where this was observed could they keep the passover. (Ex. xii. 48.)

Israel's condition under the law was that of bond-servants (Gal. iv. 21-26); they had no permanent standing before God (Jno. viii. 35): so that even the children of God among them in spirit differed nothing from bond-servants. (Gal. iv. 1.) God has always been gracious, and the just have always lived by faith; but "the law is not of faith," and the questions arising out of this contradiction between the two could not yet be settled. Under Moses the nation went on with the accuser to the judge, and the Babylonian captivity saw the glory removed out of the temple, the temple itself destroyed, and Israel branded with the mark, Lo-Ammi, "not My people." (Hos. i. 9.)

The kingdom was now committed to the Gentiles by Him who from heaven governs all things necessarily, as He always did; but with no longer any recognized throne on earth. The Gentile empires that succeed are bestial and without God; and though a remnant of Judah return to their land and rebuild once more the temple, they are still subjected to them, and the decree that has gone out is unrepealed: they are Lo-Ammi still.

So the Lord finds them; but from the Baptist-messenger who has preceded Him a cry has gone forth of recall, "The kingdom of heaven is at hand."

Matthew alone uses this term, for which the other gospels substitute "the kingdom of God." The kingdom of heaven and the kingdom of God are one substantially, whatever difference may be implied in the expression. The parables of the one are able to take their place unchanged as parables of the other. The difference seems to be that while "heaven" is the place of the throne (Matt. v. 34) it is God who sits upon it. The kingdom of heaven seems thus clearly distinct from that which had been in Israel. Then it was "the ark of Jehovah, the Lord of all the earth," that passed through Jordan. (Josh. iii. 13.) At the end of Chronicles, in Ezra, Nehemiah, and Daniel, it is of **the God of heaven** that we hear continually. And if this implies withdrawal, in a sense, from earth, where the throne is given to the Gentile, yet God's steps are never really retrograde, but in advance. Heaven is now to be opened to us, as Daniel shows us One who is the Son of Man coming in the clouds of heaven to receive the kingdom. In Matthew, in the sermon on the mount, which is in fact the announcement of the kingdom as it will yet be when Israel shall receive their Messiah, heaven is God's throne, the earth His footstool, Jerusalem the city of the great King; and if on the one hand, there are meek ones (comp. Ps. xxxvii.) whose blessedness will be in an inheritance on earth, there are those whom the world has persecuted for Christ's sake, and whose reward will be great in heaven. Heaven and earth are indeed to be linked together now, as the book of Revelation very distinctly shows us, the new Jerusalem, the heavenly city, coming down from God out of heaven, not exactly *to earth*, which is not said: there is no confusion between earth and heaven, as now so often made; and yet into such close connection that it can be said, "The tabernacle of God is with men, and He will dwell with them."

This is in the "kingdom and glory" yet to come; but there is a phase of the kingdom now, in which it is joined with another characteristic expression, "the kingdom and *patience* of Jesus" (Rev. i 9), truly the kingdom of heaven, for He sits upon the Father's throne (iii. 21), waiting to take that throne of His as Son of Man, upon which He will be able to grant His saints to sit with Him. The distinction between these two phases of the kingdom is therefore abundantly plain.

When the Lord came to His own, the kingdom was in His person offered to them; and of that therefore the early announcements, whether of the Baptist or the Lord, speak. But when it becomes plain that He is rejected by Israel, and in the eleventh and twelfth of Matthew He has declared their rejection and judgment in consequence, He disowns His merely natural ties, proclaims that His real kindred were those who did the will of His Father in heaven, and then, leaving the house, and sitting by the sea-side, He gives utterance to those parables in which the new phase of the kingdom is presented. (Chap. xiii.)

The ministers of Christ are "stewards of the mysteries of God." (1 Cor. iv. 1.) And these mysteries are "things hidden from ages and generations, and now made manifest to the saints." (Col. i. 26.) All that we have seen of the Church as the body of Christ is such a mystery (Eph. iii. 9); but there are "mysteries of the kingdom of heaven" also, which the Lord opens in these parables (xiii. 11): the parabolic form being evidence that we have in them what was hidden from Israel, according to the prophecy which Matthew quotes: "I will open my mouth in parables: I will utter things which have been kept secret from the foundation of the world" (*vv.* 34, 35).

Accordingly, we find in them such a state of things as in the coming kingdom cannot be. It is a kingdom which is brought about, not by the coming of the Son of Man from heaven, but by the sowing of seed—"the word of the kingdom"—upon earth. But here in many, in whom it seems to have taken root, there is yet no fruit. Contrary influences, the world, the flesh, and the devil, destroy much. Worse still, the enemy, not shut up as he will be when the kingdom comes in power (Rev. xx. 1–3), sows his own seed, what is not the word of God, but its semblance only, and tares are found among the wheat, not to be removed till the day of harvest. Then indeed the kingdom seems to root itself in the earth, but to become itself earthly, and shelter the birds of the air, the powers of evil. And into the good bread of life itself the "woman," the professing church, puts the evil leaven which diffuses itself until the whole is leavened.

These are the pictures of the kingdom which the first four parables present to us. Every where we see strife of good and evil in it, and even that the victory does not seem with the good, but with the evil; until indeed the day of manifestation come, and angel-hands apply the remedy when the Son of Man again appears. The first parable gives, as we might expect, the secret of the whole condition. It is a kingdom of truth (Jno. xviii. 37), into which men are discipled (Matt. xiii. 52, *R. V.*); and where discipling may mean very different things,—mere head-knowledge, barren profession, or continuance in the Word so as to be disciples indeed. (Jno. viii. 31.) Subjection to Christ may be nominal or real; they may say, "Lord, Lord," and not do the things that He says. But this lasts only till the day of manifestation; and when the kingdom comes in power, then it is written, "Except a man be born again, he cannot see the kingdom of God," and "Except ye be converted, and become as little children, ye shall in no wise enter into the kingdom of heaven."

4. THE THREE CIRCLES IN EPH. IV.

In connection with the sevenfold unity of which the apostle speaks in Eph. iv., a threefold sphere of blessing is plainly to be seen, based upon the relationships of the Godhead to us. "There is one body and one Spirit, even as ye are called in one hope of your calling; one Lord, one faith, one baptism; one God and Father of all who is over all and through all, and in all." There are here three concentric circles: that of the Church, that of the kingdom, and that of creation. Let us look at them distinctly a little.

That of the Church is plain: "one body" is, of course, the body of Christ. It would be impossible to multiply this into many bodies, impossible to have more than one Church. The "one Spirit" unites together the members of the body, and animates them, uniting them also to the head. Then, as the "calling" of the Church is distinct, so must be the special "hope."

The second circle is not less distinct, one would think, yet it is much more disputed. "One Lord" should prepare us, however, to read aright what follows. It has been seen by many that Christ does not take ever in relation to His saints now the title of King. He does not the less reign, surely; and it is His grace only that avoids the distance which might seem implied. Christians are known as those that "call upon the name of Jesus Christ our Lord." This is for us the title He is pleased to assume.

"One faith" evidently means what some would call one *creed*, not faith as the principle of dependence upon God, in which sense "one" faith would hardly be intelligible.

In connection, then, with "one Lord, one faith," we have "one baptism." This has been thought by some to be the baptism of the Spirit; but this, as what forms the body, would certainly have place in the first circle, and there would be needless, as one Spirit coupled with one body expresses already all. Moreover, "baptism" by itself naturally means the rite;

when used with other applications, other words are added in explanation. Water-baptism also, as we shall find fully as we go on, is that which is connected with the sphere of discipleship, that is, of the kingdom, as that of the Spirit is with the Church.

We have now a third sphere, one closing unity, "one God and Father of all, who is above (or over) all, and through all, and in all." This last is undeniably the reading of all the oldest manuscripts though the early versions have "in *us* all." I apprehend that the manuscripts are right, and that the "Father in us" is not a scriptural thought. It is said of Christ, and of Him alone, who was the Father's representative in the world. But if so, that would forbid the "over all and through all" being said of persons, though "Father of all" must of course be of persons. But how widely, then, does this apply? Is it of all *men*, or of all *believers?* It seems to me designedly left vague. Creation is that which gives the first ground of the title; but here the fall has brought in breach and disorder, and the Lord says to the Jews, "If God were your Father, ye would love Me." New creation must, therefore, come, and by new birth we are children of God in a nearer and more wonderful way than before. But new creation does not take us out of creation as such, in which man alone upon the earth has been the transgressor. "Over all, through all, in all," seems to take in the whole sphere of things wherein, blessed be God, we still find Him.

There are certainly here three circles. The Church is not the kingdom, whatever the comparative extent of these two may be. And the sphere of creation is different from either. But all this will become clearer as we go on: it is by the comparison of scripture with scripture that, as in the mouth of two or three witnesses, every word must be established.

5. THE PARABLES OF THE KINGDOM: ARE THEY JEWISH, OR CHRISTIAN?*

A QUESTION must now be looked at which is of the utmost importance to the whole inquiry. It has of late been taught by some that the parables of the kingdom in the gospels are Jewish, and not Christian,— that they refer to a future time, when the Church of God shall have been removed from the scene, and Israel be in the troubles of the last days, through which they shall be awakened and brought to God. Thus we must not take the kingdom of heaven as applying to the present time, with which it is in entire contrast; the kingdom now is only by the personal presence of the Spirit of God in the individual, and in no other way. Church and Kingdom now are therefore in the strictest sense conterminous: the rule of Christ is only by the Spirit indwelling, and this is what forms the Church, as we have seen.

The arguments as to the parables are these :—

(1) First, and really, as it would appear, the foundation one, the word "then" in Matt. xxv. 1, whereby the parable of the ten virgins is shown clearly to refer to the period and events of chap. xxiv. "It is *then*, when the wide world owns the sovereignty of the beast, (Rev. xiii.) that the kingdom of the heavens, comprising those who are undefiled by the universal worship (Rev. xiv.), shall be like unto ten virgins who . . . . go forth to meet Him whom their soul loveth (Song i.

---

*By those who have no question as to the Christian application, this section may be omitted without loss to the general argument. It necessarily refers to views and details of prophecy which cannot be here fully entered into, and may thus present difficulty to those not familiar with the subject.

and iii.); but in the lull which precedes the storm of the great tribulation (Ezek. xxxviii. 8, last clause), they all slumber and sleep till awakened by the cry, 'Behold the Bridegroom' . . . Then all arise to testify again in the teeth of the beast, the false prophet, and the whole world."

Now, that the "then" which begins the parable refers in some sense to the "period and events" of the chapter before will surely not be denied. If we turn to the questions of the disciples, to which the whole prophecy is in answer, we shall find that they are three: "When shall these things be? and what shall be the sign of Thy coming, and of the end of the *age* (not world)?" For the Jews, the "present age" was the age of law, the "age to come" the age of Messiah. The coming of the Son of Man would, according to Daniel, introduce the latter, and thus end the former. passing briefly over the answer to the first question, (which Luke, chap. xxi., gives in full,) Matthew dwells upon the last two. The prophecy shows us, first, Israel, then the Church, and then the Gentile nations in connection with the end, giving, naturally, along with this, sufficient of their previous history to make all intelligible. Thus, in the parable of the talents (xxv. 14), He goes back to the time of His going away to heaven, before which He delivers them to His servants. Are these also (as they should be, to make all consistent with the new interpretation,) a Jewish remnant in days yet to come? That is impossible: the Lord is speaking of Christian times; and this parable of the talents is so connected with the previous one as to make it certain that this must be also Christian.

This by itself is enough; for the "then," while it does refer to the coming of the Lord, does not preclnde the history of what precedes. But there are other things, as the *going out* to meet the Bridegroom, which is not an idea suited to Israel, who abide on earth, and are *not* caught away to meet Him. Then whose is the Bridegroom? I should agree in this with those who hold the new views, that it is Israel's; but then the virgins and the bride must be distinct, as in this case they are not, but confounded. Others have, I know, made similar confusion from the other point of view; but there is no justification of it on this account.

(2) In the second place, it is urged that "in the parable, the wicked are gathered first; in what is now, the saints are gathered first, and afterward come with the Lord. In what is now, the saints are taken out and the wicked left for wrath to come. In the parable, the scene is cleared of the wicked; in this dispensation, it is cleared of the Church; and whereas the former does not occur until the consummation of the age, the last may occur at any moment."

The fundamental facts here are in no wise a new discovery of the writer's,* although he states them in a way which is careless enough when one considers his knowledge of much that has been written. In the parable of the tares, they are gathered and bound in bundles to be burned, and then the wheat is gathered into the barn. The interpretation carries the action of the parable further,—the wicked are cast into the fire, and the righteous shine forth as the sun in the kingdom of their Father. Here, the righteous are seen to be heavenly saints, as the figure shows; and also *where*

---

*He owes them, with many others, to the labors of one whom nevertheless he does not cease to attack and vilify in the most open and shameless way, but to whom multitudes, with himself, owe the recovery of truths lost to the Church from the earliest ages. I do not defend him: his memory has no need.

they shine, for the kingdom of the Father is *not* the millennial kingdom of the Son of Man. But these *must* be the wheat of the parable, if the interpretation is interpretation at all. It must surely be, therefore, that the gathering into bundles, though an angelic act, speaks of something different from removal from the earth, as indeed the "bundles" would seem also to imply.

In the net cast into the sea, however, it is different. There, the wicked are taken out of the midst of the just; and there, by the same rule, if the interpretation is really that, then the parable must refer to something outside the present dispensation. The truth seems to be that the parables as a whole take in the whole time from the sowing of the seed of the kingdom by the Lord Himself on earth till the time He comes in glory; and thus take in the present Church-period, and that which follows it, the time of the going forth of the everlasting gospel as in Rev. xiv. In this way all is harmony.

(3) The objection that "these parables summarize all prophecy in relation to God's earthly people," and that "prophecy is not connected with the Pauline dispensation," for proof of which, we are referred to Eph. iii. 5–9, is in many ways strange enough. Of course, if they *do* summarize all prophecy as to Israel, they cannot—primarily, at least,—apply to the Church, the *heavenly* people: that is clear. But it has to be proved that this is what they do. And *if* they do, it seems strange that they should be said by Matthew himself to be of "things which have been kept *secret* from the foundation of the world." Surely that which was uttered by all the prophets could not at the same time have been "kept secret"! And the reference to

Ephesians is on this account still more strange. That *Old-Testament* prophecy does not speak of the "Pauline" dispensation is of course true, though the *New* Testament is not similarly silent.

Thus if the disciples professed their understanding of the parables, it could not be, as the writer states, from their knowledge of prophecy! That was only a knowledge of *old* things, to which the parables added now the new. (xiii. 52.) Moreover, they could understand, in general, the drift of these parables without the knowledge of the special Church-truth committed to Paul afterward, which is not revealed in them, however much it may enable us to understand better certain details of them.

(4) But it is inferred that the kingdom of heaven involves "the rule of the heavens, therefore of God, over the entire scene," and in such sort that "the bare fact of the existence and triumphant wickedness of the murderers of the upright"—Rome—"should have convinced us that the sphere called 'Christendom' cannot possibly be the sphere of the rule of the heavens and of God."

To this it is sufficient to answer that the parables themselves speak quite differently. The first four parables, which, as spoken to the multitude, and not as the last three—in the house, speak of the open, external aspect of things, present to us a constantly increasing power of evil till the end of that form of the kingdom which they picture. The devil, the flesh, and the world destroy three parts of the good seed in the first parable. In the second, there are tares, the direct growth of Satan's sowing,—not truth, but a lie, therefore,—right among the wheat. In the third, there is but *one* seed, and the general result is pictured,—the wonder being that a little seed springs into a tree, such as, in Dan. iv., the king of Babylon is compared to, and which shelters the fowls of the air, which in the first parable represent the instruments of Satan; while in the last, the woman (the professing church) hides the leaven in the meal, or corrupts the bread of life with the leaven of falsehood. Here the state of things continually gets worse, and, general as the picture is, it certainly does more than leave room for, rather it implies (if not in all her features,) the woman Jezebel of Revelation.

How, then, can her actual existence in Christendom convince us that the parables do not apply to Christendom? It is the exactness of the picture which should convince us of what it is the picture. And these four parables are exact, even as to their minutest features, in the delineation of Christendom, of those in professed subjection to Christ, which is just the sphere of the kingdom and of discipleship.

6. The Kingdom of God's dear Son.

Mark and Luke repeat some of these parables of the kingdom of heaven, just substituting for this phrase "the kingdom of God." And among these, Mark introduces another which gives plainly the present form of it (chap. iv. 26–29): "So is the kingdom of God, as if a man should cast seed into the ground, and should sleep and rise, night and day, and the seed should spring and grow up he knoweth not how . . . but when the fruit is brought forth, immediately he putteth in the sickle, because the harvest is come." This agrees exactly with the present state of the kingdom, as the fruit of the Lord's personal presence and labor in the world, now left apparently to itself, but the field to be reaped when He comes again. Nothing but Christendom can possibly answer to such a picture as this. Israel will not have the Lord *personally* to cast seed into the ground after the Church is removed, nor will they be brought in as a continuation of present gospel-work. "As concerning the gospel," says the apostle, "they are enemies for your sakes." (Rom. xi. 28.)

But if this be so, it is monstrous to contend that the kingdom of God now is "by the personal presence of the Spirit of God, and in no other way." That "the kingdom of God is not in word, but in power" (1 Cor. iv. 20) does not prove it; nor that it is "righteousness and peace and joy in the Holy Ghost." (Rom. xiv. 17.) These things indeed characterize it where real in the heart, but there are, none the less, subjects that are not really subject, and disciples that are not "disciples indeed." No doubt, where what is thus truly characteristic is spoken of, it is the "kingdom of God" that is the term employed; yet in the parables of the kingdom of heaven also, it is the "good seed" that is "the children of the kingdom." Nor can it be well maintained, with the parables before us, that there are two kingdoms, contemporaneous with one another, unequal in extent, and both of God.

The kingdom of God's dear Son, once mentioned (Col. i. 13), is evidently again simply the kingdom of God as it now exists, with the Son sitting on the Father's throne. (Rev. iii. 21.) The apostle speaks of the saints as "giving thanks unto the Father . . . who hath delivered us from the authority of darkness, and translated us into the kingdom of His dear Son," a thing in which every true child of the kingdom may unfeignedly rejoice, spite of the sorrowful fact that others, outwardly in the kingdom, have not in heart bowed to the Son, nor found therefore the deliverance. It will not do to argue from such a scripture, as the writer referred to does, that "saints only are within it." This is not said, and one has no title no say it. Condition is implied, in the kingdom in its present form, as we may now go on to see.

7. THE KINGDOM RUNNING THROUGH THE DISPENSATIONS.

THE Church which is Christ's body we have seen to be peculiar to the present dispensation; and the House of God to be, in God's thought, but the same Church in another aspect. The Kingdom, on the contrary, in what is essential to it, runs through the Jewish and the Christian dispensations both, though not without a break, when Israel became Lo-Ammi, and the throne on earth was transferred to the Gentiles.

The members of Christ's body have a place in positive relationship to Him, and as children of God, with the Spirit of adoption theirs, able to cry, Abba, Father.

With the subjects of the kingdom *as such*, on the contrary, all is conditional. In Israel there was no formal separation even between believers and unbelievers. They were one of the "families of the earth" adopted by God as His, but on that very account the true children of God not distinguished from the rest. In the parables of the kingdom of heaven we find a mixture to a large extent similar, tares not for some time distinguishable from the wheat, and never allowed to be separated by servants' hands. Under Israel's legal covenant every thing was of necessity conditional, blessing suspended on obedience simply. In the epistles we are all aware of much conditional teaching also, nowhere connected with the children of God or members of Christ as such, but in view of discipleship and a mixed profession—that is, the kingdom.

In Christianity, however, there is a notable difference from Judaism, because of the grace that has replaced law. The question is now whether this grace has been accepted, not of obedience to any legal code: but the acceptance implies that in case of such acceptance, a real change in heart and life will have resulted from it. Take one of the parables of the kingdom, Matt. xviii. 23-35: here the confessedly bankrupt debtor is forgiven freely an immense debt; but, untouched by this forgiveness, he exacts from a fellow-servant a paltry debt to himself, and is cast into prison without hope of redemption. Here, forgiveness itself is in the kingdom-view of it conditional.

In Israel a man was a Jew by nature (Gal. ii. 15), the necessary consequence of God's adoption of one of the families of the earth. Yet he must be circumcised, must receive in his flesh the token of it, or he would be cut off. The Israelite was circumcised at eight days old; infant circumcision was the rule and imperative; but if a stranger desired to partake of the passover, he could by circumcision enter the assembly, all the males of his household being circumcised with him. This was, if one may say so, the *grace of the law*.

But Israel have ceased in the meanwhile to be the people of God; the *national birthright entrance* into the kingdom has failed therefore with this. There remains but the other form, that of *proselyte* entrance; the bringing into a kingdom which is the fruit of the word of the kingdom sown as seed in the world, is "discipling." Men are "*discipled* into the kingdom of heaven," (Matt. xiii. 52, *Gk.*) The *grace* of the law is that which abides, now that the legal form is passed away. Grace reigns. Circumcision which makes a "debtor to do the whole law" (Gal. v. 3) is passed away with the law. Has anything taken its place, as an outward introduction to the kingdom of God? And in this new "discipling to the kingdom," is there a place provided for the children of proselytes, as under the law when the males were circumcised? These questions lead us on directly to the doctrine of baptism.

8. The Baptisms of the Law.

Baptism as we find it in Christianity is not an entirely new thing, but has its roots in the previous dispensation. There were Jewish baptisms more than one, which had an important place under the law; and the consideration of these will naturally prepare us for the better understanding of the New-Testament form. It is well known that "there is an universal agreement among later Jewish writers that all the Israelites were brought into covenant with God by circumcision, baptism, and sacrifice, and that the same ceremonies were necessary in admitting proselytes" (Smith's Dictionary). But of this, Scripture says nothing, and we can build only on what is found in it. Apart from this altogether there were legal baptisms, although we must go to the New Testament for the word. This is applied in Mark (vii. 4, 8) and Luke (xi. 38) to mere ceremonial and traditional "washings," as to which we have only to note that they were clearly symbols of purification with a supposed sacramental efficacy. Similarly, it is when a dispute had arisen about purifying that John's disciples come and tell him that Jesus was baptizing. (Jno. iii. 26.)

It is only in Hebrews beside, and in two passages

that we have reference to Jewish baptisms. As clearest we may take the latter first, which the Revised Version gives as follows: "According to which are offered both gifts and sacrifices that cannot, as touching the conscience, make the worshiper perfect, being only (with meats and drinks and divers washings) carnal ordinances, imposed until a time of reformation." (Heb. ix. 10.) But this is not, as to the parenthesis thus introduced, an improvement on the common version. The word (*epi*) translated "with" has indeed very commonly the meaning of "with, in addition to," but it also means "dependent on," and this removes the parenthesis and brings what is contained in it into the main argument where it surely belongs. For why are they carnal ordinances, these gifts and sacrifices? Plainly, because they depend upon "meats and drinks and divers *baptisms*"—the real word. How could offerings consisting of such things set at rest the conscience?

The "divers baptisms" belonged, then, to this service of gifts and offerings. They were, according to what we have seen already, the directly purificatory part. In a sacrificial service they can only mean one thing, and that the apostle explains to us in the verses that almost immediately follow here: "For if the *blood of goats and bulls and the ashes of a heifer sprinkling* them that have been defiled sanctify unto the cleanness of the flesh, how much more shall the blood of Christ . . . cleanse your conscience?" Here are purifications, sacrificial, of diverse character, (blood and ashes,) and those which the apostle is comparing and contrasting with what *does* now perfect the conscience in the time of reformation which is now come.

One thing only here can be objected in the face of

this decisive argument, that these "baptisms" must be in this case sprinklings and not immersions, which, it is granted on all hands, is the *primary* meaning of the word. The answer is that Scripture has changed many words from their primary meaning, and that this is one of them. The force of "baptism" in the New Testament does not depend upon the mode at all. When Israel were "baptised unto Moses in the cloud and in the sea," they were not immersed in either, and to introduce the thought into the passage would turn its solemn significance into absolute folly. In that wonderful way they were broken off from their past in Egypt and taken into Moses' school: that entrance accompanied by a wonderful lesson of the power and majesty of a Saviour-God. After all this, to turn their Deliverer into a destroyer!

Then take the baptism into one body, baptism into Christ, baptism into His death, nothing surely but very strange prepossession with an idea could make the thought of immersion in one of these cases seem reasonable or right. But we are anticipating what will be more fittingly our subject at another time.

The other passage which speaks of these Jewish baptisms is in Heb. vi. 2 : "Not laying again the foundation of repentance from dead works, and of faith toward God, of the teaching of baptisms and of laying on of hands, and of resurrection of the dead, and of eternal judgment." These things, from the words immediately preceding them, and from the presence among them of baptism and laying on of hands, have been by almost general consent taken to be the *Christian* foundation, despite the evident fact that Christ is not so much as named in it! The common version of the previous words, not bettered in the revised, reads,

"Therefore leaving the principles of the doctrine of Christ, let us go on unto perfection;" but which the margin gives literally as "leaving the *word of the beginning* of Christ." *This is Judaism*, which could not be more accurately characterized in connection with the full "perfection" of Christianity itself. Writing to Jewish converts, the apostle exhorts them not to go back to what they had left, and lay again a foundation which ignored Christ as come, though it might have many truths beside. Notice, that while repentance, faith in God, resurrection and judgment are spoken of in plain terms, the truth indeed to perfect the conscience, of which Paul speaks in the ninth chapter, is entirely wanting, while in its place we find that very "teaching of baptisms," which he shows there to be but the Jewish shadow of it! That should surely make clear of what he is speaking, while "the laying on of hands" connected with this is easily understood as in Judaism that identification of the offerer with his sacrifice which was of such importance to acceptance through it.

But these things so necessary for the soul, were but taught in type and shadow. How needful to exhort them to leave the word of the beginning of Christ and to go on to perfection! How this strengthens the interpretation of the ninth chapter is easy to be seen.

9. The Baptism of John and of the Lord by him.

A SLIGHT difference in the form of the word distinguishes the Jewish baptisms from those of the New Testament. The Jewish baptism is *baptismos*, that of the New Testament, *baptisma*. The difference in meaning is, that, while *baptismos* speaks of the transient act only, *baptisma* speaks of the *result* of the act, a state induced. The Jewish ones were transient and might be repeated; the Christian introduces into a permanent condition.

And this was true in measure of John's baptism, the forerunner of our Lord. To his baptism we next come, to learn from it what we may as to the Christian rite.

John's baptism was a baptism of repentance to prepare people for the coming Lord. Hence it was a purification —a "baptism of repentance,"—and marked out and separated a remnant from the mass of the people to escape the coming judgment. He stands himself aloof from the nation, not going up to Jerusalem, though the son of a priest, but in the deserts until the time of his showing unto Israel. In his dress and food he shows the same separateness. He preaches in the wilderness, telling the people that they must not think to say within themselves that they have Abraham for their father, because God was able of the very stones to raise up children to Abraham. The multitudes came therefore to his baptism, confessing their sins, and were baptized of him in Jordan, the river of death, as owning that all was over with them as to natural claim, and divine mercy in a Saviour alone could meet their need. They are therefore baptized for, or rather unto* remission of sins, awaiting this in hope, though not yet having received it.

John's baptism is thus a *baptisma* in bringing into a

---

* *Eis*, "unto," with a verb of motion, signifies a direction toward, generally, but not necessarily, reaching its end: "The other disciple came first *to* the sepulchre, . . yet went he not in. Simon Peter, following him, went *into* the sepulchre." (Jno. xx. 4, 6.) Here it is both "unto" and "into." "When transferred to metaphysical relations," says Winer, "*eis* is used to express a mark or aim of any kind." (*Grammar of New Testament Greek*.)

state of discipleship to John, which was necessarily however to merge into another and higher condition when He whom John heralded should appear. John's disciples at Ephesus, when they have heard from Paul the complete gospel, are thus baptised with Christian baptism. (Acts xix. 5.)

Nevertheless the Lord Himself comes expressly from Galilee to Jordan unto John, to be baptized of him. What was the meaning of this in the case of One who could indeed have no need of repentance, nor sins to confess? That the Lord could be in this a pattern of "believer's baptism" is a strange thing for any one with the least intelligence of Scripture to maintain. Was *He* baptized as a penitent believer, who was Himself faith's object,—not a Christian, but the Christian's Christ? And was it for *Him* to "fulfill all righteousness," to take His place as that He was not? Surely the Father's witness to His own beloved Son should check this strange and unworthy thought.

And yet there is a certain resemblance which we should not overlook. There is a fulfillment of righteousness in it which He plainly declares, and in which He joins others with Himself: "thus it becometh *us*." Who are intended by this "us"? It has been said that it means John and the Lord; but it does not seem as John in his baptizing others could be said to fulfill righteousness; and it does seem as if rather those who were being baptized would be associated with Him who was submitting now to baptism. It is, in fact, the first step in righteousness for the sinner to confess his sins. But how could there be any parallel to this in the Lord's case? Just in this, that He could confess for *them* the sins whose burden He was to take upon Himself! Righteous indeed was He who could diminish nothing of what was in its awful penalty to be alone His own!

The moment we realize this meaning in His act every thing comes into solemn harmony. Jordan, in which He is baptized, is indeed the river of death, and in the death He took was His confession of sin and its desert. At an after-time, He spoke of it under the same figure as here, a baptism with which He was to be baptized. (Mark x. 38.) Then the place in which this baptism takes place is just as He emerges out of His private into His public life, ending His own individual life where He enters upon His ministry for others, receiving from His Father the attestation of His own perfection, and that anointing of the Spirit by which He becomes, in actual fact, the Christ, that is, the Anointed! "Therefore doth My Father love Me," He says, "because I lay down My life that I might take it again;" and when in this symbol He pledges Himself to lay down His life, the attestation of delight is heard.

Thus it should be plain that the Lord's baptism by John signified what was absolutely unique and peculiar to Himself. It was not an example for us, but a precious witness for us of the work for us which He now took up, only to lay it down with full accomplishment.

10. The Keys of the Kingdom.

CHRISTIAN baptism was not instituted till the Lord rose from the dead. He did indeed baptize, though not personally, but by the hands of His disciples, while He lived upon earth; but this seems only to have been akin to John's baptism. We have only the briefest notice of it (Jno. iii. 22; iv. 1, 2). And it is plainly after His resurrection that we find the only commission of which we have any account, and which contemplates all the nations of the earth, and continuance till the end of the age. (Matt. xxviii. 18-20.)

There are various reasons for this, as we may shortly see; but one is apparent, that if the "one baptism" of Christianity is connected with its "one Lord," or the kingdom in its present form, it is only as risen that He says, "All authority is given unto Me in heaven and in earth," and upon this He bases the commission, "Go ye *therefore*, and disciple all nations."

Let us turn back from this, then, to examine what the Lord had said before this, as to entrance into the kingdom then not come. It is in immediate connection with His announcement of the Church, and to the same person: "And I will give unto thee the keys (not of the Church, but) of the kingdom of heaven; and whatsoever thou shalt bind on earth shall be bound in heaven, and whatsoever thou shalt loose on earth shall be loosed in heaven." (Matt. xvi. 19.)

The fact that this is said to Peter only has been misinterpreted by many so as to reduce it to comparative insignificance. It has been supposed to limit the possession of the keys to him alone, and has been applied to his double opening of the kingdom, first, on the day of Pentecost, to the Jews, and then, in Cornelius and his friends, to the Gentiles. Thus the import of the announcement is wholly in the past, and we of to-day have but little interest in it.

But can it be possible that this is all? Are the keys of the kingdom of heaven something for which there is no need to-day? Has the kingdom been just opened and then left open? Is there no need of reception into it, and no power to receive? Are people born naturally into it now? or what else?

That the keys are for admission can scarcely be disputed. It is the proper use of a key to open; and where the Lord in Matt. xxiii. 13 charges the scribes with shutting up the kingdom of heaven against men, He shows in Luke xi. 52 how they have done it: "Ye have taken away the key of knowledge." Knowledge must needs be one key to a kingdom springing out of the sowing of the seed of the Word. The taking it away must prevent discipleship. Here is one key, then, certainly, and the apostle at Pentecost and in Cornelius' house was plainly using this key to open the kingdom to them.

But were these the only occasions? And when Paul preached everywhere the kingdom of God, was he using the key any less than Peter? Or when he says, in Gal. ii., that the gospel of the uncircumcision was committed unto him as the gospel of the circumcision had been to Peter, did he mean in either case that no one else had commission from God to preach it?

Peter had in an eminent way the keys, no doubt, but no exclusive right: and this is plain; for if these words "to thee" excluded others, then the next clause gives him as exclusive right to bind and to loose; but that he had not this is proved absolutely by the Lord's extension of this elsewhere: "Whatsoever *ye* shall bind," etc.

Moreover, if Peter opened the door at one time to Jews, at another to Gentiles, this is opening the door twice, but it is not using two keys; nor could two keys be needed, if this were all. We have seen what one key is, but we must still find another: where shall we find it?

11. THE COMMISSION TO DISCIPLE.

IT is after our Lord is risen from the dead that He

proclaims Himself now in actual fact the King of the kingdom. All authority is His; and his kingdom be-ing a kingdom of the truth, He sends His disciples out with a commission to *disciple* all the nations. Here the power of the keys, then, is committted to them all, and certainly not to Peter only. Besides, it is not even as apostles He commissions them. They are not called such in the passage, and had it been intended that theirs should be an exclusive right, it would surely have been intimated. But it is not so; and the words of the commission are,—

"Go ye, therefore, and disciple all the nations, bap-tizing them unto the name of the Father and the Son and the Holy Ghost: teaching them to observe all things whatever I have commanded you; and, lo, I am with you always, even unto the consummation of the age."

It has been thought by some, because "all the na-tions" is the general expression for the Gentiles, that Israel is not in the commission; but if not, to whom did Peter apply it on the day of Pentecost? was it not to Israel? It is clear that he does so apply it, and that if Israel were, as we know they were, Lo-ammi, then they were simply part of the "all nations" to whom the gospel of the kingdom now was being sent. Thus alone can we escape from many serious difficulties, which at once disappear, if this be in fact the truth.

The common version translates "*teach* all nations," but puts "make disciples" in the margin. The revised more correctly puts the latter into the text. Strictly it is, not a verb with a noun following, but a simple verb, "*disciple*," and this has its importance: for in the former case, it would be *disciples* that would be to be baptized, while, as it really is, it is the *nations* who are to be discipled, by baptizing them.

Now, if "discipling" be introducing into the kingdom of heaven, we have here the other key that we were just now seeking. Nay, we have the two, "baptizing and teaching," and in the last recognize the one which has already been named as such by our Lord Himself, "The key of knowledge." This confirms, if it were needed, that baptism is indeed a "key," which if we look on to Pentecost, we shall find the apostle using. For when the Jews are pricked to the heart by the proclamation of the King of the new kingdom, and cry out, "Brethren, what shall we do?" he replies, "Repent, and be baptized every one of you, in the name of Jesus Christ for the remission of sins, and ye shall receive the gift of the Holy Ghost."

To this we must return. Let us notice first more fully the words of the commission: "Disciple, baptising and teaching," show in their order that the teaching is that which perfects the disciple,—necessarily, because a "disciple" is a scholar: the baptism only gives him his place as that; it is authoritative reception into the school. It is the marking off, in a world which has rejected Christ and His words, of those who receive them and thus acknowledge Him. It shows that the kingdom is not territorial, that people are not born naturally into it, that it is individual now, not national, as in the case of Israel. The meaning of it as a symbol shows much more than this. Whether this subjection to Christ is real or not remains to be determined, and is not to be settled beforehand by the baptizer; although, of course, that in which it is professed must not be suffered to lapse from its meaning and be trifled with by frivolous use. But the King welcomes freely, and the place in the kingdom is after all a conditional one.

This baptizing is "unto the name of the Father, and of the Son, and of the Holy Ghost." The *name*, not the *names*, of the Triune. This is the Christian revelation of God; and what is not done in this way is not Christian. The "name" in Scripture gives the real character of what it stands for; and the name here is the truth of the Godhead as now made known to us: thus "baptism" and the "faith" are once more, as in Eph. iv. ("one faith, one baptism,"), connected together.

"Unto" is here manifestly more correct than the "into" of the Revised Version; for baptism cannot bring *into* this or any other *faith*, but attaches one *to* it.

Thus we have also the plain confirmation of baptizing being discipling; for what else does being baptized to a faith mean but that?

We are told, however, that "Jesus *made* and *baptized* disciples" (Jno. iv. 1), and that this gives a contrary thought. But, in fact, it only emphasizes what is true, —that it is the Word, the teaching, that *really* makes disciples, which is of course true. If we think of what is implied in discipleship, the Word is necessarily the fundamental thing, the water but the formal, although that too may have importance. Who would say that the dying thief was not a disciple, although he had no opportunity of being baptized? On the other hand, to say that Jesus "made and baptized disciples" does not necessarily mean that they were disciples *first*, as the second part of the statement may be explanatory of the former, and needed to complete the idea to be conveyed: as when it is said (Ex. xxix. 7), "Thou shalt pour it upon his head and anoint him," these two things are really one, and not different acts; and the last expression but explains the former.

12. THE EXECUTION OF THE COMMISSION.

On the day of Pentecost, Peter uses the keys, as we have seen. First, he preaches the kingdom: "Therefore, let all the house of Israel know assuredly that God hath made that same Jesus, whom ye have crucified, both Lord and Christ." Then, in answer to their question, "What shall we do?" he replies, "Repent, and be baptized, every one of you, in the name of Jesus Christ, unto the remission of your sins, and ye shall receive the gift of the Holy Ghost." "In" the name here might perhaps be better rendered "at." It is that same *epi* with a dative following, which often signifies "dependent on." Hearing of Jesus as Lord and Christ, and thus witnessed to by the gifts of the Spirit, at that name they were to repent and be baptized, baptism being the confession of His authority. They would then receive themselves the wondrous gift.

Israel had formally rejected Christ, and were outside His kingdom now begun. Repentance and the open acknowledgment of His authority were now necessary that their sins might be remitted, and themselves be sealed with His distinctive seal.

It cannot be doubted that the apostle puts baptism here as something to precede the gift of the Holy Ghost. It *has* been doubted,—and denied,—that he so intends to make it precede the remission of sins. And it has been contended that, instead of this, baptism unto the remission of sins means (like baptism unto the name of the Godhead) unto the *faith* of the remission of sins.

But there is this difference, that "the name" at once indicates doctrine,—the faith; and there is nothing similar to that here. We have also the kindred expression used by Ananias, "Arise and be baptized, and *wash away thy sins*, calling on His name." (Acts xxii. 16, *R. V.*) Here one would think it would be too plain for doubt that baptism was represented as (in some sense,) the washing away of sins. It has, however, been objected that the person is active in washing away his sins, passive when they are remitted; but this is a distinction that vanishes when we take the original. Both verbs are in what is called in Greek the middle voice: hence we might as well translate "baptize thyself" as "wash thyself from thy sins"—this is the form. Yet we know, as to the first, he could only put himself into the hands of others.

But this view of "remission" is thought to be contrary to all Scripture. On the contrary, it helps much to the understanding of one passage which is Scripture as much as any other. For it was to Peter as well as other disciples that the Lord said, after His resurrection, "Whose sins ye remit, they are remitted unto them, and whose sins ye retain, they are retained." Now, if the baptism of these three thousand at Pentecost was in fact the remission of their sins, then there is a clear illustration and example of what our Lord meant. In fact, if it be not found here, I know not where in Scripture we may find it. If baptism be in any sense for the remission of sins, then it is a remission committed to disciples, and whomsoever they baptize, they in that sense remit his sins.

Perilously near to Rome, some may think; but how can we get nearer to Rome than by blinking or denying Scripture? The words are there: we have only to look them in the face as friends, to find that they are in perfect harmony with the fullest and freest gospel, —that they set it forth, not cloud it,—that sins washed away by the blood of Christ alone, and sins washed away in baptismal water are in no wise contradictory to one another, just because they are *not on the same plane at all;* as different from Romanist or ritualistic teachings as the Romanist keys of *heaven* from the scriptural keys of heaven's *kingdom upon earth.*

The Protestant thought of the keys is right, and it is not right: it is true in measure, yet is but a partial truth taken for the whole. The Romish view is bastard Judaism, wholly untrue and thoroughly mischievous: it is "the blasphemy of those who say they are Jews but are not, but are the synagogue of Satan." God has not made men heaven's door-keepers, to admit or exclude; and that remission of sins, which the blood of Christ assures to every one who in faith looks to Christ for it, needs and can have no go-between to dispense. Even in Judaism it was the cry of the convicted sinner, "Thou desirest not sacrifice, else would I give it; Thou delightest not in burnt-offering." (Ps. li. 16.) The Jewish sin-offering was of no avail to wash away sin in view of eternity; and the Jewish priest's lips could never pronounce a passport through death into eternal bliss. God reserved this ever in His own hands; and the Jews, when they heard the divine words of peace from the lips of One who could really utter them, showed, even in their unbelief, a truer knowledge than that of Rome: "Who can forgive sins," they ask, "but God alone?"

Protestantism is right, therefore, in maintaining that as to this, Christ's ministers have no higher commission than to proclaim the gospel. And yet it is in this very way plain that when the Lord says to His disciples, "Whosesoever sins ye remit, they are remitted," He cannot be speaking of the preaching of the gospel.

Whose sins do *I* remit when I preach the gospel? Whereas the words here are as definite as can be, and in the reverse order from what they would be on the other supposition: *not* "whose sins *I* remit, do *you* pronounce to be remitted," but "whose sins *ye* remit, they are remitted,"—that is, "*I* pronounce remitted."

But this cannot be, then, eternal, absolute remission; and if baptism be one of the keys of the kingdom of heaven, we have seen by our Lord's own parable, that forgiveness in it is conditional and revocable. "I forgave thee all that debt," says his lord to the uncompassionate servant; yet he "delivered him unto the tormentors till he should pay all that was due unto him." (Matt. xviii. 32, 34.) This is expressly called a parable of the kingdom of heaven. It is a kingdom which is now in men's hands to administer; and such remission is the only one that man can pronounce as to the individual, a conditional, hypothetical remission. Not indeed in a legal sense; not because, if discipleship be true, there is yet danger of not fulfilling the conditions; but because "man looketh on the outward appearance, but the Lord" alone "looketh on the heart." (1 Sam. xvi. 7.) And this, as we have seen, harmonizes with all those conditional passages of the New Testament, which are simply for the searching of the hearts of professors as such, wholesome for all, and which those who know best God's grace have least cause to be afraid of.

The kingdom of heaven is the sphere on earth in which Christ is owned, in the midst of a world which has rejected Him. There may spring up seed where underneath is still the heart of stone, and fruit never be found. If men sleep,—and they have slept,—the enemy may sow tares right among the wheat. Nay,

the whole form of the kingdom may change to the
likeness of the kingdoms of the world, and the leaven
spread in the lump till the whole be leavened. Thus
there is need of testing, where tares and wheat grow
up together to the harvest: hypothetical remission is
the only possible one, save for Him who still "knoweth
them that are His." (2 Tim. ii. 19.) According to the
mind of the Lord, however, the door of the kingdom
is that by which men pass out of the world into the
sphere in which He is openly acknowledged and
obeyed; and baptism, as a key of this door, is the authoritative washing away of their sins, that they may
come in,—conditional, because in man's hand it could
be nothing else,—yet witnessing of what is in the
Lord's heart for men, and of what His hand has accomplished too: a gospel preached in symbol to the
eyes of men, whose full significance we have yet to
inquire into.

13. THE SAMARITANS AND THE EUNUCH.

SAMARIA receives the word of God, and "when they
believed Philip preaching the things concerning the
kingdom of God and the name of Jesus Christ, they
were baptized, both men and women." (Acts viii. 12.)
Here too it is seen how clearly the remission of sins
must be hypothetical, even in the best hands. One
who with the rest "believes and is baptized" is found
to have "neither part nor lot" in the matter. Here
too we find that, even after baptism, the Holy Ghost
does not come on them until Peter and John come
down from Jerusalem, and lay their hands on them.
But there is nothing that seems to add much to our
knowledge of what is now before us.

Leaving Samaria, Philip baptizes the eunuch on the

road to Gaza; and here there is nothing to remark, except that, by the common consent of editors, with the amplest foundation in manuscripts and versions, ver. 37 is to be omitted. I do not myself attach much importance to it. If baptism is discipling, faith in the heart is what is looked for from a disciple; and "If thou believest with all thy heart, thou mayest" only puts the responsibility of this upon the eunuch. However, there is no need to discuss what is not Scripture.

14. CORNELIUS AND THE GENTILES.

THE case of Cornelius is of interest to us in this respect, that baptism here comes after the gift of the Holy Ghost; and as it is impossible to suppose that those whom God thus signally owned as His could have been yet unforgiven men, there is at once made apparent the difference between the forgiveness of sins as between God and the soul, and baptismal remission at disciples' hands. The identification of these two, as with the Campbellites, is thus absolutely set aside.

There is also here no laying on of hands to communicate the Spirit, and this precious gift is seen as no supplement of baptism, no effect of an ordinance at all. It might be before or after, it might be with laying of apostles' hands or without. And it is noteworthy that this is the beginning of the work among pure Gentiles, and that we never hear in their case of the laying on of hands for this at all. The words of the apostle in Galatians (chap. iii. 2, 5) are entirely in accord with the case of Cornelius.

15. BAPTISM UNTO CHRIST,—TO HIS DEATH.

WE will now go on to look at baptism as a symbol, and to see how its teaching in this way agrees with its place as authoritative discipling or reception into the kingdom of heaven. Its symbolic teaching is most fully developed in the sixth chapter of Romans. We will take this as given in the best translation known to me, and any points that are in dispute can be considered as we come to them.

"Are you ignorant, that we, as many as have been baptized unto Christ Jesus, have been baptized unto His death? We have been buried, therefore, with Him by baptism unto death, in order that, even as Christ has been raised up from among the dead by the glory of the Father, so we also should walk in newness of life. For if we are become identified with Him in the likeness of His death, so also we shall be of His resurrection; knowing this, that our old man has been crucified with [Him], that the body of sin might be annulled, that we should no longer serve sin. For he that has died is justified from sin."

It must not be supposed that all this is the interpretation of baptism; but it is all in close connection with it; and it is necessary to see where the line is to be drawn, and what is or what is not interpretation. In this translation the change of "into," as in most translations, to "unto" has been strongly protested against, although "baptized *unto* Moses" (1 Cor. x. 2), holds its place as generally perhaps as "*into* Christ" does here. The Revised Version indeed, even in Corinthians, puts in its margin "*Greek*, into Moses." But we have seen already that that is making the Greek more peremptory than it is. *Eis*, as we have seen, and as is confessed by all, means "into" or "unto." But "*into* Moses" gives no just sense; for there was no position "in Moses" answering to the believer's position now "in Christ;" and this alone it is, evidently, which has led to the difference in the translation of two plainly parallel expressions. Apart from all else, the single consideration that "into Moses" cannot be the meaning in the one case would naturally rule out "into Christ" in the other. The translation objected to simply brings them into harmony.

"Baptized unto Moses" has, as we have seen, the force of "set apart to Moses" as disciples. So those who were baptized with John's baptism were John's disciples. So have we found the Lord bidding to "disciple, baptizing." "Baptized unto the name of the Father" is discipled to the truth of what God is. "Baptized unto the name of the Lord Jesus" (Acts xix. 5) must be similar in meaning. After all this, "baptized unto Christ Jesus," as the true force of the words would surely seem to need no insisting on.

But baptism unto Christ is baptism to His death. It is a Christ who died who meets the need of the sinner; risen as He is His death remains in its virtue for the soul. If we put in connection with this John's baptism in Jordan, the river of death, we shall find the harmony and the difference between John's and Christian baptism. John too baptizes unto death, with the baptism of repentance; death being the wages of sin, and those baptized of him confessing their sins as justly entitling them to death the due of sin. But John could not yet baptize to Christ's death; for He had not died. Only in the Lord's significant action do we see the fore-shadow of this, when to fulfill all righteousness He takes His place in this death which these repentant ones have owned their due. But now in Christianity we come into Jordan after Christ has been in it; the death to which we come is still our due, but it is *His* death. Here the gospel-note sounds, and the baptism becomes Christian : "therefore we are buried *with Him* by baptism unto death."

Let us take another illustration,—this time from Old-Testament history : " Elisha died, and they buried him. And the bands of the Moabites invaded the land at the coming in of the year. And it came to pass as they were burying a man, that, behold, they spied a band of men ; and they cast the man into the sepulcre of Elisha ; and when the man was let down, and touched the bones of Elisha, he revived and stood up on his feet." (2 Kings xiii. 20, 21.)

Elisha was in his life in many ways a type of the Lord Jesus, and here he is so in his death. We have in the miracle a vivid illustration of baptism, just because it is a vivid and beautiful picture of salvation by the gospel. The man is dead, and so they bury him: burial is but putting the dead into the place of death. He is let down into the grave of one that had died before : he is buried with Elisha. So buried, he touches the one who had preceded him in death, and he is quickened out of it : he stands upon his feet a living man.

Let us notice, then, as to this burial with Christ: burial implies death, not life ; you bury the dead, not the living. How dead ? dead with Christ, since it is burial with Christ ? No: for it is only the one who is alive in Christ who can be dead with Him, and the man buried with Christ is buried to touch the dead Christ, and to live. Dead with Christ means dead to sin, as we see in this chapter ; but none can be dead to sin, who is not spiritually alive. Buried with Christ does not, then, imply dead with Christ, as might be thought.

Buried because dead in sins, then ? That is nearer

to, but is not yet, the thought. The death we see pictured in John's baptism is the death which is the *due* of sin, and not the inward condition, which is but the inveteracy of the sinful state itself. The death here is that into which Christ came; but He did not come into a sinful condition, but under its penalty. Hence burial with Christ is the owning of the penalty, which faith anticipates before it comes, finding Christ as having taken that place, that we may live. Baptism is therefore but a typical or acted out gospel; with a significant protest against ritualism, also: for the baptism is, as the word itself shows and the apostle's argument as well, but immersion, burial, Christ alone must give the life; and thus it does *not* go on, as Colossians in our common version teaches, to resurrection. It is the confession of death, for which we are put into Christ's sepulchre, that we may live. We are buried with Him by baptism unto death, in order that, even as Christ has been raised up from the dead by the glory of the Father, so we also should walk in newness of life. What is sought is the power for a new walk; but itself cannot give this : it is a baptism to *death* and not to life.

But we need to look closely at what follows in the apostle's argument. "For if we are become identified with [Him] in the likeness of His death, so also we shall be [in the likeness] of His resurrection."

"Identified" seems free as a translation; the word means, as a note upon it says, "grown together," and the rendering of the Revised Version, with most commentators, "united," seems preferable. There is no "Him" in the original, but it is necessarily implied; and the passage so read argues that if the truth intended by baptism be a reality in the soul, and in it—

"the likeness of His death"—they were really, not merely professedly, united with him, then the result would be seen in the practical "likeness of His resurrection,"—that "walk in newness of life," of which he had just before spoken. The resurrection of the buried man was the result of having touched Elisha; and perfectly sure is the result where Christ has been touched in faith. This touch becomes indeed a full identification, and the apostle goes on now to show the deliverance from the power of sin that would hinder the blessedness of a walk with God. Here he goes beyond what baptism in itself symbolizes, to show what identification with Christ involves, namely, the crucifixion of our old man in the cross of Christ, that the body of sin may be annulled. But this does not come within the scope of our present inquiry.

16. DOES BAPTISM SYMBOLIZE RESURRECTION.

THUS far, then, Romans; and plainly it does not go on to resurrection. Walking in newness of life, the likeness of resurrection, is what is to follow. But in Colossians (chap. ii. 12), in perhaps every version, we have resurrection included: "Buried with Him in baptism, wherein also ye are risen with [Him], through the faith of the operation of God who hath raised Him from the dead."

There is, however, an alternative rendering. The word for "wherein" in Greek also means "in whom," and Meyer and Wordsworth in their commentaries adopt this. The second "Him" in the verse is also wanting, and we may, instead of "with Him," say "together." Thus it will stand: "Buried with Him in baptism, in whom also ye are risen together, through the faith of the operation of God, who hath raised

Him from the dead." This rendering I have no doubt can be fully justified.

The primary meaning of the word *baptisma* is acknowledged to be "immersion," and though one cannot always insist upon this, as has been already urged, yet in the meaning of "burial" given to it both here and in Romans there seems good reason for accepting immersion as the mode which harmonizes with the thought. It may be said that in raising one from the water, the figure of resurrection is necessarily found. But though this follows, it is not really in itself part of the baptism.

But there are much more sufficing reasons. For, supposing it were fully admitted that in baptism we were symbolically raised up with Christ, yet how would this consist with the latter part of the sentence "through the faith of the operation of God"? Faith as the instrument would here be but a disturbing element as far as the figure is concerned. Baptism could not be a figure of anything "*through faith*" of something else!

On the other hand, if it be not figure, but reality, *then* we are really raised up with Christ through faith, but in an ordinance; which is Campbellism, but not Scripture. Nor need I take it up here.

The other translation makes all simple: we have only to remember that resurrection and quickening [or life-giving] are not the same thing. There is a double contrast in Colossians here which is instructive. In ver. 13 we have, "And you, being *dead*, hath he *quickened;*" in ver. 12, "*buried* with Him in whom ye are *risen*." As burial is putting the dead in the place of death, so resurrection is the living being brought into the place of the living. It is by faith in Him who has raised up Jesus that we step into the ranks of those spiritually alive.

17. THE PUTTING ON OF CHRIST IN BAPTISM.

FOR the doctrine of baptism, as Paul teaches it, we have but one more passage to consider. It is the statement in Gal. (iii. 27), "For as many of you as have been baptized unto Christ have put on Christ."

This "putting on" is, of course, clothing: we have it elsewhere as an exhortation,—"put ye on the Lord Jesus Christ, and make not provision for the flesh, to fulfill the lusts thereof." (Rom. xiii. 14.) Here it is evidently practical; and clothing often stands for practical righteousness,—always, I believe for something wrought out, as is a garment, thread by thread.

But when we speak of putting on Christ, this garment which covers the shame of our nakedness is, of course, nothing self-wrought. We are hiding ourselves in Another; we are arraying ourselves in a comeliness not our own. And this, we see at once, is the idea in baptism: *we* are immersed *unto* Christ. Self is owned as ruined, undone, and Christ is sought to as a refuge from self, a Substitute and Representative before God; before men also our glory and our hiding-place.

This is the *meaning* of baptism: it is not, of course, what as an act (sacramentally, as people say,) it accomplishes. It in no way supposes this, that the apostle goes on to argue that in Christ there is no distinction of class or sex, and that if Christ's, we are Abraham's seed. He gives the ideal, the profession: we are that, or else untrue to it, for Christ on His side refuses none that come to Him.

Moreover, in the words used, we have not, as so

many suppose, any implication of necessary activity in the person who "puts on" Christ. The same word, only compounded with the preposition "upon," and in the first aorist middle, exactly as here, is used in 2 Cor. v. 2 for our "being clothed upon with our house that is from heaven," and we might there speak of "putting on" the resurrection body, or here of our being "clothed with" Christ. The responsibility of the baptismal place belongs to the one in it, however the grace of God may have wrought in putting him in. To a child who has been baptized in infancy—allowing for a moment that God has given them the privilege of this,—one could say, "You were clothed with Christ."

The exhortation in Rom. xiii. 14 is not inconsistent with this. It is, what we have not in English, an *in imperative in the past* (the aorist), and means, "*be as one* that has been clothed with Christ."

18. THE BAPTISMAL SALVATION OF PETER.

ONE passage outside of Paul's writings remains to be considered. Connected with the verse before, it literally reads: "Wherein few, that is, eight souls, were saved by water; which also, a like figure, now saves you, [even] baptism (not a putting away of filth of flesh, but a request of a good conscience unto God) by the resurrection of Jesus Christ."

There is a general agreement that "the *answer* of a good conscience," upon which so much has been built, is not correct; though the word is a difficult one.*

---

* "The word has puzzled all critics and commentators. It means "a question." All the commentators speak of its use as a legal term, with the sense of contract, or rather, stipulations and obligations of a contract. Schleusner says it is never so used, but *eperotesis*, (Bloomfield, after Dindorf, denies this;) and in Latin it is *interrogatio*. Tertullian, describing the

"Question," "inquiry," "request," as variously given by commentators, will any of them give the sense, only we must get the right connection. Alford has, for instance, "the inquiry of a good conscience after God;" whereas the meaning must be rather, from what we have already seen, "the inquiry *for* a good conscience." The conscience cannot be good, that is only inquiring after God. It is, as we have seen, what baptism means, the confession of a need which God alone can satisfy, and which it requires the death of Christ to meet.

Alford reads also, "which, the antitype [of that] doth now save you also, even baptism." This makes the water of baptism the antitype of the flood, which is out of all scriptural proportion. The word used (though the original of our word "antitype") is applied in the only other place in which it occurs in Scripture to the "holy places made with hands, which are the *figures* of the true" (Heb. ix. 24)—types in *contrast* with antitypes. If any thing more than figure, then, be needed to explain the word, the rendering of the common version, a "*like* figure," is certainly right. Water in each case, with a like significance; the water of death, in the flood, yet salvation to those whom it upbore in the ark; the baptismal water similarly death, and saving because *His* death.

For this, however, you must bring in resurrection. Death, if there were no resurrection, would be awful defeat and ruin. "He was raised again for our justification." And thus in a figure baptism saves by the resurrection of Christ from the dead.

---

sponsio of a catechumen at baptism, refers evidently to this passage of Peter. But this was a much later form . . . The legal use arises from a questioning which settled the terms of the contract, hence called 'the questioning.'" (*J. N. Darby.*)

This, as is evident, is the same doctrine as Paul's. Scripture is, as it must be, of a piece throughout.

19. "Born of Water."

The *doctrine* of baptism is now complete. But there is one passage so commonly taken and by many more than ritualists, to refer to baptism, that one can hardly be excused from saying a few words about it, in proof that it does not apply to baptism at all. It is that in which the Lord says to Nicodemus that "Except a man be born of water and of the Spirit, he cannot enter into the kingdom of God." The proof may be given thus:—

1. If this spoke of baptism, it would prove that without baptism no one could be saved.

2. It would also make it a magical ceremony by which to the degradation of the Holy Spirit of God, He would be made to unite with *water* to beget a soul to God!

3. The being born of God is a spiritual process, and the one so born doth not commit sin, and his seed abideth in him. He has eternal life, not one that can perish or allow him to be the sinner that he was before (1 Jno. iii. 9), which is not true of the baptized as such.

4. Cornelius had the Spirit, and was certainly born again before he was baptized at all.

5. To be born of water and the Spirit, two elements must come together, and thus it could not be that any would be born again except in the moment of baptism.

6. The apostle Peter assures us, we are born again by the word of God preached in the gospel. (1 Pet. i. 23, 25.)

7. Which Paul tells us the washing of water repre-

sents: "washing of water *by the Word*" (Eph. v. 26) is how Christ sanctifies and cleanses His Church.

8. The Lord's words to Nicodemus refer to Ezek. xxxvi. where Israel is prophetically seen to undergo the needed change in order to enter the kingdom at a future day.

9. And the Lord uses these terms not with an ignorant man, or mere convicted sinner, but with a teacher of Israel.

10. So that He might well marvel at his want of knowledge, which He could not have done, if He were speaking of the unknown effect of a rite not yet instituted in its Christian form.

This evidence is abundant and conclusive that the "water" of which men are born again is not baptismal water, but the word of God. Another expression, "the washing of regeneration" (Tit. iii. 5), often used in the same interest as the former, says nothing of baptism or of water at all.

20. Conversion to Enter the Kingdom.

To all the preceding argument as to admission into the kingdom, Matt. xviii. 3 has been objected as decisive against it. The words are indeed as positive as to the kingdom of heaven as those to Nicodemus about new birth are to the kingdom of God. Attentive consideration will show that they both apply in the same way, that is, to the kingdom set up in power when the Lord appears. It is of this the disciples must have been thinking when they asked, "Who then is greatest in the kingdom of heaven?" A small thing comparatively to be greatest here: a very different thing to be greatest there.*

21. HOUSEHOLD BAPTISM.

WE enter now upon another inquiry, namely, as to the *subjects* of baptism. There is question really only as to one point. We have seen that in the Christian form of the kingdom, as distinct from the Jewish, the national birthright title has failed with Israel's being (for the time) Lo-Ammi. The scanty proselyte entrance of those days is become now the rule,—*discipling* to the kingdom. But this raises immediate question: if in the old form, the children of proselytes were circumcised with their parents, and what we have called the grace of the law has become the rule in the kingdom of grace, must not the families of proselytes be received still with them, as of old they were, and the baptism of households be in this way the rule in Christianity?

Here reasonings perhaps do not count for much; nor do we desire them to count for more than they are worth; but it is well, surely, to compare the past with the present, and trace, if we may, the substantial unity of the divine plan all through. In the new form of the kingdom circumcision drops out and baptism takes its place. In accordance with the larger grace of the kingdom, male and female being but one in Christ, women are baptized as well as men. What as to households?

In the meaning of baptism is there any indication that families are to be shut out now, as they were

---

*In a tract on the "Mysteries of the Kingdom of Heaven," the objection is answered differently; but I am persuaded that the above is the true as it is the most conclusive answer.

formerly admitted? Circumcision had been, in the person of the one who first received it, a "seal of the righteousness of faith" (Rom. iv. 11); yet that did not hinder its application to the thirteen-year-old Ishmael, nor to the eight-day-old Isaac. Yet if baptism were a seal of life, a life now proclaimed spiritual and eternal, there might be still difficulty. But it is burial, the confession of death, and not of life, and so understood all is easy. Then notice that circumcision is the "putting off of the body of the flesh" (Col. ii. 11); the true circumcision "have no confidence in the flesh." (Phil. iii. 3.) How near this is to the "burial" of baptism! In both dispensations the entrance into the kingdom of God is marked by the renunciation of self as worthless, that He may have real supremacy.

That baptism is discipling is no difficulty; for in a school in which Christ is Master, who can tell how soon His grace may begin to teach? Of John the Baptist it was said, "He shall be filled with the Holy Ghost, even from his mother's womb." (Luke i. 15.)

Finally, if baptism is the putting on of Christ, even this does not necessarily imply any voluntary activity; for so it is said that "this corruptible puts on incorruption, and this mortal immortality;" and man in dying puts off his tabernacle.

Yet this is all only preparatory: we must have positive Scripture if we are to go further. Here, then, the baptism of households comes in to reassure us. In Acts xvi. we have Lydia and her household, the jailer and all his, baptized. Of Lydia's household we have no certain knowledge; but the baptism of her house is put as if it were part of her own faithfulness, which she pleads: "A certain woman named Lydia heard us, whose heart the Lord opened; and when she was baptized, and her household, she besought us saying, 'If ye have judged *me* to be faithful to the Lord, come into my house.'" From the point of view already indicated, one would certainly conclude that her household was baptized upon her faith.

In the case of the jailer, who asks, "What must *I* do to be saved?" Paul and Silas answer with the assurance, "Believe on the Lord Jesus Christ, and thou shalt be saved, *and thy house*." Here the salvation of his house is clearly put as the normal result of his own believing. Nor have we any thing of *their* faith in what follows, but only of his; though we are told that "they spake unto him the word of the Lord, and to all that were in his house." He was baptized, he and all his, straightway; and *he* rejoiced greatly, with all his house,—but this is an adverb, *panoiki*, "domestically,"—having believed in God. It is "he" rejoiced, "he" believed.

In chap. xviii. Crispus of Corinth believes with all his house; and the expression is quite different.

To the Corinthians Paul writes his first epistle, learning of divisions beginning among them, and thankful he had not baptized enough of them to form a party for himself. "Were ye baptized unto the name of Paul? I thank God I baptized none of *you* but Crispus and Gaius, lest any should say I had baptized unto my own name. And I baptized also the *household* of Stephanas: for the rest, I know not that I baptized any other." (1 Cor. i. 14–16.)

Now the common thought is, that in the last statement Paul is correcting his first one. It was not just the truth that he had baptized only two of the assembly. He had baptized a family beside; perhaps more: he is not clear. But this would go some way toward upsetting the very thing he was thankful for.

If we look closer we may find that there is no mistake at all. "None of *you*" is absolute, save Crispus and Gaius. Too small a number to make a party in the assembly. But what about the perhaps half-a-dozen more? *They* were not in the *assembly;* they were a baptized *household*, in the kingdom only, And so if he had baptized even others here, it was no matter at all. The distinction between household and individual, kingdom and assembly, clears up the difficulty and gives absolute consistency throughout.

However, we learn at the end of the same epistle that the house of Stephanas had addicted themselves to the ministry of the saints (chap. xvi. 15). Were *these* not in the assembly? Surely they were. But is not here, then, a contradiction to the former statement, and a certain proof that Stephanas' house were grown men? Again, one must look more narrowly; and then it will be found that the Spirit of God uses for this word "house" or "household," two different words, although very near akin. Is it without a purpose? I, for one, cannot think so. In the *first* chapter of the epistle the word is *oikos;* in the last, *oikia :* differing only in the last two letters, but still differing.

A difference in meaning has been suggested by some, but which is not generally admitted, and must, therefore, be scrutinized with the more care. Greek has many dialects, and New-Testament or Hellenistic Greek is not the classic. The Septuagint translation is well known to be for the most part the storehouse of New-Testament words. In it *oikos* seems the word invariably used for a man's own family, the general thought indeed where "house" is used for the inmates. But there are exceptions: "house" seems also used in a wider sense, so as to include servants, and here we have the use of *oikia*. Thus in "the eldest servant of [Abraham's] *house*," "house" is *oikia*. And while at the passover they took every one a lamb according to the *oikos* of their fathers, yet (because the servants ate it with their masters) it is said, "a lamb for an "*oikia*," and "if the *oikia* be too little for the lamb." When Joshua says, "As for me and my house, we will serve the Lord," it is again *oikia:* for those who serve him are to serve with him.

The passages, no doubt, are very few in which the word is used; but the use is none the less distinct, and in the New Testament it is exactly similar. *Oikos* is used for the "house of Jacob," "of Israel," "of David," "of Judah," and in the baptismal passages. *Oikia* is never used in this way. The lost rich man in hades would send Lazarus to his father's house: it is *oikos;* for he has five brethren. The bishop is to rule his own house (oikos) well, having his children in subjection with all gravity. Noah prepared an ark to the saving of his house. And if five in one house are divided (Luke xii. 52, 53), they are father and mother and son and daughter and daughter-in-law.

Notice that Matthew and Mark speak of a house divided against itself, and here it is *oikia;* but there is nothing about the inmates in this way. Passages are much less numerous—again as in the Septuagint,—but we are told that "the *servant* abideth not in the house forever; and of him who left his house, and gave authority to his *servants* to watch; and of the saints that are of Cæsar's household—clearly not his children; and under this word comes that household of Stephanas who have addicted themselves to the ministry of the saints.

Certainly in Scripture the distinction is maintained, which being confirmed, makes all clear as to the baptism of households. It is the family of the disciple that is baptized with the head,—not the servants: a distinction which in itself suggests that the relationship rules in this matter of reception into the kingdom in the Christian as in the legal dispensation.

22. "Of Such is the Kingdom."

This might be by itself conclusive. It proves that there was a class of the baptized, at least, outside the Church altogether,—that baptism was not into the visible Church, and that the class consisted, in part at least, of the families of believers. We can go further, however, and show by the authority of the Lord Himself, that children belong to His kingdom. The words we are all familiar with, but their significance has been greatly disputed. It is, let us remind ourselves, when "there were brought unto Him little children, that He might put His hands on them and pray; and the disciples rebuked them. But Jesus said, 'Suffer little children to come unto Me, and forbid them not; *for of such is the kingdom of heaven.*'"

Mark adds that He was "much displeased;" that He took them up in His arms, showing how little they were, and that He added the solemn words, "Verily I say unto you that whosoever shall not receive the kingdom of God as a little child, he shall in no wise enter therein." (Matt. xix. 13, 14; Mark x. 13–16.)

This last expression (which Matthew omits) is nevertheless believed by many to be the gist of the whole matter. It is "of such" as children that the kingdom is, but not of children themselves! We may well ask in wonder, Are not little children "such as" little children? Or when the apostle, after naming certain sins, declares that "they that do 'such' things shall not inherit the kingdom of God," does he mean that people *might* commit *those* things, but not others like them?

Why, too, should He give this as His reason for blessing those children, that people who resembled them were fit for the kingdom?

But one need not add arguments. We see at once now how this underlies the baptism of households, which is really Christ's blessing perpetuated for those who would still bring their children to Him and beseech His blessing. Here He sanctions fully what they do, and gives the little ones a special place under His own rule and teaching. We are thus bound, in Christianity, to bring them up in the nurture (or discipline) and admonition of the Lord" (Eph. vi. 4),— that is, as disciples. For the word still holds, "Train up a child in the way he should go, and when he is old he will not depart from it." This is the practical faith, which, acting on the promises of God, secures the blessing.

And here we see why the Lord says "of such" simply. Not all children can be discipled: not because He has not love and desire, but because, if baptism imply such training, for the children of unbelievers it could mean nothing. Faith alone could realize the blessing.

Now are They Holy.

THUS we may see also why, going beyond the law, the children even of a marriage where one remains an unbeliever can be called by the apostle "holy." The words run thus (1 Cor. vii. 13, 15):—

"And the woman that hath an unbelieving husband, and if he be pleased to dwell with her, let her not leave him. For the unbelieving husband is sanctified by ("in") the wife; and the unbelieving wife is sanctified in the husband. Else were your children unclean, but now are they holy."

The use of the word "unclean" explains the corresponding word "holy." It is not *vital* holiness that he is thinking of, but external position. According to the law the children of such a marriage could claim none; but grace goes altogether beyond law. It is not said of the unbeliever that he or she is "holy," as the child is; merely sanctified *in* the believer. The child has an acknowledged place as "holy" or "clean;" and this he takes to show that the marriage stands; for if the children were unclean, the marriage itself would be. Baptism gives this acknowledged place, a place in the kingdom of God, which under different forms runs through the dispensations.

24. CONCLUSIONS.

IT remains only to add a few brief remarks upon some points not formally taken up as yet, but which it is hoped will not now present much difficulty.

As to the mode of baptism, that it should be by immersion results from the primary meaning of the word, connected with the thought of "burial" which we have plainly given to it. Yet that even sprinklings are called "baptisms" in Hebrews destroys that argument often made that only immersion can be called that. It is plain also that the word is used in other places where there was none, as at the Red Sea, and that the stress is laid not upon mode, but upon what it effects. It would be impossible, I believe, to *prove* in any single instance that immersion was the scriptural mode, much more to show that all depends upon this.

There is no command to all to be baptized, such as would render it imperative that every believer should for himself fulfill it. The universal command is only to the baptizer, leaving room for it to be differently applied in different cases. "Whosoever believeth and is baptized shall be saved" is added to the injunction to preach the gospel, which accounts for the form; but one baptized in infancy and believing afterwards, has both these requisites. That the force is on believing the gospel is plain by the close, that "he that believeth not shall be damned." No one would apply this to children.

That baptism is not into the church shows that it is not into the house of God, which *is* the church. It shows also why a difference of judgment as to it cannot exclude from the Lord's table, which is the sign of membership in the "one body" of Christ. (1 Cor. x. 17.) Baptism is individual: the Lord's Supper, a fellowship. May He give His people grace "to keep the unity of the Spirit in the bond of peace."

F. W. G.

THE BIBLE TRUTH PRESS, NEW YORK.

HOUSEHOLD BAPTISM.

A REVIEW OF OBJECTIONS.

"LET the prophets speak, two or three, and *let the rest judge*," contains a principle of great value for us all. Judgment must be exercised as to whatever is put forth for truth; and for this the means of judgment must be in our hands. Scripture, of course, is the one only standard of appeal, the measure of all truth such as we have now before us; but we cannot afford to be independent of one another's help in searching it, and especially to enable us to get rid of those merely personal influences which operate so powerfully often *against* the truth, even when they are engaged upon the side of truth. Error that we have received upon the authority of those who have rightful claim to our affection and respect finds thus, as we all know, its strongest support; but *truth* also needs often to be shaken free of just such human support, that it may stand in its own divine power. For this God would use the differences that arise among us, and which in themselves are evidence of *in*subjection to His word and Spirit, to teach us more subjection.

Controversy is only to be dreaded just so far as the personal element in the same sense enters into it, and perverts in the interests of a party quarrel the witnesses in the cause of God and truth.

Seeking, then, to avoid all mere personalities, and to bring everything to the test of the word of God alone, I shall take up briefly the arguments which have been brought forward against a former tract of mine on the doctrine of baptism, not unwilling to be given opportunity to explain further some things which may be left obscure in the former one, and to show more fully what I conceive to be the error of the views advocated on the other side. For my own, I trust I may be permitted to refer to what I have already written, and thus to avoid what for those who have read this would be mere tedious repetition.

We must still consider, in the first place, however, what is alleged as to

THE KINGDOM OF HEAVEN

before we shall be prepared to take up the questions as to baptism and the relation to it of the households of believers. Here, in fact, is the main difficulty, as I believe, in regard to the reception of this, that the confusion which exists between the church and the kingdom, and the general ignorance as to the latter, obscure what would otherwise be simple. "Of such is the kingdom of heaven" would be a text at least very easily made plain were it seen that the kingdom is the sphere of discipleship, and that baptism is "discipling." It is not the fact that this discussion is irrelevant therefore, least of all where not *household* baptism only, but *baptism as a whole* is the subject of inquiry. On the contrary, it may be affirmed that the only hope of contention for our brethren lies just here. These points must therefore be looked at in the first place, if we would be clear.

"But I shall be told," says one of our brethren (J.J.), "that I do not 'see' the kingdom. I quite grant that to 'see' it, one must be born again; nay, I maintain that is the only way to see it, or to enter into it. And I further maintain, on the authority of Scripture, that baptism is no more introduction into the kingdom than the Lord's Supper is introduction into the Church. Introduction into the kingdom is by new birth; into the Church by the sealing of the Holy Spirit."

The last sentence is the strangest, perhaps, here, where much is strange. Had our brother been asked, in time past, "How are we introduced into the Church?" I think there is little doubt he would have replied, in the very words of Scripture, that "by one Spirit are we all *baptized* into one body."(1 Cor. xii.13.) Somehow this seems now to have slipped out of his mind: he speaks now as if we were "sealed" into it! I suppose he would admit the incongruity in the term, at least; but how could he forget that the Scripture mode of expressing introduction into the body of Christ is by this term "*baptism*"? Is it not plain, at least, that here Scripture uses "baptism" as implying introduction into that which is of Christ?— and that if the kingdom were a circle of profession larger than and external to the body of Christ, then one could easily understand the analogy between the outward material and the spiritual baptism? How else can we, in fact, understand it?

Perhaps our brother would be ready to agree to this: that baptism is the introduction into the profession of

Christianity? But this is, in fact, the kingdom, the sphere of discipleship, where Christ is Master and Lord.

But he answers "No! introduction here is by new birth: to see this, or to enter into it, one must be born again."

By "seeing" it, he evidently understands such spiritual insight as could only come from spiritual life but this is not what the passage means. The undoubted reference to Ezek. xxxvi. shows that it is not to a spiritual kingdom, invisible except to faith that the Lord points, but to a kingdom which, when established, every eye will see. A Jewish teacher certainly could not be expected to know of any other. Nor does the Lord at all say that men are *born again into* it; but that they must be born again to have *title* to enter in,— a very different thing. Israel, in fact must be converted, in order to escape the judgment which introduce the kingdom. (See, for example, Isa iv. 2-4.) Thus there is NO Scripture for new birth *being* introduction to the kingdom, but the two things are quite distinct; nor is the kingdom one only to be seen by faith, but the opposite. Our brother evidently confounds the two things, stating sometimes that introduction is *by* new birth, sometimes that only the latter is necessary as a condition for the former, as if these things were the same.

Matt. xviii, 3, speaks quite similarly, not of conversion *as* entering the kingdom, but "except ye be converted, ye shall not enter" it. Here, however, it will be contended, all is admitted that is necessary to the argument: new birth is necessary to enter the kingdom; and if this be true when the kingdom is set up in power, it is "a strong reason in itself, one would have thought, for its present application. . . . The Lord Himself, however, in the immediate context, makes it of the most important present application for our conduct in the kingdom now; and it is only by applying the passage to the present that the prevailing confusion is removed, and the whole subject of the Kingdom of Heaven becomes simple."

Now no one, surely, doubts that there is to be a present *application* of such truths. The question is, *how* are they to be applied? If the long-suffering goodness of God ordain a door to be kept open now, which it is plainly warned will, bye and bye, be shut, are we to apply the future to the present by *shutting the door beforehand?*

However, the statement is definitely made that—

"The kingdom of God covers all dispensations. In all ages God has reigned; and the Lord, in John iii, gives the moral truth concerning the kingdom: "Except a man be born again he cannot see the kingdom of God." New birth into the kingdom, in all ages, is the plain teaching of the Lord. Before the cross God was dealing with man as under trial, and therefore a nation was taken up, but in the midst of this nation only those born again were *really* in the kingdom of God."

These words are by another writer (J. J. S.), but they only express more boldly the same thought—God had a kingdom in all ages. "Dealing with man as under trial," He takes up a nation. How? As His people, or not?—as belonging to His kingdom, or not? "Only those born again were *really* in the kingdom of God." In what way "really"? When Solomon "sat on the throne of the Lord," "on the throne of the kingdom of the Lord *over Israel*" (1 Chr. xxviii, 5; xxix, 23), did he "really" reign only over the "born-again souls" there? And did he "really" reign over all truly converted persons elsewhere? And when the Lord pronounced the sentence Lo-ammi, "not my people," upon Israel, did this mean that He was casting off the "born-again ones," who were those over whom alone He had ever reigned?—or what else?

"Really"! Why, who doubts that it is, and also was, only the converted people in whose *hearts* God reigned? But was that what He meant when He took up a nation? Was it not of necessity a very different thing? Was this only the kingdom "as men saw it,' or the kingdom also as God, who knoweth the hearts proclaimed it? How could men "see" what we are told cannot be seen by any but those born again?

God did not, then, make the truths of eternity—or of the kingdom set up in power—truths for His people to act upon, then,—that is clear. And our brother's "really" is something foreign to the matter in hand, or else something absolutely untrue, and plainly so. We cannot so ignore the dispensations. Thus the kingdom of God in Israel is against this view decisively. Of course it must be different now; and the same writer, speaking of the mysteries of the kingdom, bids us—

"Note in this parable, the seed are the people, and the Lord only sowed good seed; that is, 'born-again' souls. But now, as men see it, there are tares; that is, unconverted professors. Who sowed them? The devil. And so we must never forget the two standpoints from which the kingdom is seen. From God's standpoint, as He sees it in His counsels, the kingdom is composed of born-again ones only. But from man's standpoint, and as we see it, there is a mixture."

So when the angels "gather out of His kingdom all things that offend, and them that do iniquity," they simply gather out those whom men *take* to be in His kingdom, but who are *not there*. Is that just fair interpretation,— commending itself as honest and true? For this is the Lord's own account of the matter, at the end, to His disciples; and why should He say "out of" His kingdom, when we are bidden to believe that none but those born again are, or ever were, or could be, in the kingdom? Was it not easily possible to avoid words so ambiguous?

But the good seed are the "children of the kingdom"; and the tares are unconverted professors: is not that true?

It is the truth, but, as to the last, not the *whole* truth. We must go more slowly, and look more carefully, to find that. For, while the good seed in the second parable is indeed said to be "children of the kingdom," in the first parable it is as plainly said to be the "*word* of the kingdom." Of course there is not the least inconsistency between these two views: the children of the kingdom are only those in whom the word of the kingdom has grown up — the wheat. Are the tares, then, produced in any sense by the word of the kingdom?— and does Satan sow such seed as this? Clearly not. He sows false doctrine, not true, and the fruit are heretics, not mere unreal professors. All this has been often told, and cannot be a thing unknown to J. J. S. Its consistency with the whole meaning of the second parable I have elsewhere pointed out.*

Still, the good seed are the children of the kingdom and the wheat,— are they not? — gathered into the barn? Yes, the *crop*. But it does not follow that *all*

---

* "The Mysteries of the Kingdom of Heaven," pp. 42-53.

the good seed goes into the crop, as every farmer too well knows. How much *he* would like to have all the seed he sows fulfill the likeness to these "born-again souls" which J. J. S., in complete disregard of all the congruities, would import from John into Matthew. He is the more inexcusable because the *first* parable is plainly given to guard against the very thing that he is doing. *Not* all the good seed furnishes the crop, is its declaration; but here, as part of that good seed which gives the children of the kingdom, we are taught that the mere *unconverted professors* are really to be placed. In entire opposition to what our brethren teach, the "children of the kingdom" is not a term convertible with those born again. And our Lord expressly teaches (Matt. viii, 12) that "the children of the kingdom" may, as none of the converted ever can, be "cast into outer darkness," where "there is wailing and gnashing of teeth." How plain, then, that the kingdom is not what they teach, when such as these are expressly called "the children of the kingdom"!

It is one thing certain, then, the infants cannot have place "AMONG THE TARES," as our brother puts it in small capitals, and this as "bringing them into A PLACE OF BLESSING." If these were his own views when he practised household baptism, it is not to be wondered at that he has given it up.

This is a full answer also to J. J., who allows that there are foolish virgins in the kingdom "in its outward aspect,"— words that, as we have seen, Scripture never authorizes. He adds, "what makes them to be 'foolish' is their taking the place, probably by being baptized." Of course, not as infants: even our brother will acquit household baptism in this case. As for the rest, what shows their folly is their taking "no oil with them." They would not have become "wise" by throwing aside their lamps: no, nor by never having carried them.

KINGDOM AND CHURCH.

We turn now to look at the question of the distinction between the Kingdom and the Church; and here our brother C. deserves a first answer, as he has said all perhaps that can be said. As to the three circles of Eph. iv. he maintains that "even if verses 5 and 6 here could apply to something else than the Church or Assembly, we could have no right so to apply them." Why? "Because Paul's known and acknowledged subject is the Assembly, and verses 5 and 6 will apply to the Assembly." Now the Church is in the Kingdom, and therefore what applies to the subjects of the Kingdom will apply to the members of Christ's body—the Church. It is freely granted, also, that the passage in Ephesians would not decide that the Church is not co-extensive with the Kingdom.*

The relationships implied are different. All Christ's members are also children of God, but the family of God is nevertheless not identical with the body of Christ. Much that our brother says here misses the point, therefore. Moreover, the circle of the Kingdom is not "intermediate," as he puts it, between the Church and the world. This would imply that the Church was not in it, which it is. Nor do I need to discuss the question of the Church, for which the better word, as we all know, would be "assembly,"—a word, too, of various application, even to a heathen gathering.

---

* The argument as to verse 6 we need not enter into. It does not really affect our subject.

By the Church here I mean always "the Church which is His body."

Moreover, our brother is right in refusing to find room under "One Lord, one *creed*, one baptism," for those who "deny that Jesus is God." This is the Kingdom as constituted of God, not designed surely to include the Satanic work of the second parable. The enemy, "while men slept," may have introduced his followers into the Kingdom, and Christians be powerless to undo what has thus been done; but this, nevertheless, is only an intrusion. Satan's work is not Christianity, even in its lowest form. On the other hand, with those who are simply "unreal" (C. 11) the case is different. They come under the first parable, not the second,— while, of course, that does not mean any sanction of their unreality.

On this subject it is more to my purpose to quote what I have formerly said than to restate it: "The kingdom of heaven, with its message of peace and reconciliation, remains the testimony of a love which goes out to all, and would gather in to God wherever the will of man is not hardening itself in opposition. We do not, in fact, in Scripture meet with the long delay of baptism and the preparation of catechumens, which came in as baptism itself came to be looked at as reception into the Church, and the symbol of the full Christian state. In the New Testament the catecumens were inside, not outside, the sphere of discipleship. Instead of being kept waiting at the threshold, the applicants were met with a generous and unsuspecting welcome. Three thousand were baptized on the day of Pentecost: how much preliminary instruction had they? And if, as at Samaria, a Simon Magus were received, with his heart not right in the sight of God, his reception had not defiled those tender arms of mercy which had been flung around him, and from which he had, as it were, to burst, to pursue the headlong path to everlasting ruin. It is evident, upon the face of Scripture, that baptism was not then fenced round, as many now would fence it round. It was a door, *not carelessly*, but readily and with a full heart, opened to the applicant for it. No question of Christ's heart, no "if Thou wilt," was to be permitted." *

To this the meaning of baptism, and the Lord's words as to little children, unite their testimony. The doctrine of the Church as Paul declared it, and as to which our brother writes, "*To profess to be a Christian is to profess to be a member of the body of Christ,*" was unknown for years after Pentecost; and therefore, whatever may be the profession now, NONE *certainly made it then.* The power of the Spirit was abroad; and, of course, in the same proportion there was earnestness and reality, yet with proof soon afforded that the first parable of the kingdom was fulfilling too. The more reality there was the more the Church and the Kingdom would be co-extensive. The fervor of divine love in souls refused to allow any neutrality. Men were drawn along with the current that was then in full tide, or flung out as drift by the eddies along the shore. And granting, for a moment, that there were growing up with the years that went by the families that were baptized,— these, too, would be no exception to the rule. Thus the inability to find more than the "within and without" of which our brother

---

* "Mysteries of the Kingdom," page 26. Published by LOIZEAUX BROTHERS, 63 Fourth Avenue, New York. Price 15 cents.

rightly speaks. When he uses it as an argument upon his side, he simply is unable to realize the true character of that which he opposes,— that the grace of the Kingdom was not meant to promote, and did not promote, the growth of a neutral class, impossible until love slackened and zeal cooled, and that confusion which the after-parables of the kingdom indicate as so soon to set in began to appear and grow.

The idea of the open sinners in the Church being left in any "intermediate circle," such as he imagines for us (C. 19), only shows how little our brother understands the position which he attacks. When men manifest themselves as "wicked persons," they cannot be treated as neutral.

"Of Such is the Kingdom."

But the case of children shows more definitely the character of the Kingdom. Our brother C. finds abundant fault with the obscurity of my utterances on this point. This may be true, that they are obscure; but I believe it proceeds a good deal from believing that the Lord's words are *not* obscure, and may be trusted to speak for themselves. But our brother uses certainly many more words than are needed to explain the matter. "Of such," of course, means "likeness." In this I agree with him with all my heart: "'Of [persons] like these is the kingdom.' And since it cannot be physical likeness that is meant (for this would plainly imply that none but infants were in the kingdom), it must be moral likeness." Very well. Can our brother, then, conceive any nearer likeness— moral or any other—*to* little children *than* little children? He answers scarcely in a very direct manner;

"But how can the words 'of such is the kingdom' denote that children form a class in the kingdom? If they are a sample of the persons in the kingdom, all the persons that are in the kingdom must be like the sample, or it is no sample." We do not disagree. *Little children, then, "like" those little ones, and other persons like them,* belong to the kingdom.

But it will be said against this, perhaps, that I "persist in treating the word 'such' as if it necessarily implied *sameness*, whereas it only implies likeness. . . . These little babes are a sample, not of the persons in the kingdom, but of the *kind* of persons in the kingdom. . . . This is a most important distinction. It demonstrates that our Lord's words do not of themselves necessarily imply that those dear little babes were in the kingdom; and this, we humbly submit, completely demolishes our opponents' stronghold."

But *we* do not believe that the children the Lord took into His arms were in the kingdom! The kingdom of which our Lord spoke was not yet begun; and the last verses of the gospel show definitely its beginning. (Matt. xxviii. 18). No; the Lord was here looking on to the future when He spoke; and He does not say "of *these*," but "of *such*." Sameness in *some* respect there must be in every likeness; but there is not the sameness that is *individual* identity. He shows the kind of persons that were to be in His kingdom: babes and those like babes.

Consider that of old in His kingdom He had always had babes,— that cannot be disputed. Was He going now to reject them, and forbid what He had before enjoined? Do His words look like forbidding, or the reverse? He was receiving from their parents' hands those that the law enjoined to be received, and was "much displeased" that His disciples would not have suffered it. "Suffer them to come," He says, which undeniably means here "Suffer them to *be brought*," as they were being brought; and which (as undeniably, one would have thought) did *not* mean "Suffer them to *believe* on Me"(!) which is C's interpretation! *Can* he really mean that the disciples were trying to hinder the babes from *believing on Jesus?* Or would he, admitting the simple fact that "coming" means literally what it says, think it just as reasonable that the Lord should have received sheep or lambs, because it might be said "of such is the kingdom of heaven"?

No; it is He who was Israel's king of old proclaiming for the new kingdom that was then "at hand," the continuance of no less goodness than He had shown in the one passed away. He would not be less gracious in the present than He had been in the past, nor less answer the craving of the hearts of His people for the children intrusted to them.

J. J. has less to say than this, and J. J. S. no more than J. J. For both these, "Suffer them to *come*" means "Suffer them to *believe*"; and "of such" is read so as to exclude those that are most of all "such"! "If we do not bring our children to Him in any other way than by baptism, we shall not do it at all"! And if we do not eat the Lord's flesh in any other way than in the Lord's Supper we shall not do it at all. Are we, then, indeed, such poor, pitiful ritualists, that we need to be reminded of such things as these?

But can we make the meaning of the "of such" a little plainer yet, and show how the babes and the grown people like them are linked together? Let us try to get at the point of the comparison; and this will be got, I think, by considering what "the word of the kingdom" must imply for those receiving it. It implies, of course, submission to the King; that is, to His commandment, the yoke of discipleship. For this they must be as little children; for what is the little child the type of but of the learner, of one under the yoke? The will of man it is that resists the claims of the Lord Jesus,— the independence of man that refuses submission: "we have turned every one to his own way" is the inspired description of the world as away from God. For blessing, therefore, that way must be given up; and men must become like children, and take, in obedience, the learner's place.

But the children are, in some sense, already there. The state of childhood is what God has ordained for blessing, when the will is in its plastic state, and when submission to authority is natural, as it is necessary. Here the parent is the designed minister of God for good, standing in the place of authority, which most of all *represents* God among men. That "that which is born of the flesh is flesh," is, of course, true: the little child, as soon as it begins to live, begins to manifest that it is a fallen being. Still, the child's being "flesh" may be pressed in a harsh way, with which those who press it are happily quite inconsistent. Rightly, they teach their children; and we are expressly assured, "Train up a child in the way he should go, and when he is old he will not depart from it." And we are expressly bidden, "Bring up your children in the discipline and admonition of the Lord." God must be with this for any good, but He *will* be with it: and here we are bidden to put our children in the place of disciples. "I know him," God says of Abraham, "that he will command his children and his household after him, and they *shall* keep the way of the Lord, to do justice and judgment, that the Lord may bring upon Abraham that which He has spoken of him." Now we know what God had spoken of Abraham's seed; and to us He has given as comforting assurance of what His mind is toward us: "Believe on the Lord Jesus Christ, and thou shalt be saved, and thy house." But to this we shall have to return later on.

Disciples and Discipling.

C. is right as to the expression "discipled *to* the kingdom." He will find it given correctly a few lines further on (Reasons, p. 25), and the force is on the word "discipled." The phrase is the same as in Matt. xxvii. 57, where Joseph of Arimathea is said to have been "discipled to Jesus"; that is, of course, made a disciple of Jesus. It will not do, from any interpretation of Luke xvii. 21, to make the kingdom and the king convertible terms. The kingdom was in the midst of Israel, I do not question, in the person of the king; and those who were discipled to the kingdom were, of course, discipled to the king, but that is no ground for changing the one into the other. The phraseology of Scripture is always the most accurate; and in Matt. xiii, which treats of the "mysteries of the kingdom,"— things unknown before — we see at once how the Old Testament "scribe," brought to the understanding of these mysteries, would have new treasures added to the old ones. The parables show, also, if they show anything, that the kingdom is formed by the word of the kingdom being received into men's hearts: that is, it is the sphere of discipleship.

A Review of Objections.

The first parable also shows that there were disciples, and "disciples indeed,"— disciples who "continued" in the word, and those who did not (Comp. John vi. 66). This merely means, and is only taken to mean, that the word is not at all equivalent to "child of God," or "member of Christ." Our brother C. complains, as "unfair," of the use of our Lord's words in John viii. 31, "as if it implied the existence of a recognized class of disciples of a lower grade." It is simply used to show that continuance (as the wheat which had no proper root did not continue) distinguished true disciples from the unreal. C. says it "is in contrast with some who had just then (v. 30) become convinced that He was the Messiah." There is no *contrast* at all; and there was, as yet, nothing to contrast with. It is a word of encouragement, and, at the same time, of admonition; and what they might turn out to be is of no account whatever. By the fact of their professed belief in Him they were taking the place of disciples, and He spoke to them in that character. As a fact, it is well known what "disciples" meant. There were "disciples" of John, of Moses, of the Pharisees: the word is a common word for the followers of any teacher, and does not decide as to the reality of the profession even. Who can deny it?

When the Lord is risen from the dead, and the kingdom is ready to be proclaimed, He says, "All *authority*"— not power —"is given unto Me, in heaven and in earth: go ye, and *disciple* all nations." It is plain He would not say "Make children of God": this was within His own power only. "Disciple" was the suited word in reference to the kingdom; and this brings us to the commission.

The Commission and the Keys.

The words here, literally, are "Go and disciple all the nations, baptizing them . . . teaching them." J. J. S. remarks upon a quotation: "The writer admits that the grammatical construction requires that the *them* should be connected with 'disciples.'" Grammatical construction makes this quite impossible, for there is no word "disciples" for "them" to be connected with. "Disciple all the nations, baptizing *them*."

I agree with C. that "it is certain that individuals, not nations collectively, are meant." I should have thought the other view impossible. How could nations be got at "collectively"? A nation could not be "discipled" in the mass, but only by individuals. The discipling is defined, I doubt not, as to be effected in two ways,— by baptism and teaching. Our brother C. demurs, and produces passages in proof that the grammar does not *necessitate* this construction of it. Yet it is, at least, the most natural way of expressing mode: "Preach, saying"; "disciple, baptizing." But, moreover, if "teaching" must be allowed to enter into the very idea of discipling, as our brother would allow it must,— for it is what is taught that makes the real scholar,— then still more must the "baptizing," put side by side with this, serve to fill out and explain further the same thing. It was fit, where the Master was at the same time the Lord,— where the school was at the same time the kingdom,— that there should be this sign of submission on the part of those taking their place there. They are "baptized unto the name of the Lord Jesus"; and this is connected with the authoritative "remission of sins."

The "keys of the kingdom" are here clearly to be seen. "But where does it say there were just two keys?" asks J. J. S. If he can find a third we shall not object; but it surely requires more than one to make a plural. The Lord Himself speaks of the "key of knowledge"; but there needs another, if the expression be an accurate one. Our brethren are evidently shy of the question. "The real truth is," says J. J. S. again, "that Peter had the authority given him to open the door, that being what the keys represent in Scripture; and when the door was once opened it did not need to be opened again, so we don't need any man with keys to-day." This settles the matter, if an assertion can settle it; but why should not the key of knowledge be enough, then, without "keys"? Why "keys" at all? Take the commission as it reads, and the whole is clear: we see that the keys are needed still, and that the door was not thrown open once for all.

But "the keys were given to Peter, and to Peter *alone*"! It is not said "*alone*." Was the promise "and whatsoever thou shalt bind on earth" to Peter alone? Certainly as much as that of the keys. Did it hinder the Lord extending this to the assembly a little after? Why should the promise of the keys not have a similar extension in the commission to disciple here?

But, urges C., "if infants are in the kingdom, they are in it without the key of knowledge, why may they not also be in it without the key of baptism?" A fair question; and it can be as fairly answered. With regard to infants, they are received as the household of the parents, whom God has put in the place of authority over them. The key of knowledge is not set aside, but the parent acts as the guardian and representative of the child before God, charged with its interests, and not for the setting aside of the truth, but for its complete establishment over it. The exception is only apparent in this case, the spirit of the rule being perfectly observed.

Why could one only baptize among the heathen those who give evidence of some real conversion? It is because baptizing must be discipling; and where this is not meant to take the Lord's yoke really, it would be merely a mockery to baptize. For the child it is the parents' will that gives confidence as to this, and so one can "disciple." In either case the result may, alas, disappoint our hope.

One more objection only: it is that of J. J., who says: "As to baptism being one of the keys of the kingdom, if it be such it was an unaccountable omission not to give it to Paul, who was sent 'not to baptize.' But I question very much whether the Lord would have called an ordinance a 'key.'"

Now I should think that the keys being given to *all* the disciples after the resurrection of the Lord would be the very best reason why they should not be given to Paul as part of his special commission! Paul was the special minister of the Church (Col. i. 25) in its full character, and in this the baptismal commission could have no place.

Again, the simple and external nature of baptism would in no wise hinder its being a token of the Lord's authority, in its place very needful thus; and, when intelligently practised, a witness to much essential truth. But we shall have to look at this further, presently.

It is evident that our brethren cannot show us any other keys; and thus these, spite of their protests, fit the lock in this way also.

The Meaning of Baptism.

"'Scripture speaks of baptism as a 'figure,'" says J. J. "'The like figure whereunto even baptism doth also now save us' (1 Pet. iii. 20). A figure is not efficacious in itself. It is a figure of something else which is efficacious." This is simple enough, surely. It is a figure of salvation; and a figure cannot really save.

But while this is very well as a protest against ritualism, it is not the whole thing. An ordinance may accomplish something, and yet be a figure of that which it does *not* accomplish. Yet J. J. says: "Any system of doctrine which attaches efficacy to an ordinance is ritualistic, and is so far a departure from the truth. It is an unintentional but practical denial of the fact that ordinances are taken out of the way and nailed to the cross of Christ. It is to take them down again from the cross, and to assume to use them to effect what only a work of grace can accomplish. The two ordinances of Christianity — Baptism and the Lord's Supper — are not ordinances at all in this sense: they have no power whatever to 'effect' anything."

Where does our brother find this teaching in Scripture? The passage which he quotes for it does not bear him out, and his appeal to it is of the loosest kind. The apostle is speaking of "the *obligation* of ordinances (or decrees) which was against and contrary to" those in Judaism. This Christ has "wiped out," and stricken through with the nails of His cross. Without any ordinance whatever, the dying thief, according to the word of the Lord, goes to Paradise with Him. Cornelius receives the Holy Ghost, with all his company, before they are baptized. This is the grace of God in Christianity, gloriously free. But this granted fully — and the meaning left wholly unimpaired — how should this hinder that for the entrance into the company of His people on earth there should be this simple but significant and authoritative admission? Must we say, with J. J., that baptism, though to Christ, effects *nothing?* — that even though one is baptized unto remission of sins, — is baptized and washes away his sins, — still this is nothing? — and as he would not, but still we must, say that baptism is discipling, yet it accomplishes nothing?

Nor are we sacramentalists because we cannot grant this (C. 21). Our brother may find, if he please to look, whether in the Episcopal prayer-book, or the Westminster Confession of Faith, that a sacrament is understood to be an ordinance that *conveys the grace it signifies.* Thus if baptism is figuratively (as they hold) "the washing of regeneration," it imparts this grace — it *regenerates.* This, assuredly, I do not hold. And yet I do hold that there is a congruity between the figurative meaning and what is accomplished by the baptismal act.

Baptism is "discipling." It brings a person out of the outside world into the company of disciples, the Lord's followers on earth. It does not work the spiritual change which this would imply for one becoming in heart a disciple, but it does *figure* this. It does not save in *fact*, but it does in *figure*. (1 P. iii. 21.)

It is easy to see why the figure of the internal work should be found in what is external. The outward discipling becomes in this way a witness to the inward necessity, — a gospel pledge or assurance that if that be truth in the heart which is here outwardly declared, then the highest and fullest blessing which it witnesses to belongs to the disciple. But there is necessarily an "if," from the human side. God knoweth the heart; and hence the conditionality always connected with the kingdom.

Take the "remission of sins." In the absolute way we know that the Jews were right in their question, guilty as they were in their unbelief of Christ's glory, "Who can forgive sins but God alone?" Yet the Lord can say, and does, to His disciples, "Whose sins ye remit they are remitted to them"; and baptism at disciples' hands is to the remission of sins. Is this, then, the same kind of remission as His? No, assuredly: it is for the present kingdom, and for earth,— not for heaven and eternity. Yet it is the witness and conditional declaration of the other. And such conditional remission we have in the parable of the unforgiving debtor (Matt. xviii. 23–35), a parable of the kingdom of heaven.

"The reference here is *plainly*" however, J. J. S. says, "to the Jewish nation"; although there is nothing that I can see in the Lord's words to Peter to suggest such a thought. The Jewish nation never sued for forgiveness at his hands, never took the place of those forgiven; and there is nothing in the context of the parable to make it likely. The connection with baptism, which our brother cannot find, is simply that it is a parable of the kingdom.

Let us look now at the figurative meaning of baptism, and we shall find that nowhere does it figure the state, but the *process*, of salvation. Says J. J. "Baptism is a figure of Christ's death; and . . . it supplies the answer to the demand for a good conscience, because it is the figure of the death of Christ; and as He is risen from the dead, faith finds in His death all the demands of conscience met." But it is not the action in baptism that expresses this. The death of Christ is what we are baptized *to :* we are baptized *to* Christ, *to* His death. The water, like Jordan after Christ had been in it, does express to us that by which salvation comes; but the baptism proper is the immersion into it. But, again, "it supplies the answer to the demand for a good conscience"! Not at all: it is the "demand" itself, not the *answer* to the demand; and this shows that the one coming to baptism is not, in *idea*, one saved, but one *seeking* salvation. Baptism is the burial of the person himself, as judicially dead already, to meet Christ in His death. It is thus "burial with Christ,"— Christ remaining in the efficacy of His death for all who need Him, even while and because Himself risen; so that baptism is, in figure, salvation,— the process, not the state.

Again he says, speaking of those baptized upon the day of Pentecost, "their baptism was 'upon' their confession." Not exactly, either: their baptism *was* their confession. But this, too, he states elsewhere.

Again, "This forgiveness of sins was eternal remission, for it was founded upon Christ's death, upon the confession of whose name they were baptized." If this be so, what becomes of ordinances effecting nothing, as he tells us, when they were baptized to get *eternal* remission! Surely extremes meet here!

As to the gift of the Holy Spirit following, Heb. vii, 4, surely shows that it did not necessarily result that a person made "partaker of the Holy Ghost" was saved. The historical account, as in Acts, is not the record of the inward state of souls. Nor, indeed, do we know how far the signs of the Spirit's presence manifested themselves in the baptized. All did not work miracles, or speak with tongues.

Again, very strangely, J. J. quotes, "The like figure whereunto even baptism doth also now save us," and adds "plainly linking it with a saved state." But in what way? As the result of the baptism, or in order to it?—absolute or conditional?—figure or fact?

J. J. S., commenting on Rom. vi., says:—

"We are buried with Him by baptism: that surely implies death with Him. We are 'baptized unto His death'; that is, in recognition of His death. But we are buried,— not to His, but unto death; that is, an acknowledgment of our death with Him. The way our household baptists try to reason out of this plain Scripture is a remarkable instance of the really blinding effect of following human theories. The very truth it is taken up to develop — that is, in connection with sin — is enough to show it is only believers, and true believers, that could be in question here."

It is, however, "plain," if anything is, in J. J. S.'s argument, that the truth of our being "dead with Christ," which the apostle reaches only in the 6th and 7th verses, *he* implies in the beginning of the 4th; yet the apostle is carefully reasoning up to it. The truth of being dead with Christ has not been stated before at all. He reaches it in this way:—

We were baptized to Christ: [that needs no argument]; to His death then: nothing else would have met our need. Let us remember how John baptized in Jordan — death,— and that to Jordan Christ came, and was baptized. There, then, it lies before us,— Jordan with Christ in it, *His* death. Now, then, we have descended, this is our part, "buried with Him by baptism into death." Risen as He is, His death abides for us in all its value; but we need, in order to reach Him, to take the place in death ourselves,— to be buried, put into the place of death.

But the dead only can have title to the place of death: have we such title? Yes; but not because naturally dead in sins, for we could never find Jesus there: that could not be the death He took. Judicial death, then, the due of sin? Yes; this is ours; we can take this place, and Christ is in it. We must be buried with Him,— buried in His sepulchre, so to speak; to touch and get virtue from Him, that we may live.

Remember that we are baptized *to* Christ, *to* His death; and baptism is the soul on its quest for Christ, the *demand* for a good conscience, not the declaration that we have found it. The baptism is to Him, to gain Him,— ends with effecting this. The rest is His work. The life, *He* gives. The satisfaction of conscience is the fruit of His cross. Buried with Him by baptism unto death, it is that, as Christ was raised from the dead by the glory of the Father, we also should walk in newness of life. For now (mark) if we have become united to Him (R. V.) in the likeness of His death — the quest of baptism attained — we shall be in the likeness of His resurrection.

Here, now, in this new state of things, we can look joyfully around. *Knowing this, that our old man is crucified with Him* that the body of sin might be destroyed — (annulled) — that henceforth we should not serve sin."

Yes, *now* we may begin to speak of being dead with Christ: before we could not. This is the effect of what baptism speaks of — impossible before we had the effect. And now we can go on to the deliverance from the power of sin, where, as J. J. S. says, "only believers, and true believers, could be in question." But we have reached this point by a legitimate path, not implying, at the start, what was really the conclusion, as our baptist brethren do. That the conclusion is for believers, we are equally sure with them; but that does not involve the unscriptural thought of baptism being the expression of a saved state, instead of the "demand for a good conscience," and that which, as a figure, saves. These are two opposite thoughts, impossible to reconcile; and upon this rock J. J. S.'s argument is capsized and lost, without hope of recovery.

Baptism in Relation to Children.

We have learnt, then, four things as to baptism which are in direct opposition to our brethren's contention:—

First, that it is *to* Christ's death, not to show that one was dead with Christ before.

Secondly, that (as a figure) it saves, not expresses the thought of having been saved before.

Thirdly, it is the demand for a good conscience, not the answer of one already good.

Fourthly, that it is for the remission of sins, not the sign of their having *been* remitted.

All this is in clear consistency with the thought of it as one of the keys of the kingdom, a kingdom not yet set up in power, nor yet spiritual in such sort as to require to be born again to see it or enter into it. On the contrary, it is the kingdom of God in man's hand, so entirely that the Lord represents that—

"So is the kingdom of God as if a man should cast seed into the ground, and sleep and rise, night and day, and the seed should spring and grow up, he knoweth not how. . . . But when the fruit is brought forth, immediately he putteth in the sickle, because the harvest is come." (Mk. iv. 26–29.)

How unlike this to a kingdom into which God alone introduces by new birth! Oh, it is said, that is the "outward aspect,"—that is, "as men see it,—when they have just told us that it is so spiritual that not one can "see" it, except by being born again, nor one enter it except by a door safely guarded by God's own hand. On the contrary, if *men* sleep, the tares spring up in it in plenty.

But the Church, you say, has not that the two aspects? Yes; because the Church is not only the body of Christ, into which the Spirit baptizes, but also the house of God, which bad builders may extend unduly (1 Cor. iii. 12, sq.) But the history of the body of Christ has never been written; and it is never said, and could not be said, The *body of Christ* is like a field in which an enemy sows tares! Once make the kingdom of God what the body of Christ is, and such views of it become wholly and forever impossible.

But now as to baptism in relation to children.

A babe newly born has no "sins" as yet to be remitted. True; though, alas, *that* difficulty soon passes away. But the true answer lies a little deeper. For the Christian, remission of sins has in view the evil of the old nature and the practical frailty belonging to us all. And it applies, therefore, not as men soon began to think, to the past merely, but to the present ever, as the future comes continually into it. A Christian *always* has the forgiveness of sins, for it is according to the riches of a grace at all times sufficient for us. Thus the objection will be found, after all, a superficial one.

As to all else that may be objected, the answer has been already virtually given. The parent, by his God-given place, represents the child, and is distinctly

accepted of the Lord in bringing his child to Him,—
that being the "coming" which the disciples were
bidden to "suffer." It is amazing that our baptist
brethren can interpret this coming as "believing."
It is really an interpretation scarcely respectable
enough to deserve serious answer. Was it their *believing* that the disciples were hindering?—and was it
that that called forth the Lord's displeasure when He
said, "Suffer them to come unto Me, and forbid them
not"? We have surely good right to feel that there is
a veil over the eyes of those who can argue in this
way. Why, if anything is clear, it is so that it is the
parent's desire that the Lord is meeting, on the part of
those who were young enough, at any rate, to be taken
up into the Saviour's arms. Are there any who will
read this who need to be told what this desire was?
And it is to justify His granting it that He adds, as
to the babes, "of such is the kingdom of heaven."
There was, of course, no baptism; for the kingdom
was not yet; nor, therefore, baptism into it. *When*
this should come, *then* baptism for them would express
in His own personal absence, what as present He here
gives them assurance of! It is as if He said, I accept
them in this relation to Me which you desire for them.
They are Mine: you, as delegates for Me, bring them
up for Me. That is what the baptism does: it formally
admits them into the school of Christ,—*disciples*
them.

The baptism of the household expresses this. It is
the precious pledge of the absent Redeemer's love,
which is to be answered by the faith that says, in the
sense of the responsibility it implies, "Lord, they *are*
Thine, and they *shall be* Thine." Answer is easy,
therefore, to the question, why not baptize *all* babes?

— why only *believers'* households? Why, because only believers' households *can* be, in fact, "discipled." Only those who have *come* to Christ can *bring* to Christ, or therefore bring *up* for Christ. And this governs all right practice, and shows clearly how *household* baptism is the only consistent form of *infant* baptism: to those for whom baptism is to be real "discipling," clear and simple as the day!

And this, too, shows, as to those *in* the household, the rule that should govern us. The "atheist" son, of whom C. speaks, for instance, if old enough and developed enough to be such, has clearly passed from under his father's authority and care. If, in any case, the reins of authority have dropped out of the parents' hands, how can one treat the one of whom this is true as any longer of the household? As for *servants*, and in a day such as this, the thought of baptism, if any entertain it, is beyond my comprehension. Let baptism be discipling,— a thing identified with and implying the Lord's yoke for those baptized,— and the practice is simple as it is *holy:* only holy thus.

But the kingdom is the sphere* of profession? Yes; I believe so. But how can a little child profess? It is not meant that it does, or necessary that it should. It is under authority, according to God's order in the world; and, in this sense, in professed subjection, though it be the father's will, and not the child's. The term is, however, not applied in Scripture directly to the kingdom, and if thought unsuitable need not be pressed. Yet the household baptized *is* professedly Christ's, and

---

* That the kingdom is not territorial, but individual; that is, over individuals, if it were in China: this I understand, and hold. Why, "*therefore*, it cannot be a sphere," I cannot understand.

"HOLY."

I do not believe in holiness by "birth," even "of a Christian parent." The baptism *is* that setting apart to God, which alone gives in Scripture the applicability of such a title. "The child," it is said, "is already set apart by the will of God to the care of its Christian parents, and is not to be put away as unclean, even if one parent be unconverted." *Every* child is set apart by the word of God to the care of its parents, which only confirms what Nature already teaches. But this does not make it *holy;* that is, set it apart *to God.* The unbelieving wife or husband is sanctified only in the other partner, so as to make the child *clean;* but that does not make it "holy." The unbelieving wife is "clean"; that is, does not defile the believing husband: she is not "holy,"— set apart *to God.*

C. mistakes entirely the meaning here, and certainly seems to charge me with practising deception. Will he allow me to assure him that I thought everybody knew what he has explained to us — that to sanctify is to make holy? The argument is that, while the wife or husband is looked at as holy only "*in*" *another*, in such a sense as not to defile the issue of the marriage, the children are not merely clean, they are holy; and the relationship to Jewish law intimated is quite instructive. In Judaism every one knows that the children were brought into covenant relationship to God by circumcision. In the case of marriage with one of the prohibited nations, this would so defile the Jew contracting it as to deprive the child of the right to circumcision. Christianity reversed this, sanctified (so far as the marriage was concerned) the unbeliever, looked at both as (in this respect) within the covenant; and showed it did so by accepting the children of the marriage.

Thus the "holy" comes with special force,— not merely clean. "Clean" would not express for the Jew the thought conveyed by holy (*qadosh*); that is, "consecrated, dedicated, or sanctified to God"; and *hagios* is the word which would be used in Greek for expressing this. To have said "clean" would have been enough to have proved the lawfulness of the marriage. The "sanctified" and "holy" were both needed in order to express the thought of relationship to God. The use of the two words, therefore, here, is every way significant.

It is true that circumcision was connected with a nation after the flesh. That was, then, how the promises were entailed. But surely even here the spiritual relation was that ever insisted on; and apart from this the other was nothing, or brought only condemnation. How even for the Jew does the apostle press the meaning of circumcision; and that that was not truly such which was merely outward in the flesh! (Rom. ii. 28.) How, then, can one make the fleshly relation rule, as if it were the whole thing? That was, indeed, the form taken at the time by the kingdom of God. The form has passed, but the kingdom of God remains; and, according to the Lord's express assurance, the children brought in their parents' faith to Him have still their place in it. Strange it would have been if *He* had cut them off!

It is a little bold, then, to say that "no Scripture shows that the family of the believer comes in with him." In both these places the Scripture does so.

Οικος and οικια.

The baptism of households is, then, a thing of course; and our finding it only confirms what should be already clear to us. The word used for household in every case of this kind is the regular one where a man's own children are in question, οικος; and the apostle seems to put these households in a class distinct from those baptized as believers, and so naturally coming into the assembly. (1 Cor. i. 16.) Let us note again the argument, as our brethren take no proper notice of it.

There were divisions at Corinth; and because baptism is discipling, the apostle was glad to think that he had baptized but two out of the whole number, Crispus and Gaius,— too few for a party, or to allow people to think that he had been making disciples of his own. This he thanks God for: "I baptized none of you but Crispus and Gaius." He adds (lest any, it would seem, should demur to such a statement) that he had baptized the *household* of Stephanas; for the rest, he did not know that he had baptized any other. The natural inference here, and especially in view of all that we have seen already,— the argument is cumulative: it gathers strength as it goes on,— is, that here are two classes of the baptized. Of those in the assembly he had only baptized two; of the *households* (in which the numbers would soon mount up) he had baptized one certainly, perhaps more, though he was not aware of it. We can see how consistent all this is, if he is speaking of families: it was of no consequence that he should remember the number he had baptized among these: they were not the promoters of division in the assembly.

Our brother C. suggests that the family of Stephanas was away from Corinth, because Stephanas himself had been; but his coming to the apostle as a messenger from the assembly was very recent, and it is very little likely that he carried his household with him. Journeys *were* journeys in those days of old. Nor would that have hindered their being essentially a part of the assembly, if away at the time he wrote. Neither does this explain the doubt of the last words.

The "household of Stephanas," mentioned in the last chapter of this epistle, who had addicted themselves to the ministry of the saints, has been always the ready argument against those before spoken of being children. An effectual one, too, it is, if the households are the same. But a different word is used here (οικια, not οικος), which, it is contended, is *not* the word for children of a family, nor for the household baptized. But this is in question. C. contends that they are used interchangeably. We ought to be able to see if this is true.

If we turn, then, to the Greek version of the Old Testament (the Septuagint), and look first of all at what is clear, we find that *wherever* we have undoubted reference to the children of the family,— to blood relationship,— οικος, not οικια, is the word used. Thus for Noah's house saved in the flood (Gen. vii. 1) the souls of the house of Jacob that came into Egypt with him, and which are enumerated as those that came out of his loins (ch. xlvi.), the house of Israel (the nation), the house of Joseph, etc. (the tribes), the fathers' houses into which these were divided, the house of Eli, condemned for their iniquity, the houses of Saul and of David, rivals for the throne, the house of Jeroboam, smitten for his idolatry, of Baasha, of Ahab, similarly judged, of Rechab, commended for obedience, and many more that could be named,— *all* these (without exception that I know) are οικος, οικια never once. How many occurrences?

Speaking roughly, we may say, about four hundred. Is not this a number sufficient to establish pretty well the force of this word in doubtful cases?

Take now οικια. Here we have the eldest servant of Abraham's house; Jacob tells Laban he has been twenty years in his *house*,—where he was treated like a servant; Potiphar's wife speaks to the men of her house about Joseph; and although the lamb of the passover is taken according to the οικος of their fathers, the measure of eating is a lamb for an οικια, because the servants must be included here: Joshua's "as for me and my house (οικια), we will serve the Lord," naturally includes the servants.

The word is used (both words are) more for a material building — house, in that sense — than for the inmates. The latter sense has naturally grown out of the former; and one would expect to find, therefore, in this fundamental meaning of the words something of the difference attaching to them in the higher one. I think no one who examines with any care will fail to realize that there *is* a distinction, and that they are not, by any means, used indifferently. Thus, for the house of God the word is always οικος, never οικια; and the latter seems to have always a lower character. Thus, for the house of the sparrow (Ps. lxxxiv. 3) and the stork (civ. 17), the word is οικια; and this is generally used for the houses of a town, or when there is nothing noteworthy about them; while for house as implying *home*, or as the better class of abode, it is generally οικος. I say "*generally*," for there are, naturally, apparent exceptions,— which, however, seem often to carry their reason in their face. These things it would take too long to go into in detail; but there seems, plainly, a difference even in this respect, which corresponds with the difference in the higher meaning.

When we come to the New Testament, which alone is inspired and perfect, the use of these words still corresponds, even in their lower signification,— with one apparent exception, however, which at first sight may seem absolutely unaccountable, but which we must look at directly. The house of God (the temple) is still always οικος, and there are here nineteen occurrences. For kings' houses the word is οικος (Matt. xi. 8); so with the high priest's (Luke xxii. 54); and the ruler's (Mark v. 38); so where *home* is emphasized (Mark v. 19; viii. 26; Luke i. 23; v. 24; viii. 39; ix. 61; xv. 6; John vii. 53; 1 Cor. xi. 34; xiv. 35; 1 Tim. v. 4). Except "my *servant* lieth at home" Matt. viii. 6), where it is οικια; as it is in "the *servant* abideth not in the house forever" (John viii. 35), and where a man "left his house, and gave authority to his *servants*" (Mark xiii. 34). Οικια is, again, the general term for houses.

To all this there is, however, as I have said, one objection, which, at first sight, might seem insuperable. When the Lord says to His disciples, "In my Father's house are many mansions," the word used for "house" is οικια. (John xiv. 2.)

Yet for temple, or tabernacle, and the Father's house, when meaning this, it is οικος that is used; and, of course, when it is said "whose house are *we*" (Heb. iii. 6), it is still οικος.

And is not this the explanation? If so, a precious witness of the Lord's value for His people, that the higher term is thus reserved for *them!* The "many mansions" are, after all, only the Father's dwelling-place in a lesser and external sense. The Church

of God is what He counts and calls His house—
οικος.

For the rest, it is still the latter word that is used for the house of Israel, house of David, house of Jacob,—twelve occurrences; the elders are to "rule their own houses well, having their children in subjection with all gravity." (1 Tim. iii. 4.) So, too, the deacons are to rule their children and (or "even") "their own houses well" (ver. 12). The baptized households are similarly οικος. And if five in one house (οικος) are divided, they are given as father and son, and mother and daughter, and daughter-in-law. (Luke xii. 52, 53.)

But we must hear now the protests of our brethren. J. J. replies that if οικια "includes the servants," as I had put it in my former tract, it does not exclude the children: "Will F. W. G. say that when the οικια ate the lamb, the children were excluded?" No; F. W. G., as may be seen, has no such thought. But yet the term, as contemplating the servants, would naturally be used where only they might be intended; and if 1 Cor. xvi. 16 does not in itself exclude the children, the first chapter implies their exclusion.

J. J. S.'s argument that Joseph being governor over "all the house of Pharaoh" (Acts vii. 10), where the word is οικος, "clearly refers to servants only," is, after all, not so clear. "Thou shalt be over my house," says the king, "and according to thy word shall all my people be ruled; only in the throne will I be greater than thou. . . . Without thee shall no man lift up his hand or foot in all the land of Egypt." Can J. J. S. say just how far such power extended?

But the deacons ruling their children and their own houses well! "Here, also, the word for house is οικος, and is definitely linked on to servants"! Not at all. The elders show rather the reverse, as the requisitions are otherwise so similar; and the emphasis on "*their own* houses" similarly shows the ground of the repetition. Their ability to care for the houses of others must be shown by the care given to their own. The "and" may just as well be "even."

C. finds great fault with my appeal to the house divided against itself; but he is wrong. "Five in one house" (οικος) is peculiar to Luke; and Matt. x. 36, is different. Here the Lord says, "And a man's foes shall be they of his own household,"— words not repeated in the other gospels. Here the word is οικιακος, derived, of course, from οικια; and which is used again, quite in accordance with the significance of οικια in the 25th verse of the same chapter in Matthew: "The disciple is not above his master, nor the *servant* above his lord: it is enough for the disciple to be as his master, and the *servant* as his lord." If they have called the master of the house Beelzebub, how much more shall they call *them of his household"?* (οικιακος). Now in the 35th verse there is no reason to limit this to those specified in the preceding. "Five in one οικια" would be very different. It is the parallelism of *words* that we are examining, and not of texts. All the rest of his remarks I have already answered.

THE HOUSEHOLDS.

Few words will now suffice as to the "households," and our brother C. will give us all the arguments. In the case of the jailer he tells us that "having believed" *could not* be plural. Of course the *form of the word* shows it could not: I do not know what else. It is, certainly, "*he* rejoiced," and he having believed. The adverb πανοικι is hard to put in English; and that is why, I suppose, translators generally accept "with all his house" as an equivalent. But I do not see how "all-householdly" would authorize this any more than "domestically." It would rather imply, I think, "*over*" or "as to all his house."

But the remark in ver. 31 is still more strange. "It was not said 'you now, and your house by and by.'" No; there is *neither* the "now" *nor* the "by and by." But the salvation of his house is connected with his own faith, whether it were now or by and by; and just as much in the former case as in the latter. Why, then, call it "sentimentality," or "sacramentalism," to accept the connection of such blessed words with the doctrine which runs through Scripture of the connection, in God's design, of blessing to a man's house because of his faith? Is it easier to believe that God should do this once in the way and of a sudden for the jailer here, than that he should imply his desire to do it for every believer? Is it good, by making this a special and exceptional thing, to take it away from any significance that one can see for any one else? Had the jailer even expressed any desire for his children? And if he had, what would save it from "sentimentality" in his case, when it seems it would be only that in ours?

As to the case of Lydia and her house, I think there is nothing that needs more reply, as far as I am concerned. Nor do I find anything of importance elsewhere. We may here, therefore, bring this discussion to an end.

In conclusion, only, it is well to observe that the divine word tests us often by what may seem to us the triviality of a positive institution. Wherever we can show what is manifestly moral in a command, the idea of the morality comes so to enforce the precept as sometimes to overshadow it *as a precept.* If I obey only where I know the *why* of the command, that is not obedience, properly. If duly obedient I can no longer question as to what I know to be of God. Thus the whole temper and spirit of my life may reveal itself in the breach of some command which to me may seem — and just because it does seem to me trivial — a small matter, whether in this particular I do His will or not.

Cannot I present my child to God, apart from baptism? I can, surely; but is my way or His the best? Cannot I remember the Lord's death apart from the symbols of bread and wine? As to how much, may we not argue similarly? But, after all, the simple acceptance of Christ's word will be found the way of surest blessing. If the baptism in itself be little enough, at how much shall we value the Christ who is behind it?

F. W. Grant.

THE CHURCH'S PATH.

"And Peter answered Him and said, 'Lord, if it be Thou, bid me come to Thee upon the waters.' And He said, 'Come.' And when Peter was come down out of the ship, he walked on the waters to go to Jesus." (Matt. xiv. 28, 29.)

THE *individuality* of the path is what I would press upon our souls just now. How strikingly it is presented! This solitary man, amid boisterous winds and waves, forsaking the protection of the boat and the company of the other disciples, and inviting the word which bids him to a path at once so difficult and so resourceless. We often speak of a walk of faith. It is well to look steadily at such a picture as this, and to ask ourselves, have we ever realized it in our own experience? does it present really what corresponds in its features (even though more deeply drawn,) to the path as we know it?

Solitary;—but he had before him as the end of his path the gracious and glorious presence of Him who had called him, and for sustaining power the word which in its call was a promise for all difficulties that could be. If in the meanwhile he had lost the company of others, every step on this road would make the *Presence* before him more bright and lustrous; and, at the end at least, even those now separated from would be restored. Was there not abundant compensation in the meantime? Would there not be an overpayment of joy at the end?

I would press, I again say, the individuality of

it. As we look back upon the examples of faith which God has given us in His own record, how they shine separately and independently out from surrounding darkness! How seldom are they set even in clusters! Enoch, in that walk with God which death never shadowed; Noah, with his family, sole survivors of a judgment-wrecked world; Abraham, with whom even Lot is a mere contrast. They stand out from the dark background as men not formed by their circumstances, no mere natural outgrowth from that in the midst of which we find them, but plants of the Lord's planting, maintaining themselves where no power but His could avail to keep them, north wind, as well as south, making the spices of His garden to flow out. In all these the individuality of the path is manifest. Lot is a warning as to the opposite course, of unmistakable significance. A walk with God means necessarily independence of men,—even of the saints; while if it is with God, it will be marked by unfeigned lowliness, and absence of mere eccentricity and self-will.

In the scene to which I am now referring, this solitary man, in that individual path in which nothing but divine power could for a moment sustain him, is the representative, as is evident, of the Church at large. The saints of the present time are as a body called to go forth to meet the Bridegroom, leaving the "boat" of Judaism, a provision for nature, not for faith. "The law is not of faith." To faith, God alone is necessary and sufficient, and other helps would be helps to do (so far) *without* Him: hindrances to faith therefore, really. Practically, it was a Jewish remnant that the Lord left when He went on high, and to a Jewish remnant we know He will return again, we in the meantime being called to meet Him and return with Him. This company Peter, not only here, but elsewhere, represents.

At first sight this may seem to take from the individual aspect. The path is the Church's path, and belongs to the whole, not merely to individuals: and that is so far true. In fact, as a company it has perhaps never walked in it; most certainly not for centuries: and Scripture—prescient as the Word of God must be—announced beforehand what history has since recorded. If then the Church has failed, is the Christian to accept for himself this failure? or is not individuality forced the more upon him,—a good which divine sovereignty thus brings out of the evil? But in truth it never was intended that the walk of a Christian should be different in principle or on a lower level than that which characterized faith in former generations. We were not meant to seek Lot-like companionship with one another, but Abraham-like with God. He is "the father of all them that believe." If Peter here, then, represent a company, it can only be a company of such as walk, each for himself, with God: a course which would indeed secure the most blessed companionship. Communion with one another can only be the result of communion with the Father and with the Son.

In this way how striking is the path of this lone man!—a path that terminates only in the presence of the Lord, and on which every step in advance brings nearer to Him! Various as in some true sense our paths must be, it is this that alone gives them their common Christian character; it is this that makes us pilgrims; nay, as the inspired Word presents it, *racers:* our goal outside the world; our object—that which rules us—heavenly. If it be not thus with us, we are immeasurably below those of a dispensation darkness itself compared with ours, who nevertheless by their lives "declared *plainly*" that they sought a better country. And for this reason God was not ashamed to be called their God, for He hath prepared for them a city.

This path of faith is one in which we may show, with Peter, not the greatness of our faith, but the littleness of it. It will never really make much of *us*. Do we seek it? The glory of Christ is what lies before and beckons us; for our weakness, if there be rebuke, it is only that of a perfect love. Not, Wherefore didst thou *presume?* but, "Wherefore didst thou *doubt?*" And with that, the outstretched hand of human sympathy and of divine support. Is it enough, dear fellow-Christian? Is there not for all the difficulties of the way an overabundant recompense? And the end—who shall declare its blessedness?

Yet let us remember that it is to one who *invites his Lord's invitation* to such a path that it really opens. The "Come" of Christ is an answer to him who says, "Lord, if it be Thou, *bid* me come to Thee upon the waters!" The *word* for the path is the answer alone to the *heart* for the path. And what to Him is the joy of such desire so expressed? Let ours go forth, if any have not yet, with such a cry: "Lord, if it be upon the waters I must come, and that path it is which alone leads to Thee, then bid me come to Thee, blest, gracious Master, even upon the water!"

DR. WALDENSTRÖM

AND

Non-Vicarious Atonement.

I.

THE work of Dr. Waldenström may well take its place among the *Current Events* which deserve special notice at our hands. It is one of the signs of the times—sad signs of the departure from the faith which is going on every where, and will go on to the apostasy predicted as that in which the dispensation ends. (2 Thess. ii.) I do not take it up, however, merely to notice it as that, but to give full examination to the views themselves, which, having been widely accepted already among Scandinavians generally, are now being brought before the English-speaking public for an acceptance which they are but too sure to find with many. Dr. Waldenström's writings have in them a tone of piety which will attract, while they assume to deal exhaustively with Scripture on their several topics. It is something which assuredly they are very far from doing, a partial truth being very commonly mistaken for the whole, so that we have but to fill in the gaps to find the antidote. But the appearance of doing so will be enough with many to carry their convictions, at least for a time. Among his own countrymen, we are told,—

"The promulgation of the author's views on the atonement occasioned a very general and earnest searching of the Word of God by all classes of Christians, and as these so-called 'new views' were plainly found just in that Word, they were accepted by the majority of Swedes, in their own and in this country [America]; also by many among Norwegians and Danes, by preachers and people in and outside the state church. Notwithstanding the cry of heresy raised in some quarters at the time against Dr.

W——, he passed triumphantly (in 1873), by a discussion before the bishop and consistory of the diocese, his examination for admission into the higher orders of the clergy. In 1874, he was appointed professor of theology (including Biblical Hebrew and Greek) in the state college at Gefle, one of the largest cities in Sweden. This position he still holds, while at the same time he is serving his second term in the Swedish parliament."

It is with the treatise on the "Blood of Jesus," the key-note to his views as to atonement, that we naturally begin. It leads us at once into the heart of our subject.

He tells us, first of all, that if, according to the law of Moses, "almost all things are purged with blood" (Heb. ix. 22), "the purging itself was accomplished, not by the slaying of the victim, but by the sprinkling with the blood. This has a profound typical significance. In the New Testament also it is said that cleansing from sin is effected by the *blood* of Jesus—notice: not by the *death* of Jesus, but by the *blood* of Jesus."

This is true, and the reason is plain also: by the blood of Jesus our "hearts are sprinkled from an evil conscience." (Heb. x. 22.) And this sprinkling is just the *application to the person* of Christ's blessed work Useless would His death be to us if it were not to be *applied*—that is, appropriated to us; and the blood speaks of death, but of a *violent* death, not of a natural one; of a life *taken*, not merely ended. A natural death the Lord could not have died, and such a death could not have availed us, because it implies sin in the one who dies.

But, says Dr. Waldenström further, by the blood of Christ we cannot mean His bodily or physical blood; but the blood must be a *type* of something: we have to ask ourselves, therefore, what the blood typifies.

This is a very serious mistake. The blood of Christ is not a type of something else. It is used metonymically, as the rhetoricians say,—that is, to express such a death as has been pointed out; but that is a very different thing from its being a type. This would deny the blood of the cross to have any real place in our cleansing from sin at all. It would be simply in such relation to it as was Moses lifting up the serpent in the wilderness, and nothing more. Dr. Waldenström seems to have borrowed from Swedenborgianism here.

But he asks what is meant by the saints having "washed their robes in the blood of the Lamb," or our eating Christ's flesh and drinking His blood. "Every one understands," he says, "that the blood here is a type of something." I can only answer that, for my own part at least, I have never thought so. *Figurative*, of course, the expressions are; but it does not follow that *every expression* in a sentence is figurative even because some are. The washing and the garments, the eating and the drinking, may be figurative; and are, surely: but it does not make the blood simply a "type." When the Lord says, "He that eateth ME shall live by Me," is Christ Himself only a type? It is strange that a professor of theology should make so rash a statement.

He bids us, again, observe that it is not "*faith* in the blood" which cleanses from sin, but the blood itself. And that it is not the "value of the blood in the sight of God," but only the blood. And again, that the blood of Christ is never represented as a payment to God for our sins; nor in the Old Testament is the blood of the sacrifices ever represented as such a payment.

What all this is to prepare the way for is pretty clear. But is it true? and is it the whole truth?

For it is plain that if our hearts are sprinkled from an evil conscience — and sprinkling is to cleanse, as Dr. Waldenström insists,— we read, on the other hand, of God "purifying hearts through *faith*" (Acts xv. 9), and of "peace"—that is, a purged conscience—"in *believing*' (Rom. xv. 13); just as we read of justification by faith, sanctification by the truth,—that is, of course, by faith in it,—and so on. Surely it is true that faith has for its object, not faith, but Christ, and His work, and that its power for blessing is in this very thing. Thus this is just how faith necessarily must say, "*Not* faith, nor any thing in myself, but the blood of Christ cleanseth." And that is true; and yet without faith there would be no cleansing.

Now, when he says, It is not the value of the blood in the sight of God that cleanses, he makes another mistake of the same kind. Whatever the value of a remedy, of course, it is not its *value* that acts in the cure. It is the remedy itself that acts. It is indeed the blood that cleanses, and by its being sprinkled; but if we ask, *how* is it the sprinkled blood can cleanse? we shall then find that its *cleansing* power depends upon its *atoning* power,— that is, upon its *value in the sight of God*. Dr. Waldenström confounds here cleansing with atonement, while in general we shall find he makes atonement to depend upon cleansing, instead of making, as he should make, cleansing depend upon atonement. These two things are widely different. Cleansing is for man, (it is man who is cleansed), while atonement is for God. Once let us make this easy distinction, Dr. Waldenström's doctrine will appear the mere confusion that it really is.

As to the blood of Christ being *payment* for our sins, the expression, it is true, is indefensible, although those who use it have, after all, a truer thought than Dr. Waldenström. It is true that the sacrifices of old were not represented as payment for sin, and that this would be a gross, low thought, unworthy of God; yet our author seems to have forgotten that there was such a thing as atonement-*money* (Ex. xxx. 12), and that this was said to be a ransom for their souls. It is to this also that the apostle refers when he says that we "were not redeemed with corruptible things, as with silver and gold, ... but with the precious blood of Christ, as of a lamb without blemish and without spot." (1 Pet. i. 18, 19.) Here, undoubtedly, the blood of Christ is regarded as the true atonement-money.

The thought, then, is, of a price by which we are redeemed; and with this, all are *purchased*. (2 Pet. ii. 1.) Christ's sufferings are thus a price He paid for all, though only a *ransom*-price for His people. *Purchase* must be distinguished from *redemption*, although every one that will may find in the first general truth what enables him to realize the special and distinctive one. Christ tasted "death for every man." (Heb. ii. 9.) Here is the price paid, and for all: it is for faith to lay hold of this, and say, as it has title to say, "Then I am His." To him who *receives* this precious grace, the purchase is found to be redemption.

What, then, is the mistake in saying that Christ has made "payment for our sins"? This, that in Scripture the price is for *us*, not for our sins. He has bought us as that which had value in His eyes. True that the price He had to pay was really that of making atonement for our sins: here is the way open for the confusion, if we are not as careful as, in matters such as these, we should be; and yet we ought to be able easily to distinguish what is very different. Price paid for *us* speaks of where His heart is: price paid for *sin* conveys the thought of God being able to tolerate it if His demands are met. Yet no renewed soul could mean such a thing or think of it. The expression to him is only intended to convey that there was an absolute necessity for satisfaction to God's righteousness in order to our salvation, and Christ has given this. Blessed be God, He has! but price for *sin* is a different thought, and one to be rejected utterly— which every true soul brought face to face with it will assuredly reject.

But Dr. Waldenström sees no need of satisfaction to divine justice, as Mr. Princell on his part explicitly assures us ("The Reconciliation," p. 5, *n*.). Thus with him there is not merely confusion of thought, but fundamental error, as will be clearly seen in the issue.

For him, the blood of Christ is a type, as we have seen; and he thinks that very commonly "Christians hear and speak and sing about the 'blood of Jesus' without making it clear to themselves what this expression means," and so it is not "of any use to true edification"! If this be so, it is surely sad enough. Think of it, that very commonly to *true* Christians (we must suppose) all their hearing and talking and singing about the blood of Jesus is really a vain and idle thing! They do not even know what the blood of Jesus means! What then? do they not know that it is that which was shed for them upon the cross for their sins? And is the belief of that wondrous fact unedifying to the one who bows prostrate in adoration before God because it is so?

What is, then, for Dr. Waldenström the meaning of the blood of Jesus? He goes on to tell us,—

"In Lev. xvii. 11 (according to the original), we read, 'The life [or soul] *of the body* is in the *blood*, and I have given it you to sprinkle [or pour] upon the altar, that thereby atonement may be made for your lives [or souls]; *for the blood maketh atonement by reason of the life* [or soul] *which is therein.*' And again in ver. 14, '*The life* [or *soul*] *of all flesh is in its blood, and it* [the blood] *constitutes its life* [or soul]. For that reason the Israelites were forbidden to eat blood. From these words we understand that the *blood* is a term for or expressing *life*; and this immediately sheds a beautiful, heavenly light upon the language of the Bible concerning the blood of Jesus."

The blood means, then, the *life*, for Dr. Waldenström: that is evidently not death, but its opposite. And the *blood* of Jesus of course means, not the death, but the *life* of Jesus!

Let us first of all examine Dr. Waldenström's translation of the passages to which he refers us. Would it be imagined that he has more than once inserted words which are not there, but which are his commentary merely, and even *emphasized* what he has inserted, as if part of the text? Yet it is so: the words, "to sprinkle [or pour]," and "which is therein," the last of which is emphasized for us in his book, have absolutely nothing corresponding to them in the Hebrew; and the last of these additions is one of special importance for his argument. "For the blood maketh atonement by reason of the life *which is therein.*" Therein, *when?* Remember that it is the blood *sprinkled or poured upon the altar* to make atonement of which this is said. Is the life in it *then?* That would seem perhaps too foolish a question to be asked. Yet the nature of Dr. Waldenström's argument requires one to say, Yes; and he actually makes Scripture say so too! The blood sprinkled makes atonement by the reason of the life which is in it!

Strike out the interpolated words, and we have Scripture, and what is consistent with the fact. The blood does make atonement by reason of the life, but not of a life which is still in it, but of a *life rendered up.* That is, it speaks of death, as every Christian perhaps before Dr. Waldenström has understood it. If "the blood constituted its life"—the life of the body,—it is surely *in the body* that it does so, and not out of it. "The life"—not soul—"is in the blood;" or, as this means, and is said further on, it is the blood that is the life. What, then, does the blood *shed* mean but *life poured out?* and what is life poured out but *death?*

But our author would put it rather thus, that the blood being the life of the body, when shed out it still *represents* its life; nay, he says this is a very common representation in the Bible. The instances he gives are singular enough: Jonathan's words to his father, "Wilt thou sin against innocent blood, to *slay* David without a cause?" David saying (Ps. xciv. 21), "They gather themselves together against the soul [or life] of the righteous, and condemn the innocent blood;" Ezek. iii. 18, The blood of the wicked required at the watchman's hand; Pilate's words, "I am innocent of the blood of this just person;" the people's answer, "His blood be upon us and on our children;" Judas's confession, "I have sinned, in that I have betrayed the innocent blood;" and then he curiously remarks,—

"From all these Scripture-expressions we thus see that it is very common for the Scriptures to say *blood* instead of *life*; and *especially* is this very common when the question is of a LIFE SACRIFICED IN DEATH, as we have seen already from the examples quoted"!

Truly we have. So that a life *sacrificed* is still "life" for the Swedish professor, and not death at all; and we may read, "His *life* be upon us and on our children," etc., etc.! What can one say? What need one say? The life which is not death turns out to be a "sacrifice in death;" and he even ventures to quote, "The Son of Man came to give His life a ransom for many," as explaining "we have redemption through His blood," and to say, as the conclusion of it all, "*The blood of Jesus is nothing else than His life given in His death for us.*" Of course it is; but what is "life given up in death" as *distinguished from* death?

All the texts in which "blood" is spoken of here speak of death, yet Dr. Waldenström would teach that it is not death at all that is meant. What is it, then? "*Life given up* in death"!! And this is proved by the very texts which were to show us the difference.

To what is all this leading us? We shall soon see:—

"In Matt. xxvi. 28, the Lord says, while He hands the blessed cup to His disciples, 'This is My blood of the new testament, which is shed for many for the remission of sins.' In and with and under the wine He gave them His blood, made them partakers of His life, which He was now about to lay down for them in death. When He handed them the bread, He did not say, 'This signifies or represents My body;' but, 'This *is* My body;' and when He handed them the wine, He did not say, 'This signifies or represents My blood;' but, 'This is My blood.' Thus, while giving them the bread and wine, He made them real partakers of Himself, joined them to Himself as members of His body, and made them partakers of His life."

Here, then, is the key of Dr. Waldenström's position. He is, as we see, thus far still a Lutheran, though with a strange gap in his defenses as that, through which the enemy will surely find an easy way. Go back to Marburg and the table-cloth, and conceive, if you can, Luther maintaining his thesis with the admission made that the blood of Christ was a figure, though the drinking it was literal! Dr. Waldenström apparently must believe this, although the Lord actually speaks of the shedding of His blood in the text quoted; but this means, he tells us, His life laid down. Let us meet this straightforwardly, then: is it true that the Lord made His disciples then (or that He makes them now) partakers of that human life which He laid down for us? It is *not* true; or, if it be, it should be shown us plainly. It is "*everlasting* life" of which we, blessed be God! are made partakers: was it everlasting life that the Lord laid down for us? Can everlasting life become extinct in death? Will even Dr. Waldenström say so?

Thus simply is the whole argument overthrown. As for the Lutheran view itself, it is as contrary to Scripture as it is to reason; and Scripture is never *contrary* to reason, though it often transcends it. But Scripture plainly says that the Lord's Supper is a *remembrance*, and a remembrance of His *death*. The bread and the wine thus represent Christ's body and blood *separate*, as they are in death: the blood is *shed;* we show forth Christ's death till He comes. He Himself says, with reference to such a misunderstanding of like words elsewhere, "Doth this offend you? What if ye shall see the Son of Man ascend up where He was before?"—as if that would end all thought of this kind,—"it is the spirit that quickeneth; the flesh profiteth nothing: the words that I speak unto you, they are spirit, and they are life." (Jno. vi. 61–63.)

Dr. Waldenström's additions to Lutheranism necessitate an important modification of it. The Lutheran creed is, that "the unworthy and unbelievers receive the true body and blood of Christ, so that, however, they shall *not* thence derive either consolation or life." Dr. Waldenström, believing that the blood *is* the life, cannot, of course, hold that unbelievers receive it. "This participation in the life of Jesus" is "by the *believers* in Him" only. Faith he presses as a necessity, yet it is in the *sacrament* that "through the bread and wine we really become partakers of Christ's body and blood,—that is, we become one body with Him, and are made partakers of His life." Whether this is possible apart from the sacrament I cannot find that he has said. Our Lord's words are absolute, "Except ye eat the flesh of the Son of Man, and drink His blood, ye have no life in you; whoso eateth My flesh and drinketh My blood hath eternal life." (Jno. vi. 53, 54.) Dr. Waldenström may not take these words as referring to the Supper, and he would be surely right in this; but then it is possible to eat and drink thus by faith alone, and there is no ground for maintaining any other presence of Christ in the sacrament. As for membership in the body of Christ, that is by the baptism of the Spirit (1 Cor. xii. 13; comp. Acts i. 5), and not by any sacrament at all. Thus all is confusion in these views from first to last.

Dr. Waldenström lays stress in this connection upon 1 Cor. x. 16, 17, the last verse of which he translates "more literally: It is one bread; we, the many, are one body, for we all have part in that one bread." "Paul," he adds, "says, in effect, 'Here is a communion, a partaking of Christ's own life, given for us in death ; here is a uniting of believers into one body, by their partaking of Christ's body, thus making common cause with Him.'"

But it is unfortunate for the argument that the apostle as much speaks of being κοινωνοὶ, or communicants, of the devils (*v.* 20, *Gk.*), and of Israel being (κοινωνοὶ) "partakers of the altar," as he speaks of the (κοινωνία) communion of the body or of the blood of Christ. In either case, he is thinking evidently of association, and so identification, whether with the altar or worship of Jehovah, or with the devils to which under their idols the Gentiles sacrificed. And just so at the Lord's table, they were associated and identified with the wondrous revelation of God whose central part is the cross of Christ. Dr. Waldenström's views really displace the cross, turn the supper of the Lord from a memorial of the past into what is wholly inconsistent with it. True, he speaks, forced by what is so evidently there, of a "life given up in death," but it is not for him *the giving up* of life, the death itself, for participation in death (in *his* sense of participation) could have no meaning. For him, it is participation in life,—not death, but its opposite. For the apostle, in this same epistle, it is a remembrance, and a showing forth the Lord's death.

I have before said, believers are *not* united into one body by partaking of Christ's body, but by the baptism of the Spirit ; and the apostle's language, which our author builds upon, suits better the thought of partaking of the one bread being the *expression* of the one body than it does the idea of the body being *formed* by this. For it is of outward association he is speaking, and not of something entirely hidden save to faith. The *doctrine* of the body is further on in the epistle (chap. xii.), and there quite different, as we have seen.

"The life that the Son of God gave in death" becomes

thus for Dr. Waldenström the truth intended in every passage where the blood or the death of Christ is spoken of in connection with justification, remission, redemption, or whatever else has been procured for us by it. An unscriptural expression is introduced every where for the purpose of making death mean the opposite of death. True, it is admitted, He *gave* His life in death, but the necessity of that death, the meaning of it, we are never given to know. It reminds us of those who tell us, as to the old sacrifices, that the death of the animal was only needed because the blood could not be otherwise procured! Thus that which cannot be altogether ignored is annulled in its deep reality. The awful cry, "Why hast Thou forsaken Me?" finds no answer. God's making His Son to be sin for us is explained to be only this, that God "allowed Him to be treated *by men* as a sinner." In this light loose fashion, Dr. Waldenström might easily, as he promises to do, "consider briefly all the passages in the New Testament which speak of the blood of Jesus as a means of salvation," secure that if death can be only made to mean life, all is simple. The very texts which most plainly say the opposite become at once the strongest in his favor.

Thus, if the apostle says that "God set forth Christ to be a mercy-seat through faith in His blood," this is by such a process easily made to mean that "by faith sinners are made partakers of the blood of Jesus, or *of His life*, which He gave in death for them." He does not argue about this, nor need to show it from the context. We have only to bring in the new vocabulary, and read "blood" as "life," and we see it at once. It is not pretended that the passage in Romans proves that the blood means life, or that it says any thing about life. Plainly it does not, but that is no matter.

But why give any consideration to texts that can teach

NON-VICARIOUS ATONEMENT. 13

us nothing, and when we have the means of so reducing the most refractory into subjection? In this all too easy work we need not follow Dr. Waldenström. It will be only needful to look at any new argument that may present itself. And here we have what perhaps he would call that :—

"Paul says that 'God set forth Christ to be a mercy-seat through faith in His blood,—that is, God has made Him to be a mercy-seat by His giving His life in death. . . . So far from the case being such that Christ through His blood should be a shield for sinners against God and His righteousness, on the contrary, God Himself has set Him forth to be a mercy-seat for sinners, in order that He might save and bless them through Him.'"

Does Dr. Waldenström really believe that Christ's death is maintained by any of those he opposes to be a "shield *against* God and His righteousness"? Is He not uniformly presented by them as "the Lord our righteousness"? (Jer. xxiii. 16.) Can righteousness be a shelter against righteousness? At any rate, we need not, and dare not, undertake the defence of any one who does not believe that *God* "*gave* His only begotten Son, that whosoever believeth on Him should not perish, but have everlasting life."

But there is a deeper question. God gave His Son, assuredly; but why to *death?* why to the cross? why to be made a curse for us! Why *must* the Son of Man be lifted up? Why is it that "except a corn of wheat fall into the ground and die, it abideth alone; but if it die, it bringeth forth much fruit"? It is this need which Dr. Waldenström seems never to have realized.

That blood-sprinkled mercy-seat of which the apostle speaks here,—for "mercy-seat," I believe, with the Swedish translators, to be the proper rendering of the word,—should surely be the very thing to show Dr. Waldenström his error. For here, if the blood sprinkled speaks of life, it is life *taken*, not communicated. It is sprinkled *before*

God, not upon men. It is sprinkled to *make* the throne of God a "mercy-seat;" to cleanse, not sinners, by any impartation to them, but *their sins*, so that God may be able to abide among them. (Lev. xvi. 14–17.) I am aware of Dr. Waldenström's comments upon this elsewhere (The Reconciliation, p. 55), but it is not true that the tabernacle, ark, or altar represent or typify the people, as he says. No instance can be shown, and any one who reads the chapter can see the case to be as I have represented it.

Dr. Waldenström next takes up Rom. v. 9, 10.; and here he makes (rightly enough) "by His death" to be essentially the equivalent of "by His blood;" and then the usual transformation is effected. But thus he makes justification to be also grounded upon a work in ourselves, instead of the work of the cross: "In the blood of Jesus by faith they had become righteous. By faith they had become partakers of the life of Jesus, which He gave in death for them, *and thus had their justification happened.*" And he is bold enough to add, "Here again, therefore, the same doctrine. There is never in Scripture any thing about the obtainment by faith of any reconciliation or grace or righteousness acquired or purchased by the blood for the world,—no, not one single passage with any such idea can be shown to exist in the Bible"(!)

Yet even Dr. Waldenström must admit that the Lord Himself said that "God so loved the *world*, that He gave His only begotten Son, that whosoever believeth on Him should not perish," and that this refers to the cross on which "the Son of Man was lifted up, that whosoever believeth on Him might not perish," as also that He says that for this the "Son of Man MUST be lifted up." Why "must"? and was nothing in the way of grace even procured by this? It was for the world surely, for it was the fruit of God's love to the world; and many similar passages might be quoted. Here, the blood indeed is not spoken of directly, but the cross is, and is illustrated as to its meaning by the lifting up of the serpent in the wilderness : why a *serpent* lifted up ? It is a type, and we may differ about the significance, but it must mean something ; and if you say, " It just means the 'old serpent' overcome," how does the "lifting up" do this ? That is not a picture of life, is it ? it is of death, certainly. Why must the death take place that the life might be received ? Even the author is compelled by Scripture to repeat, though it seems to have no meaning for him, "life given up in death :" well, *why* "given up in death"? Could we, then, receive it in no other way than by His dying that we might receive it ? Must He lose it that we might obtain it ? Nay, He laid down His life that He might take it again ? Why was it, then, that He must lay it down ?

Dr. Waldenström cannot answer this: he *has* no answer. He catches at what is in itself true, that we are recipients of life in Him ; but if you ask, Why through death ? why "made a curse for us"? how did He "bear our sins in His own body on the tree"? how is it "through His stripes we are healed"? he does not know—has nothing that will stand a moment's question. The value of Christ's death seems for him only to win the hearts of men, if at least I read aright all that I can find upon it in this tractate : "'*By* the death,' '*in* His blood,'" he says. That Christ by the grace of God had given His life in death for them, that was what had broken their enmity, and reconciled them to God." All well ; but is there no more ?

To this we shall return, if the Lord will. The strength of Dr. Waldenström's position, it will be seen, is just the utterance of half-truths for whole ones, and the reiteration of a bald sophistry, that blood shed in death stands for life. This he repeats and re-repeats, and it would be idle to repeat the exposure of it. What makes against him, he omits to speak of: as where, in Heb. xiii. 12, the apostle dwells upon the truth that "Jesus also, that He might sanctify the people with His own blood, suffered without the gate," Dr. Waldenström insists upon what every one knows, that to be sanctified is to be "cleansed from sin." It is more, but it is that; and so when he says that "the work of Christ was to remedy just the injury which sin had occasioned," that is a truth, though a partial one. We may agree too that "neither is it said that the blood by its merit should move God to consider us holy, although we were not holy." Few, it is to be hoped, believe any such thing; and there is confusion apparently between *holiness* and *righteousness*. That God "*justifieth the ungodly*" Scripture does say plainly, *righteousness* being "imputed without works" (Rom. iv. 5, 6); but that is the very way in which God *produces* holiness,—not acts as if it were no matter.

But the gist of the passage in Hebrews Dr. Waldenström never notices at all, though it is plain enough in the verse as he quotes it. *Why* must Jesus, that He might sanctify the people with His own blood, *suffer without the gate?* It is this evidently that gives the very blood of Christ power to sanctify, as in the type he tells us that the "bodies of those beasts whose blood is brought into the sanctuary by the high-priest for sin are *burned without the camp*." (*v.* 11.) Why that? If the blood be the life, in the way the author puts it, and the impartation of life be the whole thing, how does the burning without the camp help the blood to sanctify? Dr. Waldenström has not a word—does not entertain the question. Though with the apostle of all importance, with him it seems to have none: why but that he and the apostle are not in agreement? That is the simple reality.

The apostle is speaking of death, and not of life; and

even here, he tells us, death alone would not be enough. "Outside the camp" expresses what "outside the gate" of the city of God does afterward—distance from God, because of sin! Nay, one expression of it in the cross is not enough, but the darkness which throws its pall over the scene must also testify with the agonizing words of the Sufferer which break out from it, "My God, My God, why hast Thou forsaken Me?" "Christ hath redeemed us from the curse of the law," says the apostle, "being made a curse for us, as it is written, 'Cursed is every one that hangeth upon a tree.'" (Gal. iii. 13.) The due of sin is not death alone. The bearing of our sins requires more: and to the real subject of the experience of the twenty-second psalm, the agony of agonies is that which again and again He deprecates—"But be not Thou far from Me, O Lord!"

Dr. Waldenström's system has no place for this: vicarious atonement he refuses. But why this, then?—"Our fathers trusted in Thee; they trusted in Thee, and were *not* forsaken." Why this exception in the case of the One only absolutely righteous?

Here, then, we may leave the consideration of Dr. Waldenström's first pamphlet on the blood of Jesus. There is nothing more in it that presents any difficulty, if we have clearly mastered what has been before us.

II.

WE now pass on to consider Dr. Waldenström's larger work—"The Reconciliation." "The term, 'reconciliation,'" he tells us at the beginning, "sets forth the real essence of salvation, for salvation consists just in the reconciliation of man to God." He confounds this with propitiation; or rather, expunges the latter thought from Scripture to make way for the former, as we shall see: Mr. Princell, his translator and editor, assuring us in a preliminary note to explain the author's view, that "*hilaskomai*" (to propitiate) means, "in the two New-Testament passages in which it occurs, plainly this and nothing more: I show grace, mercy, or kindness with respect to,—that is, I pardon; Luke xviii. 13, rendered 'be merciful,' and Heb. ii. 17, the *A. V.* rendering, '*to make reconciliation,*' the *R. V.* rendering, '*to make propitiation,*' plainly meaning, to show mercy with respect to,—that is, to pardon." As we are to have the passages before us, I will not anticipate what will come before us then; but it is strange if it be really so, that the "aim" of the heathen "to appease God," of which Dr. Waldenström speaks a few pages further on, should have found expression in this very word! Any Greek dictionary will satisfy us that it did so.

"All their worship of God proceeds," says the author, "from the principle that God is *angry* with them," and this is so deep-rooted in human nature, somehow, "that men often consider Christ, whom God has sent in His grace to reconcile us to Himself, as One on whom God has poured out His wrath, in order that He might be gracious to us." "Contrary to all such perverse imaginations," he goes on, "the Scriptures teach that *no change took place in God's disposition toward man* in consequence of his sin; that therefore it was *not God who needed to be reconciled to man*, but that it was *man who needed to be reconciled to God;* and that consequently *reconciliation is a work which proceeds from God*, and is directed toward man, and aims, *not to appease God, but to cleanse man from sin, and to restore him to a right relation with God.*"

Now that "God so loved the world, that He gave His only begotten Son," is the text of many a sermon and the joy of many a heart, thank God, among those who yet believe that Christ's voice it is which in the hundred and second psalm speaks of having endured God's indignation and wrath (*v.* 10; comp. *v.* 25 with Heb. i. 10–12); and it only deepens inexpressibly in their hearts the wonder of God's love. God's wrath upon sinners, Dr. Waldenström will presently himself assure us, is not enmity against them; and it is true that He does not need to be reconciled—His heart toward them needs not to be changed. There is no need for confuting what in fact is not held. Even those who do use the language rightly reprobated, as to reconciling God, do not mean by it in the least that Christ's work is the procuring cause of God's love to us, but rather the expression of that love, and that which enables it righteously to manifest itself toward us. But righteous wrath against sin there was and is, which when the soul is turned to God, needs to find holy expression also, in order that the sinner may be received. And thus Christ, "made sin for us, who knew no sin," proclaimed the righteousness of the penalty upon it, when bearing our sins in His own body on the tree (1 Pet. ii. 24), He was "made a curse for us." (Gal. iii. 13.)

"*There is not to be found,*" says Dr. Waldenström, "*a single passage in the Bible setting forth the atonement as having its cause in this, that the justice of God needed satisfaction.*" Boldly, as always, he emphasizes this. Has he forgotten that Christ "was made sin for us, who knew no sin, that we might be made the *righteousness of God* in Him"? God's righteousness is expressed in giving us our place of acceptance as the result of His taking the place of sin. Substitution is here the very thing that proclaims God's righteousness: was it yet unrequired by it? or when it said that "God hath set forth [Christ] to be a propitiation [or mercy-seat] through faith in His *blood*, to declare *His righteousness* for the remission of sins," (Rom. iii. 25) was it still not righteousness that required this blood-shedding? If the passage required is not to be found, it is by blind men that it is not to be found. The whole warp and woof of Scripture declares the same.

"But," he says, again, "love and justice are never, in the Bible, set forth as being in conflict with each other, so that one can bind the other. *On the contrary, it is right and just, both for God and men, to love—to have compassion on and to save sinners.* It was right and *just* that God so loved the world as to give His only begotten Son for its salvation." Of course, but why give His Son?—what need of that? Again and ever this utter blindness as to the meaning of the cross! Righteous to give His Son to "suffer, the just for the unjust, to bring us to God"! Righteous to "lay on *Him* the iniquity of us all"! (1 Pet. iii. 18; Isa. liii. 6.) Was it all meaningless, this? Nay: it was "the chastisement of our peace," and by *His* stripes *we* are healed. (*v.* 5.)

Yet Dr. Waldenström can quietly reply to the suggestion that God's punitive righteousness demanded satisfaction,—"It is nowhere thus written; and, as something outside of the Word of God, it is not well to assert any such thing"! And he can actually assert, "To punish in order to inflict evil on the one punished is unjust and unrighteous, and only he that is evil can do evil; but God is not evil, for He is love : but to punish in order to produce repentance is righteous, just, and good"!! What, then, was the chastisement [or "punishment"] of our peace which Christ endured? And how can God punish the finally impenitent? Alas! Dr. Waldenström knows not the glory of the cross.

I may pass briefly over the whole of the next chapter, inasmuch as there is no question either of changing God's hatred of sin, or of changing God at all, or of averting His wrath from those that go on in sin. Many of the arguments here are very much like beating the air. Late in the chapter, however, is one that cannot but create astonishment. "For the unrighteous man (as such) there is no salvation, however gracious and merciful God may be; and for the righteous man (as such) there is no condemnation, however righteous God may be." And then, after his manner, he emphasizes the words, "*Yea, it is the very righteousness of God which makes it impossible for the righteous to be condemned.*" No doubt; but who can claim for his own righteousness such recognition by the righteousness of God? The apostle says of some who imagined the possibility, that "they, being IGNORANT of *God's righteousness*, and going about to establish their own righteousness, have *not submitted themselves* to the righteousness of God." And the "righteousness of *faith*," which he goes on to contrast with "our own," is *Christ* as "the end of the law for righteousness to every one that believeth." (Rom. x. 3, 4.)

It will be said that Dr. Waldenström believes in justification by faith. Nominally, he does; in reality, rather by the change which faith produces. And this leaves Job's question (who was certainly a believer,) still unanswered: "But how shall man be just with God?" Our author would make it a very easy matter.

In the third chapter, he turns to the consideration of

the Old-Testament sacrifices; and here we must follow him more closely.

In the first place, he catches at the words of the apostle in Heb. ix. 22, that "almost all things are by the law purged with blood, and without shedding of blood is no remission," to point attention to the "almost," upon which he argues, "the apostle has laid special emphasis." But it is hard to realize this, as the apostle never refers to it again, and as his object is to insist on the rule and not the exception! Moreover, the position of the word at the beginning of the sentence merely extends the application of it, as he rightly says, to the whole verse. It is true that there were exceptions under the law to the general rule that all things were purged by blood, and without shedding of blood was no remission; but the apostle immediately goes on in a way entirely contrary to what might be gathered from the "almost,"—"It was *necessary*, therefore, that the patterns of the things in the heavens should be purified with these, but the heavenly things themselves with better sacrifices than these." What becomes, then, of the great importance of the "almost" to the apostle's argument?

To his own also it is as difficult to see it. According to Dr. Waldenström himself, apart from the communication of the life which is in the blood, forgiveness there cannot be! Why, then, insist on the "almost"? It looks as if he had begun to realize that the "shedding of blood" must mean *death*, and not life, and would as much as possible diminish the importance of a witness which is against him. Our wills often act in a way of which we are little conscious. But how much is gained by it? The law puts forward a broad principle with a few exceptions: if the law be not the very image of the things (chap. x. 1), where is the wonder?

He goes on to the question of the vicarious character

of the sacrifices. First, he asserts, in his usual manner, that God never puts forth such a principle any where in Scripture as that God's righteousness demanded that the "punishment must be endured by some one if sin should be forgiven." Now, if he means in the way of abstract statement, it is very little in the manner of Scripture to put things in that way. God speaks of how He acted or will act, and that is enough; although really the passage in Hebrews comes very near to such a proposition. If the shedding of blood be *necessary* for remission of sins, then it is certainly the blood of another, not of the sinner, that is shed, and what is that but the principle of substitution? And what are we to learn from "The Lord hath laid on Him the iniquity of us all"?

He then, as in his smaller treatise, denies the Lord's work to be the payment of debt. I do not contend for it, and need not repeat what has been already said.

He goes on to what is more at the root of the matter, that "the Scriptures never represent, in any way, that it is just or righteous to punish the innocent instead of the guilty." He is here on common ground with Unitarians and others every where; but an essential element of this case he has omitted. It is the One who has imposed the penalty who stoops to suffer it: it is His own as well as the Father's glory that is to be shown forth; the Father and He are one. Who shall forbid Him, not to execute the law upon other sinless ones, but to bear its penalty Himself? Who shall bind the hands of the Holy One, that He should not be able to sacrifice Himself? and who shall be bold enough to stigmatize it as unrighteous?

Yet Dr. Waldenström affirms, "Neither is it ever said in the Bible that God has inflicted punishment upon Christ instead upon us. Yea, the prophet Isaiah represents it as a *delusion* that the Jews believed that Christ was punished by God. The prophet says, "We did esteem Him stricken, smitten of God, and afflicted; but He was pierced through by our sins, He was crushed for our misdeeds.'"

On the other hand, Delitzsch, than whom there is no better Hebraist, and with whom few critics can compare on such a question, says of the text quoted, "Here again it is Israel, which, having been at length better instructed, and now bearing witness against itself, laments its former blindness to the mediatorially vicarious character of the deep agonies, both of soul and body, that were endured by the great Sufferer. They looked upon them as the punishment of His own sins, and indeed—inasmuch as, like the friends of Job, they measured the sin of the Sufferer by the sufferings that He endured—of peculiarly great sins. They saw in Him *nagua*, '*one stricken*,'—*i. e.*, afflicted with a hateful, shocking disease (Gen. xii. 17; 1 Sam. vi. 9),—such, for example, as leprosy, which was called *nega* especially; also *mukkeh Elohim*, '*one smitten of God*' . . . The construction "*mukkeh Elohim*" signifies one who has been defeated in conflict by God his Lord."

He adds, "In ver. 5, 'but He,' as contrasted with, 'but we,' continues the true state of the case as contrasted with their false judgment—'Whereas He was pierced for our sins, bruised for our iniquities: the punishment was laid upon Him for our peace; and through His stripes we were healed. . . . As *min* with the passive does not answer to the Greek $\dot{v}\pi\dot{o}$, but to $\dot{a}\pi\dot{o}$, the meaning is, not that our sins and iniquities had pierced Him through like swords, and crushed Him like heavy burdens, but that He was pierced and crushed on account of our sins and iniquities."

Further, he says, "We have rendered the word *musar* 'punishment,' and there was no other word in the language for this idea."

Dr. Waldenström now comes to the Old-Testament

sacrifices themselves, which, he contends, "*could* not express a penal suffering instead of the sinner." Here, first from the peace- or *thank-offerings*, he finds "something which is of the greatest importance as to the question of the meaning of the sacrifices: to wit, *that we must never draw the conclusion that a sacrifice expressed penal suffering just because it was bloody.* When, therefore, it is concluded as to the sin- and trespass-offerings, *that because they were bloody they expressed penal suffering*, then is drawn an entirely too hasty conclusion."

The "hasty conclusion" is Dr. Waldenström's alone. He should have *proved* that the peace-offerings could not express penal suffering. In fact, it is Christ's work which, as bringing to God, is the foundation of peace, as our apprehension of it is communion with God. Why could not a thank-offering, because such, speak of that blessed work, which is the ground of all our good,—for which the heart that knows it praises and blesses God forever?

The author thinks, however, there is no need to tarry upon this, and goes on to the expressly atoning offerings. And here, his first objection is, that "sacrifices were never allowed to be made *for other sins than such as were not to be visited with death or capital punishment*. . . . how, then, could any one think that the animal which was offered suffered the punishment of death instead of the offender? Why, his sin was not at all liable to be visited with the death penalty."

This is singularly inconclusive, however, and only reveals the objector's low thought of sin and its desert with God. Rome may distinguish between her venial and her mortal sins, but the Word of God proclaims, "The soul that *sinneth*, it shall die." Reason enough there was for not allowing a great offender to escape with the easy offering of a sacrifice; but God would have all men know that death has entered upon the heels of sin, and that it has passed upon all men, for that all have sinned. Dr. Waldenström's argument is worse than poor: it is a revelation of the one who makes it.

The second argument is derived from the provision of an offering of fine flour as a sin-offering in a case of poverty. It was one of the few exceptions to the general rule, for it was emphatically proclaimed that it was the *blood* that made atonement for the soul. In case of deep poverty, God's mercy abated the demand; and so where a soul might be spiritually so poor as not to know what work was needed for his sins, yet clung to Christ as meeting them, such an one could be accepted of God; not because sin needed not a true atonement, but because Christ's work has met the full need as God knows it.

The third argument is again weakness itself. Where a man-slayer was not discovered, the law decreed "that the people—mark, the *people*—should be forgiven [literally, atoned for or reconciled, *v.* 8] by the sacrifice of a young heifer." This could not mean, he urges, that it died instead of the people, for the people were not guilty of the sin, and had not deserved to die; nor for the man-slayer, for it was forbidden to take ransom (or atonement) for him!

Did atonement mean *nothing*, then? Suppose we were to argue that if atoning means reconciling or being gracious to the people or the man-slayer, should we not still have to say, the people did not need it, and the man-slayer could not have it? It is evident that if sin were not in some way imputed, it could not be atoned for, *whatever* the meaning of atonement; and that if it were imputed, God's one way of atonement was by blood?

His fourth argument is, that the laying on of hands on the victim did not signify that the penalty was transferred to the animal; first, because this took place in the case of the peace-offering, where there was no question of penalty.—This has been already shown to be a mistake. Secondly, because in Lev. xvi. 21 it is "clearly represented to be an expression of the confession of sin"! As if the confession of sin were not the suited accompaniment of the action which transferred it to a victim! Thirdly, that "on the day of atonement, the hands were *not laid on the animal which was killed, but on the one that was kept alive:*—another of the exceptions to the ordinary mode; and for a plain reason, that God would show to the people the complete *removal* of sin, which could only be done by the living animal. Yet it was identified with the other goat that had died as one sin-offering. (See *v.* 5.)

These are all the reasons given against the true expiatory character of the Old-Testament sacrifices; but before we are entitled to come to the conclusion, we have yet to see what Dr. Waldenström believes to be their actual meaning.

The first point that he insists on with reference to the meaning of the Old-Testament sacrifices is just that which we have already considered, and without which he could not get on for a moment,—that "it is never said in the Old Testament that atonement, or reconciliation, was effected by the *death* of the sacrificed animal. No; atonement was effected by the *blood:*" that is, for him, as we have seen, by LIFE, not death. To which he adds here that "not by the *shedding of the blood* was atonement made, but by the *sprinkling of the blood.*" "But what did this sprinkling signify? It signified *cleansing, or purging, from sin,* as the apostle says, 'Almost all things are by the law *purged* with blood.'" For some reason Dr. Waldenström does not complete the quotation here, "and without *shedding* of blood is no remission." I may not assume to know his reason for the omission, but it certainly would seem to need accounting for. The passage thus completed lies, in fact, in the very teeth of his argument; and it is safe to say that it is a complete refutation of it.

Why without shedding of blood was there no remission? Probably Dr. Waldenström might suggest (for, as he has said nothing, we can only suggest for him) that the blood could not be sprinkled if it were not shed; but this answer is not as satisfactory as it seems it ought to be. For, in the first place, the apostle should have said, and it cannot be conceived why in that case he did not say, "without *sprinkling* of blood," instead of "without shedding." We would insist as much as Dr. Waldenström on the exact force of Scripture words, and here plainly (for *him*), the apostle has put the emphasis upon the wrong point, and is in that measure accountable for the doctrine we have been getting from it.

But again. Suppose an Israelite who had sinned under the old economy. Should we say to him, The *shedding* of blood is not what makes atonement: it is *sprinkling* of blood; and, acting upon our suggestion, he was to go to the priest and say, "Here is the fresh blood of a newly killed animal; put it, I pray thee, upon the horns of the altar for me." Would that avail?

He might add, "And here is the beast itself for the fat to be offered, and for the priest." Still the priest would have to say, "Sir, is this beast your own sin-offering? Did you designate it as your own by laying your hand upon it, and then kill it in the place where they kill the burnt-offering before the Lord?"

All this is nothing for Dr. Waldenström. The shedding of blood is not the point, but the sprinkling of blood. One cannot see why the animal should even die at all: for the type would be much more perfect, according to his view, if it were some of the blood of a living animal than as the blood of a *dead* one; it would surely better signify LIFE!

And why need every one that sinned have his *own* sin-offering? Why must there be this solemn shedding of blood for *each one*, and the whole of the blood poured out in each case—save what anointed the horns of it—at the bottom of the altar!

The sprinkling, however, says Dr. Waldenström, is the important thing. It is this that cleanses from sin, and atonement is just cleansing from sin! Think of the Israelite again, as instructed in this new theology. He brings his beast according to the manner: it is slain, and the priest takes the blood. To do what with it? To anoint the horns of the altar, and to pour out all the rest of it at the bottom of it? The man looks anxiously. "But, sir, have you left none to sprinkle upon me? That is what atonement means; it is to be sprinkled upon me, to cleanse me." "I have none left," says the priest; "I have acted strictly according to the ritual. The animal was killed before the Lord; its blood is poured upon the ground, except what you can see upon the horns of the altar. I have no word to sprinkle any upon *you ;* but atonement is made nevertheless, and your sin is forgiven!"

Dr. Waldenström's doctrine does not consist with the facts. The blood of the *trespass*-offering is sprinkled upon the leper, as also the blood of the bird killed at the beginning of his cleansing; the blood of the covenant is sprinkled on the people in Ex. xxiv., but it is the blood of burnt-offerings and peace-offerings only; the ashes of the heifer are sprinkled upon the defiled person in Num. xix.; and to these last two the apostle refers in Heb. ix.; we shall see the significance of this shortly: but the blood of the sin-offering, or of the ordinary trespass-offerings, was NEVER sprinkled upon the person, while it was, nevertheless, again and again declared that atonement was made by it, and that the person was forgiven.

We see, then, that the apostle knew what he was saying when he declared that "without *shedding* of blood is no remission." He knew all about sprinkling, and insists upon it in the very same chapter; but had he said "without *sprinkling* of blood is no remission," the whole Jewish ritual would have borne witness against him, as now it does against Dr. Waldenström. He has made the exception the rule, and misinterpreted both alike; and Scripture, which is no "nose of wax," and will not speak as we please, but only according to the truth of God which it declares, witnesses decisively against him. The whole Levitical ritual, while it does say that atonement is by blood, unites to show that the blood is the testimony of *death*, not life, only of a death substitutionally offered to God, and so making atonement as lifted up to God upon the altar's horns. The blood is given *upon the altar* to atone. Thus is the sinner forgiven; and " without *shedding* of blood"—death—"there is *no* remission."

In what follows, Dr. Waldenström repeats what is well known, that the Hebrew word "to make atonement" is literally "to cover," and that is in the sense of annulling, —if you please, blotting out. But he is wholly wrong in interpreting this of a work done *in* the sinner: it is a thing wholly distinct. The blood of the sacrifice covers —atones for—sins, puts them away from before God, because it is the blood of a legal substitute, the type of One precious, perfect Lamb of sacrifice, upon whom was "the chastisement of our peace."

But, asks Dr. Waldenström further, "Who is set forth in the first and foremost place as one that atones for sins? Answer: It is *God*. But if God is the one who makes atonement for sins, then it cannot mean that He makes atonement for or appeases Himself in regard to sins"! A clever, bold, and absolute deception; though no doubt he is first self-deceived. If I were to ask, seeking answer from Scripture, "Who is set forth in the first and foremost place as the one who atones for sins?" I should have to answer, *The priest*, assuredly; and that is *not* God. So says the Old Testament; so says the New. "The *priest* shall make atonement for him, and it shall be forgiven him." God it is who forgives, and forgives on the ground of atonement, and the atonement is thus made to God, and to none but God. "A merciful and faithful High-Priest," says the New Testament, "to make propitiation for the sins of the people" (Heb. ii. 17). So the Revised Version; and it is undoubtedly right. The thought of propitiation cannot be taken away from *hilaskomai* here,—the very word used by the heathen every where for it. But "propitiation"—if there be such a thing at all—is Godward. The doctrine of the Old Testament and that of the New is one.

"Go quickly unto the congregation," says Moses to Aaron, "and make atonement for them; for there is *wrath gone* out from the Lord." (Num. xvi. 46.) "Every day shalt thou offer the bullock of the sin-offering for atonement." (Ex. xxix. 36.) "It is the blood that maketh atonement." "When I see the blood, I will pass over you, and the plague shall not be upon you." "He that offereth the blood of the peace-offerings." "Thou shalt not offer the blood of any sacrifice with leavened bread."

In all this work of atonement, then, is it "set forth in the first and foremost place" that it is God who makes the atonement, and therefore that the atonement cannot be offered to God, because God could not offer or make atonement to Himself? No: assuredly it is not God who offers to God, and yet the atonement *is* offered to God, or words are altogether deceptive, and there is no use in discussing this or any other matter.

But what about the passages quoted by Dr. Waldenström, as Ps. lxv. 3, for instance, "As for our transgressions, Thou wilt purge them away," where, he says, "it is literally, 'Thou wilt *atone* for them,' or 'cover them'"? Let us consider this, and we shall find assuredly that there is in it neither the difficulty which he sees for us, nor the doctrine he advances for himself.

Now it must be owned that there is a difference in some respects between the way in which atonement is presented in the Old Testament and our common way of putting it. When, for instance, on the day of atonement, Aaron goes in with the blood to make atonement in the holiest of all, and then coming out to the altar, sprinkles upon it and makes atonement for it,—though we are accustomed, no doubt, to the words, it can hardly be said that we are accustomed really to the manner of speech here. In our way of putting it these would not be separate *atonements*, but *applications* of atonement. The literal meaning of the Hebrew word (*kaphar*, "to cover,") perfectly accords with and accounts for this use, as our word "to atone" does not. In reality, for us, atonement is that satisfaction made to the holy and righteous nature of God which enables Him to manifest His grace; and that work was not done in heaven—which the holiest typifies—but on earth, upon the cross. So God says of the blood, "I have given it to you upon the *altar* to make atonement for your souls." That does not hinder, as we have seen, the making atonement with it elsewhere. This difference, it is plain, there is between the Scripture use and our own; and it accounts for the expressions which Dr. Waldenström brings forward.

When God *applies* to this purpose or that, to this person or that, the value of the atoning blood, He would, as we see in Old-Testament language, be making atonement thus. With us it would be misleading to speak so. The corresponding expression with us would be that He "purges." And this is no more difficult to understand than that any other word should have different meanings or shades of meaning. Such almost every word has, and to confound them would produce just the confusion which has resulted here in Dr. Waldenström's mind. Every translation of the Bible, I suppose, makes the difference here which he would obliterate. And yet even he, if we translated Prov. xvi. 14, that "a wise man will *atone* the wrath of a king," would rightly admonish us that *kaphar* has other meanings. So be it, then, and the difficulty is ended, this special meaning being also fully accounted for in accordance with the general doctrine, as we have seen.

We need not, then, examine at length the passages brought forward to show that atonement is simply cleansing. It is never significant of an internal work. It is by blood shed, poured out; death, not life, offered up to God as on the horns of the altar, or the mercy-seat, turning aside the wrath of God from him on whose behalf it is accepted. All this is the teaching of facts that cannot be denied, and ought not to be misinterpreted.

But we must look more closely at what is said of the day of atonement, though I cannot agree with the statement that the sacrifice on that day was "the sum of all the sacrifices that were offered for sin." The atonement for the holy place, for the tabernacle, and for the altar, Dr. Waldenström urges, is not that "God should thereby become gracious toward" these, (who ever thought so?) but "to *cleanse* and *hallow* from the uncleanness of the children of Israel."

He anticipates, however, an objection:—

"Some one objecting may say: 'But the holy place could not really have any sins from which it needed to be cleansed. Answer: The cleansing of the tabernacle was a type of the cleansing of the people. Therefore, also, it is said that the holy place, the tabernacle, and the altar should be cleansed *'from'* [thus, literally; the versions have it "because of"] the transgressions of the children of Israel." (*v.* 16.)

This is surely arbitrary enough; for the verse quoted can scarcely be contended for as *proving* that the tabernacle represents the people of Israel! It should, on the other hand, (if only he had quoted it entire,) have taught him better: "and so shall he do for the tabernacle of the congregation which *remaineth amongst them* in the midst of their uncleannesses." The tabernacle that is specially marked as remaining *amongst* them cannot rightly be confounded with the *people amongst whom* it remains. And it should be plain that no typical significance of the tabernacle is at all in question, but the simple fact of God dwelling thus in connection with sinners.

But we have come to what is indeed utterly opposed to Dr. Waldenström's system, and which he seems to have no capacity to see. "The holy place could not really have any sins from which it needed to be cleansed." True, but could not the sins of the people defile the holy place so as to make it no fit dwelling-place for a holy God? Surely, it is plainly asserted here; but then the difficulty for Dr. Waldenström results: *how could atonement meet such a case as this?*

For him it could not; for atonement with him is the cleansing of people, and this is expressly stated to be for the tabernacle itself. Look at the full specification in the thirty-third verse: "And he shall make atonement for the holy sanctuary, and he shall make atonement for the tabernacle of the congregation and the altar; and he shall make atonement for the priests, and for all the people of the congregation." The mention of all these distinctly in this way precludes the thought of the one being but the type of the other.

But here, then, as there are confessedly no sins belonging to the sanctuary itself, atonement *for it* is not the cleansing of sins, but of *defilement* from the sins of the people; and this is accomplished by the bringing before God the precious blood which vindicates His righteousness so entirely that no patient going on with sinners in grace can raise a question of it.

But for Dr. Waldenström no atonement of this kind could be needed. God is *always* righteous, he would say, in going on thus with men; just as it is also righteous of Him to show grace when they turn to Him apart from atonement altogether. How, then, can His tabernacle among men be defiled? The author's incompetence to explain such a thing is shown by his having to make the tabernacle only the type of the people themselves. The apostle's interpretation is, "It was necessary, therefore, that the patterns of *things in the heavens* should be purified with these;" although the blood could scarcely be the figure of life communicated in the case of "things in the heavens"!

The scape-goat, however, is to make all plain, it seems. There is confessedly a difficult phrase in connection with the scape-goat, that he is to be "set alive before the Lord, to make atonement with him, to send him away for a scape-goat into the wilderness." So the common version; but the revised gives, "to make atonement *for* him," and this is allowed to be the regular use of the Hebrew words This appears to suit Dr Waldenström, who claims that "atone for" means here the same thing as at other places,—to wit, *make holy*, *sanctify*, or *cleanse*. "That atonement should be made for the goat meant, therefore," he adds, "that in a typical or symbolical way he should be *sanctified* [separated or dedicated] for the purpose of carrying away the sins of the people."

But surely this is a strange reading of atonement. First, it means "to cleanse;" but where in Scripture do we hear of a sacrificial animal—and the two goats are one sin-offering (*v.* 5),—needing to be cleansed for such a purpose? This "cleansing," therefore, has to be attenuated into a "dedication" with no thought of cleansing in it! But certainly *kaphar* never means this. Indeed the only "cleansing" by it is, not *inward* cleansing, but the removal of guilt—a very different thing. Moreover, this removal was by blood; but no blood was shed for or sprinkled upon the scape-goat, and it would have been an extraordinary thing indeed in such a case.

But what are we to make then, of an atonement for the scape-goat? We must leave the phrase as it stands in the Revised Version, I believe. It is the regular force of the words: "atonement *with*" is not correct; "atonement *upon*,"—the resort of many translators,—has no clear meaning, and what it might have scarcely seems consistent with the facts.

But what, then, does "to atone *for* it" mean? The facts will, I doubt not, themselves explain, if we will follow them only with attention.

The *two* goats are, as already said, but one sin-offering; and the object of the sin-offering is to atone: the two goats illustrate atonement; they are a double type, like the two birds in the cleansing of the leper. One bird only dies, as one goat only dies: in each case the second one of the two is needed for a purpose for which its death, without a miracle of resurrection, would have incapacitated it; and this is the only reason why there are two at all.

Thus if atonement be by blood, only one furnishes the blood, *only one properly atones*. The atonement, illustrated by the two, is yet but actually made by the one, who in *this* sense *atones for the other*. And thus the words following in this case are explained,—" to make atonement for him, *to let him go* for a scape-goat into the wilderness." This is why the other must die, in a sense, for him, that he may be sent away alive, as, in fact, he is.

This, which is plain, is a complete answer to Dr. Waldenström's real perversion.

The Old-Testament doctrine of sacrifice is clear. It is the shedding of blood by which comes remission, and the blood shed is all poured out at the bottom of the altar, save what is put upon the horns in testimony of death, not life,—a death offered to God, as the blood upon the altar shows, for it is upon the altar, the place of offering, that it atones for the soul. It is not ordinarily sprinkled upon the person at all, but upon the altar; and thus the wrath of God is removed from the sinner that turns to Him. He sees the blood, and passes over. He says as to Noah, that He will not curse; or as to Abel, gives testimony that he is righteous, testifying of his *gifts*.

The sacrifice is substitutional. The hands of the offerer mark it out as this. It is henceforth his *sin*, or sin-*offering*, for the words are the same. Death is entered into the world through sin, and "the soul that sinneth, it shall die,"—so the victim dies. The sword of judgment is sheathed, for the ransom has been found. The Old-Testament doctrine of sacrifice is the doctrine of *vicarious atonement*.

But we have still to inquire as to the New Testament: will it reverse or confirm what we have gathered from the Old?

No one of those whose doctrine Dr. Waldenström is opposing would think of denying that Christ's blood cleanses from all sin. If they were bold enough or ignorant enough to do so, it would certainly be easy work, with but a single text such as he quotes, to refute them. As it is, his first arguments, when he comes to the New Testament, are but another instance of the strange half-sightedness which so constantly afflicts him. *Why* should it result that because the blood of the Lamb cleanses, it cannot atone? or that cleansing and atoning should be but the same thing? Surely it cleanses, purifies, sanctifies (we affirm it with all our hearts), and yet it atones! And more: its power to atone is just what gives it power to cleanse, as we shall see.

Even as to cleansing, the washing of water and the sprinkling of blood have to be distinguished as he does not distinguish them; and likewise the sprinkling of blood upon the *person* from the sprinkling of blood upon the *altar* or upon the mercy-seat. All this he entirely confounds; and to disentangle the confusion is enough completely to destroy his system.

He begins with what is indeed an important text—Heb. ii. 17, 18, where the common version gives, "to make reconciliation for." The Revised has, rightly, "make *propitiation*." He says, Christ's "work as High-Priest was to make *propitiation* for the sins of the people." The apostle does not say, "to propitiate God," but "to make propitiation for the sins of the people." Dr. Waldenström turns back to the Old-Testament sacrifices to explain this in the manner already familiar to us, adding, "As John says, 'The blood of Jesus, His Son, *cleanseth us* from all sin. (1 Jno. i. 7.)' But to cleanse is to cleanse, or purify, and nothing else. . . . and when once all His work shall have been consummated, then there shall stand around His throne a great multitude which no man can number—a multitude of human beings, pure and holy like Himself. And were you to ask how they have become so pure, they would answer that they '*washed their robes, and made them white in the blood of the Lamb.*' (Rev. vii. 14.) Mark, mark, not that they by the blood of Jesus have *appeased God;* no, but that they, in the blood of Jesus, have *washed their robes.*"

The style of argument I have already indicated: "The apostle does not say, 'to propitiate *God*'"*!* Not, it must be confessed, in so many words; but does he say, to *make propitiation?* It is the only possible rendering of the text. WHOM, then, does He propitiate, if not God? How did He make propitiation at all—that is, *appeasal,*—if there were no one to *be* appeased? If there were, who was it but God? Surely, if He is not named, the reference is, plainly enough, to Him.

Mr. Princell, as we have seen, is bolder than his leader. *Hilaskomai* here "plainly" means only "to show mercy with respect to"—that is, "to pardon'! But this is only assertion, against which we have the whole doctrine of the Old Testament, as we have seen, as well as the regular use of the word. In Luke xviii. 13 the correct force of the passive is also "be propitiated." The sacrificial system shows any thing rather than simple "forgiveness" without atonement made, and the sinner's repentance was not the atonement.

Then the quotation from John can scarcely, one would think, be meant for proof. Of course, to cleanse is to cleanse, but "to *make propitiation*" is not "to cleanse.' The latter is the *effect* of the former—not the same thing. And even to *cleanse* here is not to make inwardly pure, in the sense of regeneration, or communicating a new life, but answers to Heb. x. 22—the" heart sprinkled from an evil *conscience.*" The meaning of purging by the blood Hebrews will presently show us.

As for the blood-washed throng in Revelation, they

are witnesses *against* Dr. Waldenström, not for him. For the white robes are (δικαιώματα) "the righteous acts of the saints" (Rev. xix. 8, *R.V.*), which cannot be meant, therefore, to have been internally purified, but freed from the imputation of the evil which had been in them after all; the washing here was from *guilt*, and it is by its atoning power that the blood of Christ avails for this.

But the doctrine of cleansing by the blood is in the ninth and tenth chapters of Hebrews, to which Dr. Waldenström now goes on, having quoted chap. ix. 13, 14, he asks, "What, then, according to the idea of the apostle, were the sacrifices of goats and oxen meant to do? Answer: To appease God? No; but *to sanctify the unclean unto an outward cleansing*. To effect any spiritual cleansing, or to make the worshipers perfect as touching the conscience, that they could not do. (*v.* 9.) 'For the law made nothing perfect.' (chap. vii. 19.) But the sacrifices of the Old Testament were only types. In the New Testament, there is a better sacrificial blood—the blood of Jesus Christ, who, through the eternal Spirit has offered Himself unto God; and what was its significance according to the idea of the apostle? Did he say, "How much more, then, shall the blood of Christ appease God, so that, again, it may be possible for Him to be gracious unto us?' No; but he did say this: 'How much more shall the blood of Christ cleanse your conscience from dead works to serve the living God.' . . . To cleanse, to cleanse from sin, *that* is the power of the sacrificial blood in the New Testament."

Now, what is the theme of the apostle in all this part of Hebrews? It is the cleansing of the *conscience*, so that we can now do what under the law they could not—draw nigh to God. The vail before the holiest showed that under the law,—that is, by its works,—this was impossible. The vail is now rent, and Christ has, by His own blood, entered into the holy place, having obtained eternal redemption. What does this mean, entering in as high-priest by His own blood? Does it mean power in the blood Godward, or simply manward? How has He obtained redemption? Does the blood speak of death here, or of life? Now, *immediately following* the verse which Dr. Waldenström has quoted we find this: "And for this cause He is the mediator of the new testament, that, *by means of death, for the redemption of the transgressions* that were under the first testament, they which are called might receive the promise of eternal inheritance."

Why has not Dr. Waldenström quoted this? Would it have helped his argument, or spoiled it, to have done so? And the apostle goes on to insist upon the necessity of death, and to connect with it what was, indeed, the testimony of it—the blood so necessary even under the law, and without *shedding* of which was no remission? We see that this shedding of blood does not stand alone in this chapter; but that it is connected with the doctrine clearly announced, of the necessity of the *death* of Christ for redemption, and that the shedding of blood must (of course) furnish the blood which now sprinkled upon the heart purges it from a bad conscience. The knowledge of redemption through Christ's death sets the soul at rest, and enables us to draw near to God.

But more: by the same precious blood the heavenly things themselves are cleansed for us,—"that is," says Dr. Waldenström himself, "the heavenly sanctuary." He catches at this to say that whatever may be meant by it, "yet surely we must see that [the apostle] sets forth the meaning of the sacrifices to be that of *cleansing*." If he had said '*a*' meaning, who would have contested it? But he thinks he has gained all when he states thus a half-truth for a whole. Nay, it is no matter to him what the heavenly sanctuary means; nor, therefore, what the cleansing itself is, for that must be affected by it. His view imperatively requires, as we have seen, that it should be internal cleansing,—the communication of life, for the blood is the life; but how can the heavenly sanctuary be cleansed thus? It cannot, and cleansing from defilement has no real place in Dr. Waldenström's thoughts.

Yet he can venture to tell us that the apostle "explains this cleansing as meaning that Christ once for all, now at the end of the ages, has been manifested '*to put away sin by the sacrifice of Himself* (*v.* 26);'" and that "in verse 28, he repeats the same thought, saying, '*Christ was once offered to bear* [that is, for the purpose of bearing, or taking away] *the sins of many.*' Thus, what in other places is called atonement for sins through sacrifices, that is here called a *putting away* of sins, or a *bearing them away*"!

This is bold enough: the two words are quite different, the "putting away" of sins the effect of atonement, the *bearing* of sins, the essential element of atonement itself. The last is the same word that Peter uses when he says, in a text which seems, like some other important ones, to have escaped our author, "Himself bare our sins in His own body on the tree . . . by whose stripes ye were healed." (1 Pet. ii. 24.) Is this the same as 'bare *away* our sins in His own body" and that "on the tree"? Even if it were, awkward as would be the conception, it could scarcely obscure the vicarious character of atonement here; but it is not, as Dr. Waldenström must know it is not: it is "bare up," "sustained," bore the burden of. How nearly the repetition of Isaiah's words: "He shall bear their iniquities; . . . He hath poured out His soul unto death; and He was numbered with the transgressors; and He bare the sin of many"!

Thus alone could sin be taken away, "the chastisement of our peace" being "upon Him." How vain to deny it! how terrible to slight or deny the need and value of a work so precious! It is needless to follow Dr. Waldenström into the tenth chapter of Hebrews, where his argument is but a monotonous repetition of the same half-truths. The sacrifice cleanses, therefore it does not atone! it sanctifies, therefore it does not atone! What is supposed to be a part of our intuitive knowledge he does not seem to have apprehended, that a whole is greater than its parts. Let us repeat it for him, that it is just because the blood of Christ atones for us that it can cleanse,—that it is just because He bare our sins upon the tree that they can be taken away from us. The truth he refuses is the natural, necessary complement of the truth he sees.

Nor does it need to take up the passages cited from the first epistle of John, which even all his effort cannot make otherwise than clear. It is only when he introduces such thoughts as that of "propitiating sinners from their sins"—to which he rightly enough appends the doubt, "if we could use such an expression"—that there is any difficulty at all. He does not, as we have seen, even mention the passages in Peter. His arguments, with the most wearisome reiteration, do but affirm and reaffirm these two things, that because the blood is the life, blood *poured out*, or sprinkled is still life, not death; and secondly, that once prove that the blood sanctifies or cleanses, you have *dis*proved vicarious atonement. Meanwhile, he has scarcely attempted to meet the arguments on the other side, or looked even at the texts upon which they are founded! And while he admits, in a general way, that Christ died for us—I suppose, for our sins,—yet why He should have died, we cannot, in the two books we have been examining at least, understand at all. It may be that it was for the moral effect of it: *Scripture* says it was "for redemption." That "the chastisement of our peace was upon Him;" that "the Lord laid on Him the iniquity of us all;" that thus "He was made sin for us," "bare the sins of many," "bare our sins in His own body on the tree," "suffered for sins, the Just for the unjust," "redeemed us from the curse of the law, being made a curse for us;" that He "tasted death for every man;" that "the Son of man *must* be lifted up, that whosoever believeth in Him should not perish,"—all this, and much more, must be for him as inexplicable as, in fact, by him it is unexplained.

We do not propose to follow him into the last three chapters of this book, where, from the common confusion between reconciliation and atonement, he gains some points against those who make it. In this there is little interest for us, and in much that he says we should have to agree with him; but it is striking and characteristic that, when he has shown us how, in those who are ambassadors for Christ, God beseeches men, as it were, and they pray, in Christ's stead, Be ye reconciled to God,—there, as if a mountain lay across his path, he stops and goes no further. From his book you would never learn that the *ground* of the appeal for reconciliation lies in this, that "God has *made Him to be* SIN for us, who knew no sin, that we might be made the *righteousness* of God in Him."

And this mountain, though with the eternal dawn bright upon its summit, lies still as an insurmountable barrier across the path of Dr. Waldenström and all those who plead the cause of non-vicarious atonement.

FRUIT OR ROOT?

SOME THOUGHTS UPON JOB'S "DITCH."

(Luke xxii. 31-34.)

I HAVE in my mind, beloved brethren, a subject which has been much upon my heart of late and which here and there I have taken up in different ways. I believe it to be a matter of importance for our souls, a subject in which there is much encouragement.

We have in the verses before us, no doubt, a typical case, of how the Lord makes sin to serve Him. I dare say in the way I put it, it may seem a strange statement to make, but after all it is a very simple one. God has His hand upon all, and God makes all things serve Him. "He makes the wrath of man to praise Him, and the remainder of wrath He restrains:" He does not permit one particle of the wrath of man anywhere which He can not make to praise Him. That is, clearly, He makes *sin* serve Him. It does not, in the least, alter the nature of sin, it does not make it less hateful; but it makes God what He surely is, the perfect Master of everything, and it gives us the only comfort that we can possibly get as we look at evil, as we realize its terrible prevalence in human history. What comfort would there be for us, if we were not able to look at it and say, God can get glory out of all this? In a true sense, therefore, God has ordained it to His glory.

Here in Peter you get an instance of this,—a sample of the principle of which I have been speaking. Here is a sin on Peter's part, that the Lord foretells to him: he is going to deny Him thrice. Satan has asked to have this disciple of His, as the trier of God's wheat. He has asked to have him in his sieve that he may sift him; and the Lord has not prayed that he might not be sifted. That was necessary in a certain sense. Satan claims to be the trier of God's wheat, and the words express that, much more than appears in our version. It is not exactly, "Satan has *desired* to have you." It is much more than that. It is, "Satan has *demanded* to have you,"—"Satan has demanded to have you, that he may sift you as wheat." But how can that be? What does it mean? Why, it means that Satan is the one who is the accuser of the brethren and who, if he accuse them day and night before God, must of necessity accuse them on the only possible plea which could avail him there —the plea of righteousness. Thus when he accuses Job, even when God puts him before him and says, "Hast thou considered my servant Job, that there is none like him on the earth?" he says, "Does Job serve God for naught? Hast Thou not made a hedge about him?" And he gets Job into his hands upon the plea that Job is professedly God's wheat; so let it be tried if he is really this. He does not believe that Job is just all that he seems to be. Job is in very good circumstances. Everything goes fair with him, and how can he be tested in fair weather like that? Very easy for a man to be good when all circumstances are in his favor! In opposite circumstances let us see, he says, what sort of a man Job will appear. It is all right, take Job into your hand and do so and so, is the divine answer.

I don't doubt there is an instructive type of Satan, in that way, in the book of Joshua, in a very remarkable person who is the first in the league against Gibeon, when Israel is entering the land. Adonizedek, king of Jerusalem, is the person I speak of. Adoni-zedek is a very striking counterpart, in some sense, of Melchizedek, king of Salem. In the first place, it is the same city, with almost the same name. Salem, which means "peace," is the same as *Jeru*-salem. Jerusalem means the "*foundation* of peace." Then look at the personal name. Melchizedek is "king of righteousness," and the other man's name is Adoni-zedek, that is "lord of righteousness,"—almost the very same thing. But there is one thing as to Melchizedek that you do not find about Adoni-zedek. Melchizedek is priest of the most high God. Adoni-zedek is not that at all. The priest of the most high God is the one who blesses Abraham, the father of these Israelites, when he has conquered the kings and comes back from his victory. Adoni-zedek is the head of a league *against* the children of this very Abraham. Melchizedek is for; Adoni-zedek is against. Melchizedek acts in priestly character. There is no priestly character about Adoni-zedek. Adoni-zedek is the very picture of Satan himself. How everything about him proclaims that he is standing apparently for righteousness. He is the lord of righteousness. He is the king of the "foundation of peace," and the foundation of peace is righteousness. Such is Satan. He is the accuser of the brethren. He is the one who takes them up on the very ground of righteousness. He is Adoni-zedek, with no priestly character about him, but the very reverse. He is the awful contrast to the Lord Jesus Christ, the tender intercessor for men.

How much that affects the state of things upon the earth! What we have here in Luke is only a sample of the way in which Satan is busy. And I believe we all of us have personal interest in it; for I believe there is not one of us that Satan has not accused, and is not accusing, before God, and, I tell you what, beloved, we give him plenty of opportunity to say of us, "These people are not all they profess to be."

The moment you take your place as wheat with God, you take your place, as it were, in Satan's sieve for him to sift, according as God may permit it, and see if you are what you profess to be.

What is the effect of it for Peter? He is terribly bruised in the sieve. The Lord has prayed, not that he may not be sifted, not that his faith might not fail. He does not pray that he may not break down, or that he may not sin: He *predicts* the sin. He says, "Peter, you are going to deny Me thrice."

What does He say in connection with that? "When thou art converted, strengthen thy brethren." What does that mean? Of course, "conversion" here does not mean that which we generally call by that name: that is, the great primary turning to God from sin, from the world. It speaks of the turning of a saint, the "conversion," if you like, of a saint, and not the conversion of a sinner. That is plain; but then, how is he converted? Converted from his sins? No: *we* might imagine that. He has to be converted *by* his sin, and *from* his self-righteousness. The Lord has ordained the breaking down of a self-righteous man.

Peter answers, "Nay, Lord, I am ready to go with Thee to prison and to death." That is the point; that is the very thing he needed to realize he was *not* ready to do. That is the very thing he needed to be converted out of, the self-confidence which is the ruin of men wherever they have it.

Therefore it is that the very sin into which the Lord allows Peter to fall is to be the means of ruining that self-confidence in him and so of turning him to another mind. We make great mistakes in regard to those things. We are apt to look upon some outward evil, some sin that a man has committed, perhaps a gross one, as if it were the whole matter, or at any rate the great thing; that which is only the fruit of the tree we look at as if it were the tree itself, and we say why did God permit it? when that really means why did God permit the tree to show its fruit? Well, why *did* God permit the tree to show its fruit? Because the fruit makes manifest the tree, and men need, beloved, to be made manifest in that way. They need to realize what they are. If a man does not realize what he is, he may be going on apparently just as Peter was, full of love to the Lord, right in conduct and all that, and you think of the man as going on well. Suddenly he falls, and you look at *that* as the departure, when the fall is only the *fruit* of the departure which has been going on long before; and then the fall is the very thing which may be used to make the man conscious of his weakness and nothingness, — therefore to bring him back; to make him humble that he may now really be strong; that he may find his strength in Another, and that he may perhaps be even the means of strengthening his brethren.

God must break down before He can build up; in order that He may deliver us from sin He must deliver us first from righteousness, and that is a great principle in God's ways. It is a sample of how He uses sin. Sin, of course, is the abominable thing He hates, but while it is that (the thing that He is going to put in hell out of His sight forever, because He hates it), while sin is that very thing, there is not an atom of it God permits on the face of the earth but because He can make it serve His purpose and glorify Him; otherwise He would not permit it. What a comfort it is to realize that God's strong hand is upon things and upon people after that manner. What a comfort it is that we can look into the most awful pit of darkness that can anywhere be, and see there the glory of God! What a blessed thing to know that there is not a corner of God's earth that is out of God's reach; and, beloved, He makes the thing He hates to serve Him, but that does not show that He loves it, or that He is indifferent about it. We make our criminals serve in jail, and God makes His criminals as all else, serve Him, whether good or bad.

I would like to apply that now a little. If we look at man away as he is from God, we see not in him how sin began. In him the stream is far on in its course; before men fell there was a host of beings above them that had fallen. Satan, the devil, was in existence then. We know that, of course, because he was the tempter of man at the beginning. What a question it is, and how naturally we ask it: "however did sin come in?" For man, of course, it came in through Satan: man listened to Satan. But to whom or what did *Satan* listen? who tempted Satan? who made Satan Satan? Why, there was no one at all to do it outside of himself; and how could *he* have made himself that? how could an angel become a devil?

Scripture tells us in that remarkable way in which we have many other of the most important truths brought in, quite incidentally, as it might seem, that Satan fell through *pride*. You have, I don't doubt, the description of him in the king of Tyrus in the 28th of Ezekiel, and there you find it in detail. The picture can hardly be mistaken: "Thou sealest up the sum, full of wisdom, and perfect in beauty: thou hast been in Eden the garden of God . . . thou art the anointed cherub that covereth . . . thou wast perfect in thy ways from the day thou wast created till iniquity was found in thee. . . . Thy heart was lifted up because of thy beauty: thou hast corrupted thy wisdom by reason of thy brightness;" —thus we see the very process of such a perversion as has taken place in the fallen angel,—Satan becoming the awful creature that he now is. And how? By self-occupation, self-admiration,— pride. The text we have in Timothy, where in his direction in regard to bishops the apostle tells him that a bishop must not be a novice, "lest being lifted up with pride he fall into the condemnation of the devil:" that is fall into that for which the devil was condemned.

That is how all the sin in the world came in. "Being lifted up with pride:" that was Satan's snare,—the only possible thing, we may well think, by which a being created in perfect uprightness and apart from any temptation, or from any circumstances of evil, could become evil: at least, it was the original departure from truth and uprightness. There was no evil around to solicit him. There was no evil self in him for him to be taken up with, but there was a *good* self; and the being taken up with that *good self* made him the horrible creature he is! I wish I could ring out that lesson far and wide among men. I wish one could make the people of God learn that lesson by heart. For I tell you what, it is one of the most necessary lessons to learn that possibly can be.

When God creates man and puts him upon the earth after this fall of Satan, you can see that it is constantly in His mind: He alters His methods in order to avoid, if possible, so great a collapse. Satan had been, just as the angels are, one that excelled in strength. Measurably, he was a being so far complete in himself, and independent of others. He was thus a being who could look at himself with admiration, for beauty and strength; and now the problem is, (if from our human side we may call it so,) how could God make another creature who should be free from the snare of self, and yet a good and a reasonable creature?

God could not make anything but a good being; He must make him reasonable, worthy to be a creature of His hand. He must be tested also; at least, he is to be. All this meets in Adam in a way which should have deepest interest for us, and which shows the divine care and love, in a way to call out our answering adoration.

First of all, He does not make him a creature to excel in strength. He puts him upon the earth in the midst of numerous creatures stronger than himself, a naked, defenseless being. He puts him upon earth in such a condition as to mark his dependence very strongly. His life is to be continued by his eating of the tree of life. Life is not in himself; life is in the tree of life for him; he is warned in the most distinct way of his dependence and put straitly under condition. The tree of the knowledge of good and evil is placed in the garden, and that which we are accustomed to think of as the very thing which helped his fall, is that which in fact should have helped him to remain upright, for it was the constant warning of the danger of forgetting his dependence. Yet it was a very small thing to be forbidden. What was it for one who had all the trees in the garden to eat of besides, to refrain from just one tree?

Again, if he looked at himself, he found himself, as to his body linked with the animal creation; in a certain sense, I may say less perfect, as far as strength goes, than many others. He finds himself thus in every direction encompassed with the witness of his infirmity as a creature. God would "hide pride from man." The angel's snare he must, as far as possible, be shielded from. Beautiful it is to see the tenderness of God in this respect.

You would think He had fenced him around so that it was impossible for him to be touched. Nor only so, but when temptation comes to him, God ordains that it shall only come to him from below, not from above. He shall not be tempted by a being manifestly above himself. Temptation shall not come in the form of an angel of light, but in the form of a beast of the field, one of those that Adam had looked at and seen that there was not a helpmeet amongst them all for him. How carefully God had provided for the creature of His love!

With it all, what you find is that the devil tried upon man the very method by which he had been ensnared himself. He turns his heart away from God by putting his very dependence and deficiency before him, instead of the strength he has not; yet still to lift him up with pride in the insinuation of what he may be—of the capacity he has. That is a marked deficiency that he has not the knowledge of good and evil. If he eats of this forbidden tree, he shall be as God, knowing good and evil. Alas, Satan had aspired to be as God, and he knew well what had come of that.

Awful it is to see him practising the devilish art, which he had learned in that way, upon another. "Ye shall be as God," he says, "knowing good and evil." Thus man falls; but how carefully God had guarded him so that he should not!

After the fall he is still more compassed about with the witness of what he is. Men are continued upon the earth by means of the woman. Eve becomes "the mother of all living." But how are men brought into the world? In the utmost feebleness indeed. An adult man is a feeble creature after all. Put him outside among the beasts without any of the things which he has slowly accumulated about him, out among the beasts of the field; and see how he will fare. But feeble as he may be in his full grown strength, how feeble is he as he comes into the world, dandled in his mother's arms, slowly and painfully acquiring the wisdom he is so proud of, learning through years of feebleness to submit himself to the will and care of others. Debtor to the love of others for all that he is, he could not possibly live, if he were put out to live as others, not so far from kin. How God has borne witness to him of his nothingness, how God would abase him in his own eyes, and hide pride from him!

Yet, after all, man's constant snare is still himself. When a man turns to God, what do we find? he has to be brought down from this, down into the dust, down to learn not only that he is a sinner, but that he is an *impotent* sinner too, a sinner and without strength. How do men find that out?

Constantly by struggling to deny it; constantly by fighting with it, as hard as ever they can; fighting until they have to surrender. How does God help us to this end? by allowing sin in man, just when he wants to be very righteous and very good; just when he wants to come to God, and say, "God, I thank Thee I am not as other men," God has to humble him and smite him into the dust (Job's history over again); and when he comes up again, and washes himself and thinks he is never so clean, God plunges him,—so Job has it,—into the ditch again, and his very clothes abhor him. God is using sin against sin, using sin to defeat itself. If in the devil it might seem as if goodness was its own snare, God says, now sin shall be its own destruction. He lets the man sin. He tumbles him into the ditch; and when he finds at last that he is without strength, *then* he finds, blessed be God, that "*when* we were yet without strength, in due time, Christ died for the ungodly." What a long while it took for that due time to come! what a long history of man in the Old Testament, and what comfort do we get from it? Not much I fear; and in truth the comfort comes out of discomfort; what carefulness there is through all God's history of man, to show the poor creature that at best he is! God's righteous men are still sinners; none of them without some flaw, in which they become warnings, and not for imitation. It seems as if a painter were at work to make a beautiful painting and then some other hand had splashed the color over it. Scripture biographies are unlike all mere human ones; but they are written in divine wisdom—to prevent man from glorifying man, to prevent man's goodness ministering to man's besetting sin.

God seems often afraid of man's goodness, as He is not of his sin. For man's sin Christ died, and not his goodness. In God's wonderful grace, man can come to God and say, "O God I am a sinner and Christ died for sinners," and find his resting place there upon the solid, immovable rock. Thus the same method prevails, God is using sin itself against sin, in His grace to man.

The lesson is thus learned as to righteousness: it is found in Another—in Christ. And he who has learned it says, "Thank God, I know my righteousness to be in Christ; God has taught me wisdom." All well, and so it is indeed. But the same man starts now on a fresh quest; and here his old lessons seem to avail him nothing. He is now after holiness; and if righteousness is in Another, *holiness* at least must be in himself: true, but not all the truth. But with that word up comes afresh a busy, earnest self, attractive in its search for holiness,—alas, too attractive—once more the good self, fatal to an angel once. Holiness is to be realized in a self-conscious way; and in this self-consciousness lies the evil and the snare. He wants to be able to look at himself, and realize himself to be just the thing for God. God's grace ought to be fruitful in him; he ought to find power in it against evil, and for good: all true, surely; but with so much true, he cannot see the deception that yet lurks in it,—the potent Pharisaic spell under which he is.

So the old remedy is ordained for him,—the stain upon all human glory. Job's ditch is ordained to save him from the greater precipice; and, once again, God makes the sin He hates to serve Him. The law of sin is in his nature. Nor can he in this way find deliverance from it. When he would do good, evil is present with him; and how to perform that which is good he finds not.

There is no hope in this direction. The cry can only be, "Oh wretched man that I am, who shall deliver me?" And now, in the infinite grace of God, he finds, not deliverance merely, but a Deliverer. Sanctification is, after all, in Christ; if the holiness resultant is yet to be in us: just as surely as the sunshine is in the sun, by which we are brightened. So now the soul is turned from the impracticable self of experience, to find for faith the true self in which we abide before God. Here is the satisfaction for our hearts as for the heart of God. Here is communion with Him fully attained. Here is a heavenly Object to draw off the heart from the world and from the snare of self together. Here holiness is found, but found in self-forgetfulness; or if self be revealed in connection with it, it is for the Spirit of God to show us by contrast with the true Man for God, our own mere unlikeness and evil. We learn to "rejoice in Christ Jesus" and to "have no confidence in the flesh."

There is not a truer sign of a man walking with God than this utter self-forgetfulness. God has provided for it in His grace, when man turns in upon himself again, and sees this horrible thing within him. How can God go on with that? But, says the word of God again, God has not gone on with that. He has put that away by the cross of His own Son. God has put away sin altogether away from before Him, root and fruit in the cross of His own Son; and now then you are in Christ before Him. Look up there. You can never see yourself aright except as you look out of yourself; and if you do that you shall find the most attractive self you could possibly have. You shall find a self that you can glory in. So says the Apostle, "I knew a man in Christ, of such an one I will glory." Yet it is himself, it is the man *in Christ*. It is himself in Another, in the Christ before God for him; and finding himself there, he can fall in love with himself as much as ever he likes; but the self he falls in love with is that OTHER self who *draws him out of himself*.

How perfect is God's wisdom! how beautiful it is to see that He has ordained by the very evil in man to antagonize the evil in man. No wonder we ask, how is it possible? A great many Christians think it is not possible. Why should it be that it is impossible for me to get rid of this sin within me? how is it, I have got a nature that I cannot get rid of, like a dead carcass strapped to me, a "body of sin?" If it be really so, there must be some way of justifying it. There must be some good in it after all. The very evil must be some good in some way. God could not allow it, unless it was good for us; good to carry about with us the thing we hate; good that we should get exercised about it, have to look at it, and see what a horrible thing it is. Thank God, as I have said, in this way we learn to turn from ourselves because whenever we don't turn from ourselves we find it there. It confronts us; it frightens us from ourselves.

I have often said, that a man taken up with the kind of self-cultivation so natural to us, is just like a man who is cultivating his garden in the crater of a volcano; and it may be very productive soil for awhile, as long as the mountain will keep quiet. But when the mountain will not keep quiet! a little shake, a rumble of the mountain! the evil hidden within bursts out, and the garden is spoiled. That which seems but evil is God's way; it is God's own remedy; it is God's own way of victory over evil; just because it is God's own way of turning the creature away from himself forever, and giving us lessons which shall last through all eternity. It is a lesson which we learn here upon earth and which we could not learn anywhere else, which we learn as sinners, learn from the very sin itself, and carry with us through eternity to His praise and for our own sake.

God is not working merely for time, and it is not merely a question of how He will keep us clean for the few years we are here. I do not want to make light of that, not at all; but yet there are worse things than even the outward sins which soil our lives alas, so much. He who can make light of sin makes doubtful the truth of his own conversion; for the man in the experience of the seventh of Romans, though he has not power over it, *hates* the sin he does. He may be sin's slave, *but not its free man.* He who serves it freely will get its wages. And "the wages of sin is death."

But yet a worse thing than the outward sin is that pride of heart which by making us something, puts us in the way of repeating the awful history of the first sinner, Satan.

That is something worse, and in a Christian is what necessitates the other. The spirit which was in Peter here could only be got out of Peter by that awful fall in the High Priest's palace; the awful sin of denying his own Lord with curses; that was to teach him what Peter the Saint was; what Peter who loved his Lord was, and in spite of his true love for Him. It was to destroy in him his self-confidence and self-righteousness; it was to manifest his weakness, but to reveal to him His strength; to make him utterly weak, and then to lift him up in the arms of Eternal Might and enable to go forth to strengthen others.

If we look at the Old Testament history with its sad picture of man, we naturally say, the people were under the law, did not know God's grace; they were an earthly people, a nation in the flesh; but now then, if we turn to the history of Christianity should it not be quite different? And has it been so? God's history of it has been written—briefly, no doubt,—beforehand: is it a comforting one to look at? In the apostles' days the "mystery of iniquity" was already working. When John wrote his epistle there were already "many antichrists"; and by this he knew it was the "last time." The time since, therefore, could not be different; and in the last days we are assured that "perilous times" should come. They close with apostasy and the man of sin, "whom the Lord shall consume with the breath of His mouth, and destroy with the brightness of His coming."

Man's history of the Church has doubtless been badly enough written; but the main features of it are nevertheless quite unmistakable. The whole Church has fallen into fragments; the largest of which is morally the worst. The dark ages were the time when the Church ruled the world, and when the world found its yoke an intolerable tyranny. Protestantism enlightened by the Word is the most painfully divided. I do not dwell on it; but what a history it is! Does it not repeat forever the discouraging text, "Cease ye from man"? And discouragement, discouragement, discouragement, seems to face us everywhere. Yet God is the "God of all encouragement!"

After all, do not these things go together? Let us reach but this point, and what is all this discouragement about the world and the Church, about man, even if he be a saint, but encouragement to hold fast to God alone?

Blessed be God, if we are losing confidence in ourselves altogether! Well we may: we have had superabundant proof of what we are. Had we thoroughly learned to "have no confidence in the flesh," we should be learning indeed the corresponding joy of "worshipping God in spirit" and "exulting in Christ Jesus," and should take a new start in divine things. God grant that we may do so! As man counts for much, God counts for little. As man descends in the scale of our estimation, God proportionally acquires the glory that is His own. In the knowledge of the new man, as we find it in Colossians, "Christ is all"; and the sum of wisdom is to maintain this. That "God shall be all in all" is the expression of the glory of the eternal state, and of its stability as well. The creature can no more come into competition with Him: the necessary end of which is the darkness of hell, as the opposite pole is the glory of heaven.

CREATION IN GENESIS AND IN GEOLOGY.

I.—THE SCRIPTURAL STATEMENT.

THE questions involved in the first chapter of Genesis are those which lie at the bottom of the whole controversy with what men are pleased to call science in the present day. "Science," alas! and knowledge are getting to be widely separated, although originally the same thing. A mere hypothesis is "scientific" nowadays, and hypotheses are coloring, to a large extent, the very statement of what should be facts. "Eyes of faith" (to use the language of a well-known man of science,) are getting as necessary for the observation of facts as they could possibly be for the knowledge of Scripture. "A working hypothesis" is indeed a fact; what it may work is another question. To those who have their eyes open, there cannot be a doubt that men are working themselves into a delusion which Scripture has been beforehand in prophesying, and which therefore, spite of itself, must fulfill Scripture.

On looking at the questions which our subject indicates, our first business is with Scripture itself. The book of Genesis is a fact, at any rate, whatever may be its significance. It is a fact that what purports to be a record of creation has come down to us from time so far back as to antedate all other human writings of which we have knowledge. It is a fact also that the character of this record stands in the most striking contrast with all that may seem in any wise to compete with it in point of age. The various national myths which deal with this subject few would have any difficulty in dismissing as such. But although there are those, no doubt, who think as cavalierly to dismiss the book of Genesis amongst them, it is easy to see that even for themselves this is impossible. The book has its hold upon them whether they will or no. They may talk of the effect of education, no doubt,—of the influences under which they have been brought up, and so on; but they have not found it hard to break through bands of this kind, times without number. Their very opposition to Scripture makes it evident how much they feel its power. No one thinks it worth while to fight with a Chaldean cosmogony, however ancient. They can look at and discuss it with the most scientific equanimity; Scripture they cannot so discuss. And this too is a fact in the moral realm which is worth considering.

When we turn to the first chapter of Genesis, we find nothing, at least, that wears the aspect of a myth; no obscurity; no seeming exaggeration. The style is simplicity itself, and this simplicity is sublimity. It is the style of one entirely at home with the subject of which he is speaking. Wonderful as the nature of the subject is, he is not dazed, not awe-struck; nor on the other hand reveling in mere imagination. The language is intelligible even to a child. There is no attempt at lengthy explanation, or at explanation at all. There is no argument, as having to prove any thing. The writer is above his theme, not under its power; and, when we consider what the theme is, *who* is the writer? People may deny its truth; they can scarcely deny its similitude to truth. It is the language of one who has nothing to gain by proving his point; no interest, in fact, one may say, at all, except it be an interest in man, which indeed shines out every where. The words may seem to give too human a picture of divine ways; but in it many at least have discerned the manner of One who, seeking to draw near to man, must adopt human speech, even with its defects. Can this be shown unworthy of Him?

Even for a scientific man one would think there should be interest in what, the moment he looks at it, corresponds strangely in certain of its features with what the facts of geology announce. Take, for instance, what to a writer of this antiquity would be strange enough, the fact of the dry land emerging out of the water. No geologist doubts that all land has, in fact, so risen; but it is a discovery of later days, anticipated here before the science of geology was born. Take, again, the progress of life from the lowest to the highest—from the denizens of the water to those of the dry land, and last of all, man. Every one knows that upon this very progress have been based some of the theories most current among men of science as to the development of life. Yet the writer in Genesis, while denying the development (at least, the genetic development), is aware of the fact of progress, and states it. How many scientific men are disposed to give him credit for this? Yet is not here again a fact noteworthy for the man of science?

The Christian, who is able to go deeper, notices, on the other hand, both in Genesis and geology, how remarkably the natural typifies the spiritual, and how God has thus given witness to Himself and to His record in the very book of nature with which the man of science deals. What means this strange fact which Genesis announces and geology confirms, that creation as we now see it, is in fact a birth out of a world passed out of being? Creation to the open eye is every where indeed a type of the new creation; but we shall be able better to dwell upon this at another time.

And now, to look somewhat in detail at the history before us. History it is, if it be any thing at all; it is at least not given as a speculation. It is not an argument, as I have already said; nor is it poetry, as some assert. All the basis for this assertion is found in the grandeur of the genesis which it relates, and the simple sublimity of the relation. But it is a history, if it is not an audacious fiction. "God created"—"God said"—"God made." Such are the statements. Is not this the offense in the eyes of some, that every thing here begins with God, and every thing belongs to Him? Yet there is no attempt to make an impression. Opposition to the prevailing idolatry is only marked by the fact of every thing being made and claimed by the one God before us. The style is the ordinary one of familiar speech, truer after all than much that may be more pretentious. It describes, one may say, appearances—phenomena; not meaning by this any thing in contrast with reality, but things as they would appear to, or be apprehended by, the mass of men. The God of Scripture seeks every where to be known by His creatures. He never affects the language of philosophers; never shuts Himself up to the learned and the wise. The greatest blessings every where (if we may still speak of blessing,) are the widest and most common,—sunlight, fresh air, water, and such like things. Whatever restrictions man may make, God means these for all. The very life we live is no better lived by him who understands the natural processes than by the man who scarcely knows that he has lungs to breathe with. These things go on independently of all our thought or intelligence about them, which may indeed often act, as the facts prove, rather as hindrances to than promoters of them. "To the poor, the gospel is preached;" for the poor, Scripture is written. The wise and learned not being excluded on this account, any more than they are excluded by sharing with the common man their sunlight and fresh air.

But however familiar the style, this must of course be implied, that if the history be from God, as such a history, to be true, must be from none other, then no imperfection of human speech must be allowed to interfere with the perfect accuracy of every statement. Scripture, if not intended to teach science, as of course it is not, must nevertheless be as accurate as any science. There is no inaccuracy in saying, for instance, that "the sun rises, and the sun goes down," for these things are always phenomenally true; and the man of science uses this language of necessity as others do, and there is no deception really in this. To us—from our stand-point, it is really true that the sun rises. It may not be the whole truth, but it is in fact that from which the truth back of it has been inferred. The sun's rising is, we may say, the primitive fact; the scientific account would be the explanation of the fact. Scripture does not and needs not to go beyond the primitive fact. Thus it is every where intelligible, and yet every where true. The men of science must be allowed to bring all they can against it if they will. If they can prove untruth, we will not shirk this by any quibbling about Scripture not meaning to teach science. God cannot be deceived; He cannot deceive. These are first principles upon which all others are built, and with which no other can be contradictory. It is in this spirit that we are to examine the account before us.

"*In the beginning God created the heaven and the earth.*"

WE are here brought at once face to face with one of the great questions of the day. Was there such a thing as creation? Does the word "created" even mean that which we ordinarily take it to mean? The reverse is now commonly asserted, and this at least must be allowed, that the making out of nothing is not necessarily intended by the word which we translate "created" here. It is nevertheless used in a sense sufficiently distinct from any mere making or fashioning. These two last words have their proper representatives in the language. The first word, "*Bara,*" is only used of God; He alone is "*Bore*" —Creator; and in the chapter before us alone the employment of *Bara* is very distinct and significant. In this first verse, the words "In the beginning," taken absolutely, necessitate that it should be a making out of nothing. We find it only three times used besides in the account. First, when the "living creature" is brought forth, it is said, "And God created great whales, and every living creature that moveth." Then again, when man comes on the scene, it is said, "God created man in His own image." The last place in which it is used is in the third verse of the second chapter, where, in the original, there is a distinction between "creating" and "making." The term used is really there, "created to make," as in the margin, "He had rested from all His work which God had created to make." So, justly, the Vulgate—"*Creavit ut faceret.*" Here, the making is rather the final purpose of the creating; and in the creation of the beast and of man, two other elements of being appear for the first time, which would seem to give the word the strict force of creating.

Of course, when I say this, I found it upon Scripture entirely. Scripture asserts as to the beast that it is not merely matter, as man would make it now, however wonderfully organized, but that it has and is a "living soul." Man, again, is distinguished from the beast by the fact that he possesses, not alone a soul, but a spirit also, and by this spirit he is in connection with God, as his God and Father, as the beast is not. God is said to be the "Father of *spirits*," not of souls. Angels are spirits, and are therefore also called, as men are, "sons of God;" and if we take this "spirit," as explained by the apostle in the first of Corinthians ii. 11, as that by which a man knows human things, as the intelligent part, in fact the mind, we can easily see that God is indeed only, in a strict sense, the God of those who can thus recognize Him. The beast is necessarily without God. "Man being in honor and understanding not, is *like* the beasts that perish." Yet, as I have said, the beast is not mere organization. "Every thing wherein there is a living soul," is said, in the thirtieth verse of this chapter, of "every thing that creepeth upon the earth." Even self-direction, if I may so say, never comes from the most skillful combination merely. All the instincts, the appetites of the body even, are referred, in Scripture, to the soul. The beast which has these has therefore a soul. Man too has a soul, of course, but in him the spirit characterizes and controls (or ought to control) it. A broad distinction is thus made between man and beast—a distinction which no development could possibly bridge. God Himself came in in both these cases; first of all in the creation of the beast—the living soul, and again in the creation of man (spirit also, and not soul alone) we find this word used, inferring the distinct step upward which is in each case made. With these exceptions, the word is "made," not "created." All mouldings of mere material, in whatever wondrous way, are here distinguished from the living thing, and even the plant is thus distinguished from the moving creature.

In all this, we are of course speaking of Scripture merely.

Men may deny the truth of it, but Scripture at least is self-consistent throughout; and such self-consistency, in view of the facts, is surely the self-consistency of truth.

The first verse, then, speaks of a primal "creation," which, as to its *general* character, the six days' is not. We find elsewhere that "in six days the Lord *made* heaven and earth, and all that in them is." It does not say "created." The first statement is that He "created," and not "made;" and this primal creation is surely distinguished plainly enough from the six days' work itself. The first day begins with the calling forth of light. But before this, the earth is already in being, but "waste and desolate" (as the words "without form" rather mean), lying in darkness, and buried under the waters. The second verse thus points out the state of ruin into which, through causes unexplained, the primitive creation had lapsed. It is not chaos, according to the old idea which Milton has popularized for us. The earth, buried under the waters, comes up upon the third day at God's bidding. It had existed all through. The six days' work was but calling it into new order, not into being. It has been said that this is but a fiction to meet the facts which geology has brought out. It is so little so that it has been advocated by others before geology was even in being. But I would rather appeal to the record itself. Scripture *never* says that the earth was created in six days. And the *first* day begins—where? *Not* with the chaos, as some would make it. The "evening" of the first day still implies, what the account necessitates, that light was there when it began. "God called the darkness *night*," but "*evening*" is the darkness already modified by light.

Besides, on the first day God evidently calls forth the light only—but where? Certainly with reference to a particular scene, a place from which it was absent. In the second verse, no hint of any act of creation is to be found. The words "waste and desolate" imply ruin, not creation. We must go back to the first verse to find this last. But the moment we do this, we find what Scripture itself assures us cannot be connected with the ruin into which it afterward lapsed. "For thus saith the Lord that created the heavens, God Himself that formed the earth and made it; He hath established it, He created it not in vain"— not "*tohu;*" the very word translated in the second verse of this chapter as "without form." God did not, then, create the earth in the chaotic condition which the second verse describes. That is not a primitive state, but a lapse; and the six days' work is a new fashioning—a bringing out of this state of universal ruin—universal, I mean, as regards the earth itself, and which is carefully distinguished from one affecting the heavens. "God created the heavens and the earth." "The *earth*," not the heavens, "was [or became] without form" or waste.

It is quite true that on the second day we find the firmament made, and called "heaven," but this is plainly a different "heaven" from the first spoken of. It is the heaven of the earth simply—the atmosphere, as to which we shall see more particularly when we come to it. The lapse is proved, then, a pre-existent state before the six days' work began; and a state in which, according to Scripture itself, it had not been created. No apology is therefore due here from revelation to science. The Bible, whatever questions may be raised as to its chronology, does not assert that the earth is but six thousand years old; nor does any statement imply, on the other hand, the antiquity of *man* to be more than about six thousand. How long this state of ruin continued, how many changes the earth may have passed through before this waste and desolate condition came about, we have no knowledge of from Scripture. Science may come in and supply the void in whatever way it will. Scripture says nothing for or against; nor is it a failure on the part of revelation to leave a void. Its object is not science, but moral and spiritual dealing with the spirit of man.

The agents in the six days' work are the Spirit and Word of God. "The Spirit of God moved [or brooded] upon the face of the waters; and God said." This language is anthropomorphic, if you will; we have spoken of that before. God, if He would gain man's ear, must use man's language. But the terms are simple enough as to their import. In the first place, it is no natural birth, this genesis. Just as the Spirit and Word unite in order to give life—true life to man individually, so the Spirit and Word unite here in order that there may be a renewal of the face of the earth. There is no energy of this kind inherent in matter. The evidence of science itself also is all the other way. There are plenty of signs of wearing out—*extinction* of species, not origination of them. To produce a *cosmos*, a world of form and order, an organized whole, in which part should be fitted to part in proper harmony, there must be the working of *mind*. I do not dwell on this here, for at present we are only occupied with the Scripture statement, not with the scientific one. Scripture asserts, as plainly as possible, that if a state of ruin were "natural," the interference of God was necessary to bring out of the ruin.

Thus comes the first day and light. Observe how simple are the terms used. It does not say, God *created* the light, nor even "made" it. It does not speak of light as a substance in itself. "He said, 'Let there be light,' and there was light." The words do not even show that the thing, "light," was first originated here. It is manifest only with reference to the scene before us. "Darkness was upon the face of the *deep*"—locally *there*. Every thing through the universe was not necessarily in darkness when God said, "Let there be light." Thus there is no ground whatever for the assertion that Scripture would confine the being of light to six thousand years or so. It makes no such statement. The light clears up the darkness which was upon the face of the deep. This may seem with some to lower the statement. They have been accustomed to attach to the words the idea of a primal creation of what was brought into being this first day. But whatever our thought may be, Scripture must be judged by its own statement.

This light is of course without the sun. It is no partial breaking through of what, in its source, was hidden; it is *not* sunshine. The sun, if not created, is certainly "made," on the fourth day. Light, apart from sunlight, on this first day of the week, is plainly asserted. However unscientific he may have been, Moses—if no higher—stands responsible for this statement; and if it be no higher, it is strange that even a "Hebrew Descartes" should have made a needless difficulty in this manner. To the nations of antiquity, light would seem much more inseparable from the sun than the discoveries of science will allow us now to believe; and there can be conceived no reason for the idea that is here given, if from a human source only. Truth might require it to be stated, but only truth.

On the second day, the "firmament" is made, or the "expanse." The word, after all quibbling about it, simply means that. I need scarcely pause to explain what has been so often explained. People have imported into a very simple passage ideas which have, at least, been elsewhere gathered. There is nothing at all about any thing solid. It is that in which the "fowls fly." "The way of the eagle is in the heavens." The clouds are "the bottles of the heavens." Nay; "the heavens are stretched out as a curtain." This word, "curtain," being so called, as Gesemus remarks, from its tremulous motion. All this is simple language, easy to be understood. It is not the common man who would make any mistake about it. The birds do not fly in a solid vault; nor do winds blow in it, or the clouds belong to it. And these clouds—not any holes in a crystal sphere, or any thing of that kind— "drop"—according to the sacred writer and the common man alike—"drop and distill upon man abundantly." The reservoir of the waters is therefore not, in Scripture, considered to be above the expanse, but in the expanse itself, and the clouds which float in the expanse.

Talking of the clouds, a remarkable witness to the science of Scripture has just come into my hands. There are two words for "fine dust," which are used in connection with the clouds. In Hebrew, *abaq* is, "small dust," such as is fine and light, easily driven by the wind; hence distinguished from *gnaplar*—thick, heavy dust. In Nahum i. 3, we find, "The clouds are the dust of His feet." In the case of the other word, it is not a comparison merely, but the word for cloud itself. *Shachaq* is, "dust, finely divided." It is used in Isaiah xl. 15 for the "small dust of the balance;" yet it is the word commonly used for "*clouds*," and also for *sky*. Is this any thing more than a figure of speech? One might have supposed not, but a recent discovery of science seems, however, to put it differently. Mr. J. Aitken—as quoted in a recent number of "*Nature*," in an article on "Dust, Fogs, and Clouds,"—remarks, "These would seem to have but little connection with one another, and we might think they could be better treated of under two separate and distinct heads; yet I think we shall presently see that they are more closely connected than might at first appear, and that *dust* is the germ of which *fogs* and *clouds* are the developed phenomena." From experiments with filtered and common air, he deduces,—"First, that whenever water condenses in the atmosphere, it always does so on some solid nucleus. Secondly, that dust-particles in the air form the nucleus on which the vapor condenses. Thirdly, therefore, that if there was no dust, there would be no fogs, no clouds, no mists, and probably no rain; and that the supersaturated air would convert every object on the surface of the earth into a condensor, on which it would deposit itself." Also "it is suggested, and reasons are given for supposing, that the blue color of the sky is due to this fine dust."

This is but by the way. As to the nature of the work on the second day, it is as plain as possible. The expanse that separates the waters from the waters is not even exactly the atmosphere itself. It is *by* the atmosphere, no doubt, that it is produced; but that is a different thing. The words give, in truth, a description of a fact, not of what causes the fact; and the waters above the expanse are but the clouds themselves. There is no hint, as strangely suggested by some, of watery bodies (such as Jupiter, etc.) being intended. The whole applies, not to occult matters of science, but to a simple and intelligible phenomenon, of immense import, however, to us.

The second day accomplishes a similar division between the land and the water. The waters under the heavens are gathered together in one place, and the dry land appears. Nothing is said here as to the elevation of this land, much less as to the fashioning of the mountains.

The thought is not mountains being raised, but of the water, one would rather say, subsiding. In the one hundred and fourth psalm, which has been called "The Psalm of Creation," the language, too, is similar—"Who laid the foundations of the earth, that it should not be removed forever. Thou coveredst it with the deep as with a mantle; the waters stood above the mountains. At Thy rebuke they fled; at the voice of Thy thunder they hasted away. They go up by the mountains; they go down by the valleys unto the place which Thou hast founded for them. Thou hast set a bound that they may not pass over, that they turn not again to cover the earth." Here, plainly, the mountains are already formed while yet the waters stand "above" them. The eighth verse has been taken rather to say that the mountains go up and the valleys go down, but this is against the plain sense of the passage. "The place which Thou hast founded for them" is plainly the "one place" of the first of Genesis, and is the place for the waters, not for the valleys. The following verse, again, plainly applies to the waters, and not to the land. Thus the whole connection seems to show the application to be to the waters themselves. No attempt is made to explain by what agency this gathering of the waters is effected. The dry land appears,—that is all that is said about it; and this dry land God calls "earth," a fact which, as has been remarked by another, may well help to explain the difficulty that some seem to find in the earth having foundations. It is the *dry land*— "earth" in that sense—which has them, not the earth as a whole.

We now come to that which is more really a *new* production,—grass, herb, and fruit-tree springing out of this dry land. Again, if we look at the words, we shall find no scientific division,—no care for science, in fact, but abundant care for man. It is that which is conducive to his welfare that God is considering and speaking of; He is furnishing man's earth for him.

Distinctness of kinds, however, let us observe, *is* here asserted: the proper distinction of species. Let science overthrow it if it can. It is not the place, however, to discuss this; and the words are so simple, we may pass on.

On the fourth day, God furnishes the heavens with "luminaries." The word is perfectly distinct from that for "light," as on the first day. These luminaries are candlesticks, so to speak, to hold the light; and here, again, with direct reference to man, and for his blessing; not only to divide the day from the night, but to be for "signs and for seasons and for days and years." The mention of *signs* shows, of course, that man is in question. The seasons themselves may have reference to the animal creation, or even to the vegetable, but not the "signs," and we shall have to look at the importance of this on a future occasion. So they are for "luminaries in the expanse of heaven, to give light upon the earth." That is the great point. They may serve a multitude of other uses. These are not denied, but they are not in question here. God has His eye on man. The two great lights, of course, have reference to him. The words are phenomenal again. No scientific measurement of distant orbs: they speak of what is plain to every common eye, and in the proportion of importance which, with regard to man, admits of no controversy. The moon, to us, is of infinitely more importance than Sirius.

"The stars also," appended to the account of the two great luminaries, is the only notice that we have with regard to the other heavenly bodies. They are introduced in a way which defines little. They are connected, evidently, with the preceding statement, as giving light upon the earth, along with the sun and moon. It is not said, even as to these, that they are now for the first time created. The sun is made a luminary at this time. Its body may have before existed—nay, *may have given light before*. Our knowledge of variable stars gives us more than a hint as to the extinction and lighting up again of such bodies. But at any rate, the sun is no more created on the fourth day than the earth upon the first; and the words translated "set them in the firmament of heaven" are, "*gave* them in the firmament of heaven," and that for a specific purpose—to give light upon the earth. If this be so as to sun and moon, still less is any creation of stars asserted here. The sentence, in fact, seems purposely left vague, doing nothing more than connecting these small luminaries, as such, with the larger ones.

On the fifth day, however, we come, as already noticed, to what is strictly "creation." "The living soul" is introduced. The words literally translated are, "And God said, 'Let the waters swarm with swarms—the living soul; and let the flier fly over the earth in the face of the expanse of the heavens;' and God created the great sea-monsters, and every living soul that moveth, wherewith the waters swarmed after their kind, and every winged flier after its kind; and God saw that it was good." There is a still more precise statement in the thirtieth verse, to which we may here refer, in which it is stated, "As to every moving thing upon the earth, wherein is a living soul." Thus every animal, even to the lowest grade, is called "a living soul," and for this reason, that a soul is in it. It is characterized by its higher part. Bodily organization is one thing; it is very far from being the whole thing in this case. Not merely is it a soul, but a soul is in it. In other words, the soul is not confounded with the body, but expressly distinguished from it. The soul, too, is definitely *what lives;* the body, of course, permeated by it, is alive also; but the source of its life is the soul. All Scripture shows this. The words for "soul," both in Hebrew and Greek, are the words for "life" also. Yet there are abundant passages which show that this is not merely what we call "vitality," but a life which is, in fact, dependent upon the presence of a soul. There are other uses of these words, (whether *nephesh,* as the Hebrew, or *psuche,* as the Greek,) derived from these. Into this I need not and cannot enter here. The Scripture is plain, that *in* the bodily organism is that which, distinct from it, animates and governs it.

Man, too, is a living soul, as the animal is; but man has a spirit also, as the beast has not. The distinction of these in Scripture furnishes the real key to that distinction between man and beast which is so puzzling the naturalist. To the spirit of man Scripture ascribes (1 Cor. ii. 11.) the knowledge of human things. Spirit and mind are thus far identical; while soul stands for what we ordinarily call (speaking figuratively, of course) the heart. But the soul is more than this. It is not only the seat of the affections; it is the seat also of the instincts and appetites of the body—things which are never referred to the spirit; while with the spirit, God connects Himself, as the "God of the spirits of all flesh," and the "Father of spirits." To have said, The Father of souls, would have made Him Father of beasts also; but it is man who alone is made in His image, and is "His offspring." Angels are also spirits and sons.

The beast has no God. It can have no knowledge of God; no real knowledge of itself. Reflection, moral judgment, conscience, have no place with it. Perfectly fitted for the sphere for which it is made, it exhibits a capacity within certain limits which may seem to outdo reason itself; but the very perfection of this shows its character. As there is no failure, so there is no improvement. The wasp lays up food for an offspring that it never sees, and can have no knowledge of. Reason in it would be unable to accomplish this; but it is not a power higher therefore than reason, but lower. It is what we truly call instinct; and in spite of the poet, reason and instinct are very far asunder.

Man, too, has instincts, for he has a soul; but in him, these are subordinated to a higher purpose, and he is left to exercise the intelligence God has given him, and improve it by the exercise. The dependence of the psychical powers upon organization merely is very easily disproved. The brain of a baboon is far inferior to that of the higher apes; yet their so-called mental manifestations are exceedingly similar. The bees and the ants, of a comparatively low order of life, manifest surprising powers, which those of their own kind, somewhat *higher* in organization, cease to manifest. But it is, of course, impossible to enter into details upon this subject here. I have already said that when we come to the living soul, we find the use of the word which from the first verse on we have not found hitherto—the word, "creation." God created the heavens and the earth at the beginning;

on the fifth day, He created the living soul. What is indicated by this is, that a new element of being was introduced here, as implied in the word, "created." Of these creatures, again, there is no scientific classification. It is wholly impossible to gather such from the words, "The waters swarmed with swarms—the living soul." The flying creatures are not at all distinguished, as to whether birds or insects or what else. Nothing of this kind is needful to the completeness of a revelation such as Scripture gives us. The whole earth is God's, and from God. On the other hand, it is for man, subordinated under his hand by God, as we shall find expressly stated presently.

For on the sixth day there is another "creation;" as such, carefully confined to man, although upon that day the *earth* brings forth "the living soul after its kind, cattle and moving thing and wild beast of the earth after its kind." Of these it is said, God *made* them. But though He says, also, "Let Us make man," He adds to that, "in Our image, as Our likeness," and He terms it "Creation."

Here, therefore, the spirit of man, which God "formed within him," as the prophet says, is a new element introduced. God is a Spirit, and spirit alone is in the likeness of spirit. The words here are, as often remarked, really poetry—the first poetry of Scripture. It is as if God's heart rejoiced over His new creature, as we know it did; we know that His delights are with the sons of men. Alas, for what this favored creature—dropped out of knowledge and thought of all this love—has become!

Man, then, exclusively, is formed in the likeness of God upon earth; and under him is subjected "all fish of the sea, and the flier of the heavens, and cattle, and all the earth." That he is to have them in subjection, implies, on his part, a control which shall keep them so. In point of fact, man, seduced by a beast, or what appeared such, vacated his place and lost it. He is now in a world of adverse influences, which God's mercy indeed may and does temper to him; and where, of course, divine grace can make, for the objects of it, "all things work together for good;" but where now God's **interference**, so to speak, is necessary for this. The miracles, which man denies, are thus the necessary tokens of the grace which would deliver him from the fruit of his own way.

Let us notice yet, what has been so often noticed, the pains with which God would impress man with the sense of his importance to Him. He takes counsel as to man's creation; He says, "Let Us make man." And, when we come to the more detailed account of His creation in the second chapter, we find God breathing into his nostrils the breath of life, and thus man becomes a living soul. His body had been formed before. His organization was complete and perfect. It was that which coming from God, not from the ground, and by that actual inspiration which, however anthropomorphic the language may be, speaks surely of a more direct communication from Himself:—it was that by which he became a living soul. We have seen that the animals also are living souls, and man, it may be pleaded, is only on common ground with them. It does not follow indeed that the soul of man is just what the soul of the beast is; and its connection in him with the spirit, which the beast has not, would alone go far to prove its higher nature. But a "living soul" he is. It is this which distinguishes him from the pure spiritual beings, which Scripture shows us also as God's creatures and His sons. Still, I repeat, it is by that which comes from God in a way his body does not that he becomes this; his life is higher than the beast's, and much more than the result of the superior bodily organization that is his. With this, then, we may close our preliminary examination of the scriptural statements, which I have separated as far as possible from questions called scientific, in order that we may arrive at a simple and unprejudiced apprehension of what it is that we have to compare with, and test, if you please, by science. We need not fear the result of testing. The pure gold will stand the refiner's fire and show no dross.

II.—THE SCIENTIFIC ASPECT.

Turning now to consider the scientific aspect of these questions, there is one thing that I would say, however, by the way of preface. We must not think that Scripture is waiting upon science to get its credentials thence. Thank God, for many it has proved itself so thoroughly to their souls that no scientific issue could possibly affect its authority for them. This the men of science themselves cannot with any justice object to. It is only saying, with an emphasis proportioned to the importance of the subject, what they themselves would say with regard to the different branches of scientific research. Connected as these are, they have their independent proof, which no one hesitates to take as proof, apart from all other testimony whatever; as well as their margins in which they overlap each other. No scientists refuse to consider any point established because all possible connections with every other point have not been ascertained; and it would be entirely too much for any one to imagine that Scripture is to be tested, as if for the first time, by the discoveries or the theories of the nineteenth century. If Scripture be a revelation from God at all, there must be some nearer way to ascertain its truth than by the slow and devious one of geological research—a path, moreover, which is open to the few alone, and not to the many; which excludes altogether the more simple and less educated, except as they may be supposed to take for granted the conclusions of others. But this would be no proof. It would be that very faith in authority which people now deprecate.

Scripture, written for all, appeals to all. It refers for its proof to man's own heart and conscience. It offers itself as that which, as light, manifests itself to those who have eyes to see; as truth, to those who are of the truth; as a revelation which reveals; and he who has used the light knows for himself the power of it. "He that believeth on the Son of God hath the witness in himself." This is not credulity; this is not blind confidence in authority. Light is its own evidence, and it is the evidence which faith in Scripture hath in abundance to justify itself to us.

But I pass from this. It is not my purpose now to dwell upon Scripture-evidences; while the very examination that we are upon will furnish, I do not doubt, many. Let us now take up the main points in which scientific teaching may be thought to come in collision with the Mosaic account of creation.

1. CREATION.

AND here the first point will necessarily be the fact of creation itself; although we are continually told that we may choose it as a hypothesis, if we will. It must be, however, at the cost of all reputation for wisdom. For as Prof. Tyndall tells us, "as far as the eye of science has hitherto ranged through nature, no intrusion of purely creative power into any series of phenomena has ever been observed." We shall be glad to learn from him how it could be. Scripture certainly knows nothing of creation as a process now going on. It declares that "the works were finished from the foundation of the world." The products of creation are alone, then, what science can deal with; and it would be interesting to know just what amount of proof of such a fact Dr. Tyndall would require.

Yet the only objection to the Scripture-statement seems to be that "it invokes forces and processes" of which science can give no account. Natural causation, therefore, is preferable, by reason of its greater simplicity; and as to the sufficiency of natural causation, Mr. Huxley has told us it is presumptuous to doubt it. To deny its sufficiency, he says, "It is obviously necessary that we should know all the consequences to which all possible combinations, continued through unlimited time, can give rise. *If* we knew these, and found none competent to originate species, we should have good ground for denying their origin by natural causation; until we know them, any hypothesis is better than one which involves us in such miserable presumption." "The hypothesis of special creation," he remarks, therefore, "is a mere specious mask for our ignorance." And this is the usual plea. Evolution, in the non-theistic form of it, is nothing else, in fact, than natural causation. But here we may be permitted to appeal to what Prof. Tyndall speaks of as *vorstellung-faehigkeit*, a term which he says, as used by him, means the power of definite mental presentation; of attaching to words the corresponding object of thought, and of establishing these in their proper relations without the interior haze and soft penumbral borders which the theologian loves. He will be the last, of course, to blame us for insisting upon this here.

What, then, is nature?—this word upon which men of science ring such countless changes? Nature is what is *natus* (born)—the inherent quality of a thing. To use it in Mr. Huxley's sense may be poetical enough, it surely is not scientific. The penumbral borders are deep and broad enough for any theologian. Nature is the nature *of* something; it is dependent and derived; it is no creator. It could never produce the thing of which it is the nature. If you mean by it the nature of the universe, you postulate the prior existence of the universe by the very term. If you mean, in fact, the nature of any primary atoms, these must be postulated; and nature cannot add the smallest atom to their company. The penumbra here, it would seem, is not a "border" merely. Was life among these primary atoms? Dr. Tyndall perhaps would tell us, —nay, he has told us, as to the earth, that "the elements of" it were there, which grouped themselves together into their present form as the planet cooled." Does he know any thing—does science—of these elements? All is confessedly hypothesis here. But it is plain that Dr. Tyndall could not account even for these elements of life by natural causation. He must have the elements first, before he could have the nature at all.

Is natural causation, then, the simpler thought? It is well that it should be understood here what scientific men deem to be the duty of science. I quote from no writer of extreme views when I quote the following: "It may sound strange to some of our readers to be told that it is the duty of the man of science to push back the great first cause in time as far as possible; nevertheless, this accurately represents the part in the universe which he is called upon to play." A very important part this, no doubt, but this is the best reason that can be given why we are bound, for instance, to prefer the gradual condensation of a solar system from a nebula, to its immediate production by the hand of God. When theistic writers commit themselves to such principles, it is no wonder that many may be found to carry them to their legitimate result; and having been able from the very commencement of things to do without God, should propose to do without Him altogether.

This is, in fact, the benefit which such a writer as Mr. Huxley almost openly professes to be derived from Darwinism. Mr. Darwin "has rendered a most remarkable service to philosophical thought," he says, "by enabling the student of nature to recognize to their fullest extent those adaptations to purpose which are so striking in the organic world, and which teleology has done good service in keeping before our minds, without being false to the fundamental principles of a scientific conception of the universe." He has explained the difference a few sentences before:—"Far from imagining that cats exist in order to catch mice well, Darwinism supposes that cats exist because they catch mice well; mousing being not the end, but the condition of their existence." Again, "For the teleologist, an organism exists because it was made for the condition in which it was found; for the Darwinian, an organism exists because, out of many of its kind, it is the only one that has been able to persist in the conditions in which it is found." This is, of course, the annihilation of design, and, at least, of all proof of a designer. I only quote it to show what he considers to be an important service to science. We can understand now why natural causation should be the more "scientific" thought, but it is scarcely the simpler for all that. Once admit God, and you have admitted all that is necessary really to the complete existence of the cosmos as it is; admit natural causation, and every step toward this is accompanied with further difficulties. The competent thought is simpler than the incompetent, assuredly.

Spite of the Darwinian theory, design, however, is evident; and Scripture appeals to it as such.—"For the invisible things of Him from the creation of the world are clearly seen, being understood by the things that are made, even His eternal power and Godhead; so that they are without excuse." This is not only Scripture, it is notorious fact. They would scoff at the idea of some chipped flints not being a sufficient proof of man's existence. Like any other mortals, they would speak of design in their formation, and be teleologists in the ordinary and not in the Darwinian sense. If you spoke to them of natural causation, and of its sufficiency to account for all things, they would rebuke you on the other side with the same confident assurance they ever possess. They have no doubt that in this case they have the work of mind, and can detect it without mistake in the very low forms in which they supposed it to have existed in the anthropoid animals whose existence may be indicated. Here they seem to allow what we contend for. But on the other hand, if these flints were only able to make other flints— if the design in them were only by a good many degrees higher in quality, then they would at once reverse their decision, and see nothing but laws of matter and natural causation, incompetent to make the lower forms. The consistency here is possibly too profound for an ordinary mind to apprehend it, or the *vorstellung-faehigkeit* is at fault, and cannot present it to the ordinary mind. In either case, the result is the same. We shall go on to suppose that we find design in nature, and take comfort in the idea that physicists can favor the cool retreat of penumbral borders as well as theologians.

Nay, there is a revolt in the ranks of science itself. People are beginning to speak now of an intelligence which they qualify (very penumbrally) as "*unconscious* intelligence." A popular philosophy in Germany at the present time is, the "philosophy of the unconscious;" which, for Hartmann and his followers, is what the "unknowable" is for others amongst ourselves—a kind of God that can be owned or disowned at a breath, and whose worship being, "for the most part, of that silent sort," will not interfere with the researches of the devotee of science. It is hard to know what is unconscious intelligence, and more hard to realize how, by any inductive process, man arrives at the unconsciousness. Just as hard as it is to realize the "unknowable" of Spencer, or how he can exhibit such very precise knowledge where he proclaims none attainable.

If design, then, proves a designer, faith in creation may have grounds to justify it, even apart from Scripture; and Scripture boldly claims it as a matter of faith, and nothing else. "By faith we understand that the worlds were framed by the Word of God." The time is past when even naturalists can afford to sneer at faith. Huxley's faith in natural causation we have seen. In the discovery of those very chipped flints of which we have spoken, the discoverer professes to have been guided by "eyes of faith." Nor need we speak more of miracles on the one side than on the other. Creation cannot be against natural law, or at least against any known, for there is none known. The evolution of life as we find it now is invariably from life. Its elements do not group themselves together according to any law that Dr. Tyndall can make evident; nor is natural causation as competent now, in the days of its decrepitude, as Mr. Huxley knows it to have been in the days of its lusty youth. Why should we not, then, believe in creation? The faith of the Christian is not built on what he gets by induction from accumulated facts. That, the truth of which he has proved so well, and is daily proving,—the Word of God, as he surely knows it, is to him above all the groping of reason in the things transcending it. But when he proclaims his belief, nothing that can be truly called science, has one word of dissent to utter.

2. Life in its Various Grades.

The next question that will come before us is that as to

the nature and introduction of life upon the globe. The nature of life is the great puzzle with the physical school. At present they are determined to classify it, if possible, as part of the universal "force" which they recognize as pervading nature. From the crystal to the living organism, they agree, is but, at any rate, a very small leap; and in the region of the unknown from which they get so many treasures, they can as well as not hypothecate some combination of molecules by which this leap may be effected. Hypotheses are scientific enough, and imagination, as we have been told at full length, has its lawful place in connection with science. It is more simple to assume natural causation than divine; and this at once settles the matter in favor of the molecules. Facts, however, are stubbornly against them; and we must here glance at the facts which are on all hands admitted.

It is usual to recognize various kingdoms in nature, with some higher divisions which it has been proposed to call "empires." The inorganic must be thus distinguished from the organic. In a mineral, for instance, there is no combination of parts to form a whole. Its atoms are alike throughout; and it grows, if it grows at all, not by any internal principle, but by mere accretion from without. The forces that are manifest in it are those of gravity, or chemical ones only. The properties of the atoms furnish the conditions under which these forces act. Spontaneity is no where present. From such and such a combination such and such results will assuredly follow, and may be calculated on with most definite precision. All is material, and yields itself, as matter will, to the control of mind without resistance. When we come to the vegetable kingdom, we find at once that we are in another sphere. Here too there is matter; here too gravity and chemistry are recognized forces; but there is something which, at present, at any rate, cannot be resolved into gravity or chemistry. With conjectures we have nothing to do. That this is the fact all must acknowledge perforce. Here there is a principle of growth, whatever it may be—an internal principle which is absolutely characteristic. There is power of reproduction, a power different from any thing that we can possibly find in the mineral. There is a correlation of parts, which act together for the welfare of the whole. There is a plain mastery exhibited, in a certain measure, over the merely material and chemical forces. This is shown strikingly when death takes place; for then the chemical forces escape from such control, and reduce the organism to mere inorganic molecules.

When we turn to the animal kingdom, we find the exhibition of a still higher power; to which the lower, though there and manifest, is again in more or less evident subjection. We can readily recognize the forces of gravity, chemistry, and vitality as all present; but there is now a true spontaneity—a power of self-direction, which is not apparent in the vegetable. Descending to the region of infinitesimals and invisibles, we may find more or less difficulty in distinguishing, as people have pointed out, the animal from the vegetable. It is usually more difficult to see in the dark. But in the higher forms there is no such difficulty; and the higher forms, and not the lower, show us the true character of what is here. What we call, in a loose way, *mind* has come in. For "mind" in a strict sense, we have to rise, spite of the physiologist, to a higher kingdom—we must come to man. But this we cannot as yet enter into: we must return back to look at these three grades of life a little more distinctly.

It is in connection with the plant and with life, therefore, at its outset,—present wherever life of any kind is found—that we come in contact with that mysterious thing for which the name now popular is *protoplasm*. A very remarkable thing is protoplasm. Mr. Huxley has done his very best to present it to us as a mere compound of certain material elements; but manifestly, the moment he employs chemistry to decide this question, the life must have escaped. He is arguing as if there was no difference between the dead and the living. From all that we can gather of it, looked at as a living thing, protoplasm is now well known to be structureless to the highest powers of the microscope. It is every where the great organizer: it has itself no organs. It has been so commonly talked of, that every one knows that these little masses of protoplasm, invisible save to the microscope, lie imbedded every where in all the tissues, whether of the animal or of the vegetable. They are the living part of these organisms. All the rest is what is called "formed material," and material which the protoplasm itself has formed. Wonderful to say, this has the power of receiving from without the nourishment of whatever kind which is supplied to it, transforming it into its own likeness, and then building up the different structures from itself.

These little masses have power of growth, of multiplication, of movement; and we have, many of us, seen pictures in which they are presented moving in a given direction, as along the strand of a muscle, and leaving behind them as they move a sort of a spider's web of formed material. No difference can be discerned between one mass of protoplasm and another. Nay, all of them, in any one body, are derived originally, so far as we can see, from a common mass. Yet in spite of this apparent identity, they are, in the more developed organism, very manifestly different in the work that they perform. Each in its place builds up the tissue which is required by the plan of the whole structure, and it builds up no other. That which is set apart to build nerve tissue will not build muscle, and that which builds muscle will not build bone. The division of labor is perfectly understood by these little workers, but the labor is steadily devoted to the good of the whole. Each works independently, and yet in fullest harmony with all the rest. Here, surely, there is a thing very different from what we ordinarily apprehend as chemical, inherent in the protoplasm itself, that renders it absolutely necessary to speak of vitality and of vital action. This vital action, as has already been said, controls and counteracts even the chemical action, as death shows; when chemistry prevails again, and putrefaction is the consequence.

As I have said, protoplasm is found wherever life is found. It does not distinguish the animal from the vegetable; although the structures built by it in the animal may be and are more various and complex. But the plant is thus a living thing. As compared, however, with the animal, we find very readily that ordinary lifeless forces have a larger part in it. The plant is nourished simply by what is called endosmose,—a law by which two fluids upon the opposite side of a membrane will diffuse themselves through it in proportion to their different density. The plant is passive here: no animal but what is more or less active in its quest of nourishment. Endosmose has, of course, its place in the animal frame, as I do not forget; but it is a different place. Life, however, in itself does not separate between the animal and the plant. When we come to the animal, we find, if we take Scripture, something more than life, however connected with it. The plant, as we have seen in Genesis i, is a thing "made," not a fresh "creation." The living soul, or animal, is a "creation;" but here we rise out of the sphere of pure physics into a higher one.

The animal has a soul. The soul, however, is not all that it is. It is but one of its constituent parts—the highest; from which, in contrast with mere matter, or with even the vegetable, it gets its name. "Every thing wherein there is a living soul," says Scripture. The soul is a higher power inherent in the bodily organism, closely connected, as is evident, with the life of the body; directing and controlling, to a certain extent, the bodily powers, just as we have seen vitality itself controlling the chemical. It is the order of nature that the higher should in part control the lower, and yet only in part. There are thus certain bodily functions which we may easily recognize to be under the control of vitality alone. We have seen that bodily structures can be built up without a soul at all. It is important to realize this. It is certain that we have no consciousness or superintendence of what goes on in this way. Nay, in ourselves, any control that we have over it tends often to act injuriously rather than the contrary. Vitality has its own sphere, and an important one. The soul is an added entity which, however now indissolubly connected with the life of the body, has also its own sphere, overlapping to a larger or smaller extent the bodily one.

Again, let us take the animal at its highest, not in its

lowest forms. No one but the naturalist would go to the germ in order to find out—just where the microscope and every thing else fails—the character of what is presented. The development of the germ is what makes manifest what is in it. How worse than foolish is it to argue from any apparent identity of the germ at the beginning, that that which develops into an oyster is yet the same as that which develops into a man. Surely the simple fact of development is a clear proof that something, and that the most important for a true definition, must have escaped the microscope or the chemical analysis. Nay, if we even take the lower forms that are developed, how *many* tendencies are there in these which would never be discerned in their true character except by comparison with those of a higher grade! To find, then, what the animal is, we should rather go to the *highest* animal than the lowest and least developed, and here we shall find, I doubt not, that Scripture and science agree most perfectly.

Anatomically, the thing which we may consider distinctive of the animal organism is the nervous system. It may be hard to trace this in the lowest forms, but I have said we shall prefer pure daylight to what is obscure. The nervous system is evidently that by which the self-directive power is manifested in the higher animal. It is necessary to spontaneous movement. But there is more than this; we have a whole range of things beside, which imagination itself can hardly ascribe to the most developed plant. Sensation is the basis of all these—one thing apart from which none of them can apparently exist. We may distinguish the animal as a sensitive being. It has sensations, and it responds to them. Sensation is not a quality which depends upon the mere possession of life. Life, as we see it in the vegetable, can exist perfectly without it; whereas in Scripture, sensation is ascribed to the soul, and to the body only as connected with it.

This may suffice to distinguish the animal from what is below it. But in order to understand clearly what the animal is, we must learn to distinguish it also from that which is above it, which, in spite of materialism, man is. There is a *human* kingdom, better perhaps called an empire, as distinct as possible from the animal, although in distinguishing it anatomy and physiology may altogether be at fault. Just as the phenomena of life do not suffice to explain to us the animal organism, which of course man is possessed of, and in which he resembles other animals, so the powers of the animal, while yet he possesses them, do not suffice to explain the highest powers of man.

Man, if we still cleave to Scripture, has a spirit as well as a soul; and with this spirit is identified the "knowledge of the things of a man,"—reflection, judgment, the moral faculties. It will be objected by some that Scripture also speaks of the "spirit of the beast." (Eccl. iii. 21.) There is one place alone in which it does so, but not as giving any positive doctrine upon the subject. It is, as the large part of the book of Ecclesiastes is, human conjecture and reasoning only. It is what a man, though he might be the wisest of men, said in his heart at a certain time. It is given as that, to put his condition of perplexity into which he had fallen, and into which every one else will fall who seeks, with him, simply "to search out by wisdom concerning all things that are done under heaven." Man's wisdom is here at fault, just as in the book of Job man's goodness is found wanting also. The wisest man here, the best there, has to confess his folly and his vileness before God. Looking at things in this human way, death is for us the great mystery—the thing which levels man with beast and wisdom with folly. Here, then, is his thought at this time: "Man has no pre-eminence above the beast." It is just because "that which befalleth the sons of men befalleth the beast; as the one dieth, so dieth the other." He adds, "Yea, they have all one *ruach*"—the word which in Hebrew stands for both breath and spirit. Its vagueness, therefore, here answers his purpose better than any more precise definition. Death is before him, and, as far as the eye sees, "all go unto one place: all are of the dust, and all turn to dust again." Now comes the question: "Who knoweth the spirit [*ruach*] of man that goeth upward, and the spirit [or *ruach*] of the beast that goeth downward to the earth?" It is human conjecture, not divine knowledge;

and whether the human *ruach* (*which is, in fact, spirit*) is distinct from the *ruach* of the beast (*which is, in fact, breath*) he knows not. At the end of the book there is, however, distinctly given to us the exact opposite of this. It is of man that he says, speaking of death also, "Then shall the dust return to the earth as it was, and the spirit shall return unto God who gave it." Thus the spirit does *not* go downward to the earth; it is distinguished by this fact from the *ruach* of the beast.

The passage here, then, if duly weighed, will only make more manifest the Scripture-distinction between man and beast.

The mental or moral powers are ascribed to the spirit in Scripture; although in man the region of the spirit overlaps that of the soul, just as we have seen the soul overlapping the vital sphere and the vital overlapping and governing the chemical.

Let us take a few passages as to the soul and spirit, that we may see how differently Scripture characterizes them. Thus the soul is the seat of the affections (Gen. xxxiv. 8.)—"The soul of my son longeth for your daughter;" "The soul of Jonathan was knit to the soul of David" (1 Sam. xviii. 1.). Hatred is ascribed to it, as is love,—"The blind that are hated of David's soul" (2 Sam. v. 8.); "My soul loathed them" (Zech. xi. 8.). The soul is the seat of the appetites of the body (Ps. cvii. 18.)—"Their soul abhorreth all manner of meat;" (Prov. xxvii. 7.)—"The full soul loatheth the honeycomb;" (xxix. 8.)—"He fainteth, and his soul hath appetite:" (Lam. i. 11.)—"Meat to relieve the soul." So the derived meanings of the word, as given in our ordinary version, are, "appetite" (Prov. xxiii. 2; Eccl. vi. 7.), "pleasure" (Deut. xxiii. 24; Ps. cv. 22.), "desire" (Jer. xliv. 14; Mic. vii. 3.), and "mind;" but in the sense of will or intention and not of the understanding, 1 Sam. ii. 35; 2 Kings ix. 15.

The spirit is used in a very different way. I have before quoted the main passage in 1 Cor. ii. 11,—"What man knoweth the things of a man, save the spirit of man which is in him." It is also the common word for "mind" (Prov. xxix. 11.)—"A fool uttereth all his mind;" (Ezek. ii. 5.)—"I know the things that come into your mind;" (Dan. v. 20.)—"His mind hardened in pride;" Isaiah xi. 4, it is translated "understanding."

Thus there is a uniform sense which these words have in Scripture, and we can understand well its consistency with that which has been before noted,—that God is the "God" and the "Father of spirits," and not of souls. He is the God of those able to apprehend and to respond to Him: He is the Father of those who have in their own spirit the likeness of His being which is spirit.

If we turn to what science says, or what we can gather naturally from things, we shall find the same distinctions, if we do not find the things which are the basis of them. I prefer at this point to use the language of another rather than my own—the language of one whose scientific competence can hardly be questioned, and who evidently has in no wise the scriptural statement before him when he uses it. Prof. Mivart distinguishes two classes of powers in man. The highest class he characterizes as follows: "First, a power of directly perceiving and reflecting upon our continued personal activity and existence—sensations and perceptions being reflected on by thought and recognized as our own, and we ourselves being recognized as affected and perceiving—*self-consciousness*. Secondly, a power of actively recalling past thoughts or experiences—*intellectual memory*. Thirdly, a power of reflecting upon our sensations and perceptions, and asking what they are and why they are; of apprehending abstract ideas; of perceiving truth directly or by ratiocination, and also goodness—*reason*. Fourthly, a power of, on certain occasions, deliberately electing to act either with, or in opposition to, the apparent resultant of involuntary attractions and repulsions—*will*. Fifthly, a power of giving expression by signs to general conceptions and abstract ideas; a power of enunciating deliberate judgments by articulate sounds—*language*. These powers result in actions, which are deliberate operations implying the use of a self-conscious, reflective, representative faculty."

Besides these highest psychical powers, he enumerates

the following powers and activities also: "First, *vegetative* powers of nutrition, growth, and reproduction. Secondly, a power of responding to unfelt stimuli by means of nervous interconnections—*reflex action*. Thirdly, a power of inadvertently performing appropriate actions in response to felt stimuli; such actions, termed *instinctive*, being provided for beforehand by the special organization of the body. Fourthly, a power of experiencing sensible pleasure and pain. Fifthly, a power of indeliberately perceiving sensible objects, of which some start or exclamation may be the sign—*sensible perception*. Sixthly, a power of effecting the coalesence, agglutination, and combination of sensitives in more or less complex aggregations, and so simulating inference. Seventhly, a power of automatic or *organic memory* which may exhibit itself in unintellectual imitation. Eighthly, a power of responding by appropriate actions to pleasurable and painful sensations and emotions—*organic volition*. Ninthly, a power of experiencing vague pleasurable and painful feelings—*emotional sensibility*. Tenthly, a power of expressing such feelings by signs or by gestures understood by our fellows, and replied to by corresponding sounds and gestures—*emotional language*."

The first of this latter class of powers—the vegetative ones—is, as the name implies, the result simply of the possession of life. The rest are as characteristic of the soul as Scripture defines it as the former class of higher powers are of the spirit as defined in Scripture also. I might quote others with regard to these distinctions, but this will suffice. Mr. Mivart remarks that as to the instinct of animals, "their highest psychical faculties appear to answer very closely to the above indeliberate human faculties; and thus we come to see, not only what instinct differs from, but also what it resembles." We are thus able to differentiate the soul from that which is above it, as we have already seen it differentiated from the mere vegetative life which is below it.

Life, soul, spirit, are thus without much difficulty to be distinguished from one another. It is remarkable that if we take the brain itself, which, of course, we have in common with at least the higher beasts, the latest science of the day makes it doubtful as to whether the cerebral lobes themselves, and even the frontal which are most in question, have any thing directly to do with the higher class of faculties which Prof. Mivart has described to us. For the expression of them outwardly, they are of course necessary, as the nervous system generally is. Prof. Ferrier, the latest investigator, speaks only conjecturally here; and his own researches, since confirmed by those of many others, show conclusively that large portions of the brain are devoted to mere muscular motions of the face and head. It is little, therefore, for Mr. Huxley or another to compare the brain of an ape with the brain of man. Even here there are great differences, although all the parts in the one are doubtless to be found in the other. But this is no more than saying that man has the animal structure which the beast has. That which makes him "man" is above the analysis of the knife or microscope.

No one who will reflect upon what we have had now before us, but will observe that sort of consistency which belongs to truth, and which nothing short of truth could be expected to have; and yet, as already remarked, what we have in Scripture is no labored argument to prove this, nor any argument at all. It does not even dwell upon such things as these, or bring them into any special prominence. It is content to leave them where man, if he chooses, can search and find; and if those who have busied themselves so much with the investigation of nature had only taken half the pains to investigate *Scripture* upon these subjects, they might have found, not only the harmony which they deny, but the real key also to many things which, for the want of the key, remain, and are likely to remain, questions merely.

I pass on now to other things.

3. Kinds.

Scripture commits itself definitely to the doctrine of species. There is here, as I believe, no uncertainty or ambiguity at all. The seed is "after the kind" of the herb which yields it; the fruit also "after its kind." God created also the living creatures "after their kind," "every winged fowl after its kind, and cattle after their kind, and every thing that creepeth upon the earth after its kind." There is no room to doubt the doctrine in all this. The question of the origin of species is vital to the truth of Scripture. Let us see briefly what are the points which are in contention as to this.

According to the most pronounced system of evolution in the present day, there are three things which we must especially consider in connection with the question of origin.

There is first of all the principle of *heredity*. This, by itself, is what Scripture-doctrine plainly asserts. It is the principle by which the kind preserves itself upon the earth; it is that by which the offspring resembles its parent in all essential features. It has been strangely misused, as we shall see directly, by evolutionists. It is a principle which, as far as Scripture is concerned, we have no difficulty with at all.

Next, we have to consider the principle of *variation*. It is as undoubted a truth that the offspring seldom or never *exactly* resembles the parent. Throughout the world, scarcely two individuals can be compared without bringing out satisfactory points of difference. The usefulness of this is easily to be understood. Were there absolute resemblance, the very fact would breed confusion. Individuality is as marked on the one hand as kinds on the other.

Along with these two principles we are to place, according to Mr. Darwin and his followers, a third, which he calls "natural selection." Mr. Spencer's synonym for it is, "Survival of the fittest." This natural selection is the fruit of a "struggle for life" which is going on every where through nature. Were but one kind left to multiply itself upon the earth, in the end the earth could not hold it. Mr. Huxley has shown us how if a plant produced fifty others in a year, in nine years, the whole surface of the earth would be overspread with it and something more. But in this way, at least, as all could not live, a struggle for life must ensue—a struggle in which the hardiest and best fitted to survive would naturally do so. The result would be, the *selection* of the varieties which thus proved themselves the fittest; and, supposing variation to be indefinite, the development, by degrees, of indefinitely higher kinds.

It is mainly in virtue of these three principles that it is supposed the different species, whether of animals or plants, have had their origin; granting, of course, the first species. Sexual selection has been added latterly in order to reinforce them when their weakness became rather awkwardly apparent. But it is evident as to the lowest forms this could have no place whatever; at least it is hard to imagine it in an oyster, or in the various forms of hermaphrodites. If natural selection cannot thus far, at least, advance alone, it will be out of its power to call in the help of the other principle. In point of fact, the question is not so much of the existence of such a thing as natural selection, which may be allowed without much trouble, and which might have its use to maintain the vigor of a species, if not to improve, at least to adapt it to varying conditions; but whether there are no limits to variation, which it may be impracticable for it to override, is another point, and is the main one.

The principle of heredity, which evolutionists strangely appeal to in their own behalf, is really that which is powerfully against them. No doubt there are variations, and plenty of them; no doubt that these are most useful in adapting a species to fresh conditions; no doubt that man can, to a large extent, both multiply and preserve these variations. We know, however, that skill is required on the part of breeders to preserve them; and we know too that they are to be found mainly in *domesticated races.* Let these but run wild, and they will most surely return, if not to the primitive condition, yet at least to be sufficiently homogeneous, and with as little tendency to variation, as the primitive one itself. The facts as to hybrids also are allowed by Mr. Huxley himself to have great importance. "The formation of hybrids naturally," says M. Quatrefages, "is so rare that eminent naturalists have doubted its reality. There are, however, according to M. Decaisne, a score of well-proved examples among plants. What is this number compared with the thousands of *mongrels* produced every day under our eyes? and yet the material conditions of fertility are identically the same with races as with species, and our botanical gardens, which group numbers of species side by side, facilitate crossing still more.

"Among wild animals living in liberty, hybrids are still more rare. It is unknown, for example, among mammalia, according to Isidore Geoffroy, whose experience has here a double value. The order of birds alone presents some facts of this kind, nearly all of which are in the order of Gallinæ. According to Valenciennes, they are unknown among fishes. In domestication and captivity, spontaneous crossing between different species is a little less rare.

"The intelligent intervention of man has multiplied unions of this kind in a remarkable manner, especially among plants, *but without being able to extend their limits.* Linnæus thought crossing was possible between species of *different families;* but in 1761, Koebreuter showed that he was mistaken. From these investigations, which were carried on for twenty-seven years, and from those of M. Naudin, his worthy rival, it appears that artificial crossing between species of *different families never* succeeds, and *very rarely* between species of *different genera;* that it is always very difficult, and demands the most minute precautions to insure success; that it even fails between species of the same genus closely allied in appearance; and finally, there are whole families amongst which hybrids are impossible. Amongst the latter, figures the family of the cucurbitaceæ, so thoroughly studied by M. Naudin, where the most perfect mongrels were produced spontaneously, we could not imagine evidently a more complete contrast. . . . . All experimenters agree, further, in declaring that even in unions between species which have been most successful the fertility is constantly diminished, and often in immense proportions. The head of the *Papaver somnifera* generally contains two thousand seeds or more. In a hybrid of this species, Goertner only found six which had been matured; all the rest were more or less abortive.

"Hybridism in animals present exactly the same phenomena as in plants. Man has been able, by diverting and deceiving animal instincts, to multiply crosses between species; but he has not been able to extend the very narrow limits at which these phenomena cease. Not one fertile union has taken place between different families. They are very rare between genera, and even between species they are far from being numerous; a fact the more remarkable, as animal hybridation is an ancient institution. . . . . We may draw this conclusion from known facts, that there are only two species of mammals —the ass and the horse, the crossing of which is almost universally and invariably fertile."

With regard to hybrids, M. Quatrefages further remarks that "in the vegetable hybrids the physiological equilibrium is destroyed in favor of the organs conducive to the life of the individual, and at the expense of those conducive to the life of the species. The stalk and leaves are always developed in an exaggerated manner relatively to the flowers. The most common animal hybrid, the mule, is an entirely similar case, being invariably stronger, more robust, and more hardy than its parents, but *sterile*. This sterility is not absolute, however, among all hybrids of the first generation. . . . . In a small number, the elements which characterize the two sexes remain capable of reproduction. Nevertheless the fertility is always immensely reduced. From his hybrids of the datura, M. Naudin only obtained five or six fertile seeds from each plant; all the others had completely failed, or were without an embryo. The capsules themselves were only half the normal size.

"If two of these first hybrids are united, they produce hybrids of the second generation. In most cases, however, the latter are either sterile, or present the phenomenon of a *spontaneous return* to one or other of the parent types, or to both. M. Naudin crossed the large-leaved primrose with the *primula officinalis* and obtained an intermediate hybrid between the two species, having seven fertile seeds. When these were sown, they produced three primroses of the male species, three of the female, and *a single hybrid plant, which was perfectly barren.* . . . .

"In order to establish a series of generations presenting a certain amount of uniformity, the hybrid must lose some of its mixed characters and resume the normal livery of the species, as M. Naudin says; in other words, it must return to one of the parent types.

"The same facts which we have just noticed amongst plants occur also among animals. . . . . There are, however, some examples among birds and among mammalia of hybrids which have propagated *inter se* for several generations, four or five at the most. . . . . But can these hybrids, of which so much has been said, maintain themselves without reverting to the parental types? M. Roux evidently believed it, and it is still asserted by M. Gayot. But the testimony of those who have established and impugned their assertions, leaves scarcely any room for doubt. Isidore Geoffroy, who had at first believed in their fixity, and had spoken of it as a conquest, did not hesitate afterward to admit the reversion. The fact has been established in Jardin d'Acclimatation, and M. Roux himself, upon the assertion of M. Faivre, appears to have abandoned his previous assertions. The observations and experiments made by the Agricultural Society of Paris clearly show that the *leporides* sent or presented by the breeders themselves, had entirely reverted to the rabbit type. Lastly, M. Sanson, discussing the anatomical side of the question, has arrived at the same conclusion."

M. De Quatrefages sums up the characteristics of hybrids as follows: "Infertility as a general rule, and, in the exceptions, a very limited fertility; series suddenly cut short, either by infertility, by disordered variation, or by reversion without atavism."

The reality of species from the scientific side can scarcely, therefore, be doubted, except by those whose theories blind them to facts such as have been stated. Heredity appears in these, whatever its nature, not as a principle which would preserve variations, but as a principle rather which tends to prevent their indefinite extension. It is a truly conservative principle. It controls and limits variations within certain degrees, within which it may be, and is, no doubt, of the greatest utility, but beyond which it would breed but utter confusion.

4. The Day-Period Interpretation.

Returning, now, to take up the six days' history more in order, we are confronted at once with the fact that there are two modes of interpretation of these, which have been ordinarily represented as contradictory of each. Carried out as they have been by various writers, whether from the side of Scripture or of science, no doubt they are so; yet in spite of this conflict, those who have looked carefully at what is said on either side, instead of finding no force in either, will find force in *both*. The resemblance of the six days' work to the geological periods is not merely an ingenious fancy, but has a foundation of fact. It does not follow from this that the days *are* periods as given in Scripture. To me, it is evident indeed that they are not so; but there is a real analogy, which, pushed beyond limits, as it has been by many, is nevertheless a true witness to the inspiration of the narrative. It surely should be no wonder if whether working upon the larger scale of periods or upon the smaller one of days God should preserve the one plan of working. Those who realize the unity of the plan in the things created will have no difficulty in realizing it in the order of creation. The fact, however, should speak for itself, that an analogy there is, and which needs but little dwelling upon for any one acquainted with the facts of geological science accepted every where now. Let us look at this first, reserving the question as to whether it be the whole truth for examination afterward.

Scripture, then, presents to us evidently, at the outset, before life existed upon the earth, a *reign of water*—"Darkness was upon the face of the deep:" and buried in the deep, to emerge from it only on the third day, is that which is dry ground afterward.

A view of this kind is by no means, at first sight, natural or reasonable. We are most of us familiar with the wonder that was produced when men found the shells of the ocean upon the mountain-tops. We may perhaps remember that Voltaire, not so very long ago, suggested that those that were found upon the Alps had been dropped by pilgrims on their journey over them. Moses, nevertheless, (if it were no higher than Moses,) declared long ago a primitive reign of water, which science has so abundantly confirmed. The mountain-chains are mostly of comparatively late geological formation. As we go back through the history as presented by the strata, we find the land becoming less and less elevated, more and more, in fact, subsiding under the waters. The carboniferous epoch presents us with a time when immense tracts of land were so near the water-level that oscillations of no excessive character alternately plunged them underneath or raised them to the surface. The Silurian seems to speak of little dry land any where, and that, probably, mere archipelagoes of no great extent. Every geological formation has been formed under water. No one acquainted with the facts doubts, I suppose, that it was at first universal.

The second point, that may seem more doubtful, is the the existence of dry land before there was life. It is certain that the first forms of life that we find are exclusively marine, and the distinct evidences of land-vegetation are still scanty in the Silurian, perhaps not to be found in the preceding "Cambrian." If the contested *Eozoon* be accepted as a reality, the first primitive being that we have knowledge of, long before the Cambrian, was still marine. Yet at that time there are evidences, at least, though not unambiguous, of vegetable life existing in such a form as ordinarily argues the existence of dry land. The graphite of the Laurentian is apparently near akin to coal, and the inference is that it was formed in a similar manner. This exists in large quantities, so altered, however, by the action of heat as to have lost any trace of vegetable structure which it may have once contained. Further, the graphite, we are told, occurs "in the way in which we should have expected it to occur, if of organic origin. It is found disseminated in the limestone just as bituminous matter is found in unaltered rocks of this kind." We have also, according to Dana, the occurrence of anthracite in small pieces in the iron-bearing rocks of Arendal, Norway, which are probably rocks of the same age. Geologists do not consider this evidence to be absolutely decisive, but it is all the evidence we have on the subject.

Nearly connected with this last point is the precedence of animal life by vegetable. In the Laurentian, if the presence of graphite is conclusive at all as to the existence of the latter, it would be evidence of the existence of it already in a comparatively high grade, while such an organism as *Eozoon* shows only the very lowest form of animal life. To this is added, in argument, by Prof. Dana, "Secondly, the fact that a cooling earth would have been fit for vegetable life for a long age before animals could have existed; the principle being exemplified every where, that the earth was occupied at each period with the highest kind of life the condition allowed. Thirdly, the fact that vegetation subserved important purposes in the coal period, in ridding the atmosphere of carbonic acid, for the subsequent introduction of land animals. Such is a valid reason for believing that the same great purpose—the true purpose of vegetation, was effected through the oceans before the waters were fit for animal life. Fourthly, vegetation being directly or mediately the food of animals, it must have had a previous existence." Here again all the evidence that the case seems to admit of is in perfect agreement with the scriptural statement.

We are upon more certain ground, however, when we come to the next point of agreement. According to Scripture, upon the fifth day the waters produced the living creature, and not until the sixth day, the dry land. Geology is in complete accordance with the order of production announced here. The Laurentian, Cambrian, and lower Devonian, so far as the records of the rocks have been deciphered hitherto, speak only of marine life. The middle Devonian presents for the first time an insect said to be allied to the modern May-flies. There is also a shell which we are told may possibly be that of a land-snail. The course of discovery is continually carrying back indeed the supposed dates of origin of all classes of existence. It is not however in the least probable that the conclusion here stated will ever be overthrown. Land vegetables began only in the carboniferous or coal period. There, comparatively speaking, in their lowest forms.

A progress in the development of life necessarily follows from all this—a progress which Scripture indicates, while it does not dwell upon it It is plain, from the Word of God and nature together, that there has been an "evolution," but an evolution of a plan in the Creator's mind alone—an evolution of what was first involved, as all real "evolution" must be.

The final and last point of similarity that needs to be insisted upon is that in both records the whole animal creation is in existence before man. That is not questioned any where. For man, as indeed the head of it, "all creation waited." When it had advanced near this its culminating point, its special adaptations to his need began to assume the multitudinous shapes he finds now around him. For him indeed, long ages before, the immense masses of coal were packed away with a manifest design which causes even Mr. Huxley himself to break out into admiration of nature's thrift: he will allow nature to prophesy, however little he will allow God. But the intelligence which looked so far forward we may surely attribute to a higher source. If man, however, had existed in that carboniferous period, he would have found little, if any thing, of "the fruit-tree yielding fruit," so necessary to his existence; he would have found little trace, apparently, of that which now furnishes him with bread; he would have found none of the flowers which now adorn for him the face of nature. We must wait long in the geologic ages before we come to these. To quote the words of another, "we miss in the species of plants of the primeval epochs those distinguished for their utility at the present day. Doubtless the earth formerly yielded ferns, firs, cycases, and palms; and plants of the same families supply useful products. The New-Zealander and Tasmanian derive some substance from the subterranean stems of a fern. We ourselves owe much to the firs of our own forests; and the natives of northern Europe sometimes use the green bark of a pine, as well as of other trees, to eke out their scanty meal. Some of the human family can, by a troublesome process, extract nourishing matter from the stems or seeds of a cycas; and certain palms do furnish valuable products, constituting, in fact, a vegetable bazar, yielding food and clothing, and luxuries besides; but how small a part, after all, of the families of man in our world do the aforesaid plants support, and that part is the least civilized and intellectual! . . . . We find few traces in the Tertiary epoch, which immediately preceded man's, of plants belonging to families from which he derives his necessary food. In that Tertiary age there were, so far as geology reveals to us, few or no species yielding 'cinnamon and odors and frankincense and wine and oil and fine flour and wheat.' There are few evident indications of any vegetables from which man derives food and valuable fibre, and, in a word, of species which support and clothe, by far, the larger proportion of the human race. Scarcely any Gramineæ (grasses) appear in the list of extinct forms. May we not conclude that the principal cereal plants are characteristic of man's epoch—that barley, oats, rye, wheat, millet, Indian corn, and rice were special provisions in order to man's appearance? From the lists of Pliocene vegetation we miss the labiate plants, which so charm us by the beauty of their flowers, and which yield essential oils to regale us by their perfumes. Of Rosaceae there are few traces; and in the list of finally-added species we must include the roses, which yield us their precious 'Attar,' and the delicious fruits which characterize our more temperate climes."

Thus does geology itself show that divine "delight in the sons of men" to which Scripture alone gives adequate expression.

Brief as this account is, it will suffice to show us that the Day-Period interpretation is not without much aprarent justification. There is at least in the analogy between the geologic ages and the six days' work sufficient to show that they have one author. Instead, therefore, of seeing in this view of things an insuperable difficulty, we see a real harmony which it reveals, to lose which would be a loss indeed. When we ask ourselves, however, Does the Day-Period interpretation as a whole really agree with Scripture? we shall find plenty of reason for not accepting it as the full thought there.

The first and most evident argument is that which is derived from the thought of "days" themselves. It is quite true that the word may be used in other senses; but when "evening and morning" are defined to be the day, this sort of use is much more questionable. That even these terms may be used poetically may be conceded; but the first of Genesis, as already said, is certainly not poetry. The seventh day, moreover, can hardly cover the whole period from man's creation until now; and to speak of the work of redemption as the work of it, the day being a day of *rest*, seems still worse confusion. In the ten commandments, that one which ordains the keeping of the Sabbath has been rightly brought forward as against the period theory. "In six days God made heaven and earth, the sea, and all that in them is, and rested the seventh day, and hallowed it." Is this seventh day not the day which He commands in this connection to be kept? If so, it is not an age, clearly; but just what we ordinarily mean by day. The attempt of some to make the first evening include the period of darkness preceding it breaks down manifestly when we consider that for "evening" itself light is necessary; and light dates only from a certain point when the earth, waste and desolate, and under water, was nevertheless there.

If people contend for the analogy, I have no objection. But analogy is one thing, literal application quite another; and it would seem very hard to prove the literal application to the geological ages,—nay, it would be hard to prove that these six days as defined periods have any proper representative in these.

But this is not the whole matter. Indeed, there are

arguments much more decisive. The evident reference to man which runs through the inspired account is a stronger one. Take, for instance, the fruits of the third day. They are surely those which are given to man for his use upon the sixth; and it is quite impossible to find such fruit, or to think of such a use of them, in the carboniferous period for instance. How can we suppose that this vegetable creation which God speaks of here is only that belonging to a by-gone time, and of which no trace remains at present? Does Scripture give any hint of such destruction or renewal as this would involve? I do not say that destruction and renewal have not taken place, but it is merely impossible to read them into the simple narrative of the first of Genesis.

So too with the living creatures of the fifth day. How is it possible to imagine that they were nearly, if not totally, blotted out of being before the sixth day came; and that a new generation of creatures should, in fact, coexist with the beasts of the sixth day? Still more, how is it possible to suppose that all these very creatures of the land, or at least the major part, had passed out of being before man, created upon the *same* day with them, came into existence?

Turning back again to the fourth day, where we find sun and moon appointed for "signs" as well as "seasons" —for signs, which could have no significance except with regard to man himself as the beholder of them. How can one with any reason imagine that they could be given as signs for ages before there was any one to behold them? To import such things as these into the simplicity of the Scripture-narrative is to destroy it. An analogy is all that I believe can rightly be urged—an analogy the importance of which I have already admitted, nay, insisted upon; but for the traces of the real fulfillment of the six-days' work—the geological traces—we must look elsewhere.

5. The Literal Day Interpretation.

The character of the Scripture chaos which precedes the six-days' work we have already seen. The terms "waste and desolate," which apply to the earth in this condition, speak of a lapse from the primitive state. The land is buried under the waters, and darkness rests upon it. We have reason to believe, as I have before said, that it had already acquired, in the main, its configuration. "The waters stood above the mountains," says the book of Psalms. The mountains, therefore, are recognized, and geology plainly indicates that they were outlined, as we say, from the beginning. The continents have been gradually formed, the mountains gradually upheaved, that is plain; but there was no destruction of continents, so far as we can find, and formation of others in their place; no subsiding of mountain-ranges, to be replaced by others. Thus in the period of desolation, already we find the earth materially finished in the form which it at present has.

Again, we are not to think of a total want of atmosphere; for, as I have pointed out, all that the second day indicates is the creation of an "expanse," not an atmosphere. Nor is it necessary even to suppose that before this the sun had not acted as a luminary to the earth. There is no necessity to deny that it had so acted, but, so far as Scripture is concerned, we scarcely expect to find this confirmed. That the mass of the sun existed is not at all against the Scripture-statments here, but rather in agreement with them. Life, on the other hand, seems clearly stated to have been absolutely extinct; that is, supposing it to have formerly existed, which we may reasonably believe that geology has proved.

If we take, then, the chronology of Scripture, allowing, as we may, for various estimates of that chronology, the period of man's existence upon the earth will not at any rate exceed seven thousand years; and this should give us dates whereby we might reach somewhat definitely the time of the six-days' work. The question here, then, occurs, Can we find any thing which answers to such a state of the earth as has just been described immediately preceding man's appearance upon it? To answer this, we must first of all dismiss from our minds indeed the thought of such periods of time as are being claimed by geologists. It is easy to show that the claim they make on this score has no real justification. The basis of such calculations assumes what can never be proved, and what is indeed against all probability, that the rate of change which is at present taking place upon the earth can be rightly taken as the rate of changes of its surface from the beginning. Into this I cannot, of course, enter now; but it is an admitted fact for most that all evidence of man's existence upon the earth dates from the *Glacial period*, and not before. It is the estimate of a recent writer that this period ended, "somewhat suddenly," some where about from five to seven thousand years ago. This, at any rate, is the estimate of scientific men, totally apart from any theories of Scripture-interpretation.

This glacial period, when we first look at it, gives us some apparent extraordinary coincidences with Scripture. It is a time during some part of which at least the whole of North America to the fortieth latitude, of Europe to the fiftieth, Siberia mainly if not entirely, are found to have been covered with water. Strata which had not been submerged from the earliest periods then were overflowed. As the land emerged, it left the evidence of this in the sea-beaches of the terrace-period, found far up upon the mountains. This time of submergence was preceded by another—the true glacial one, as to the exact nature of which opinions are divided—some contending it to have been a time rather of elevation than of subsidence, while others take the opposite view. In any case, it was a time when the whole surface indicated was covered with ice. The evidences are found in boulders of foreign material left, as on Mt. Washington, at an elevation of six thousand feet; in Scotland, at Ben Uarn More, at an altitude of three thousand five hundred and eighty-nine feet, and elsewhere similarly through the northern part of North America and Europe. On Mt. Lebanon, boulder-drift has been observed, according to Dr. Hooker, six thousand feet above the level of the sea. In South America, similar evidences have been found from Tierra del Fuego to about forty-one degrees south latitude. According to Agassiz, glacial deposit from the Andes has been found throughout the valley of the Amazon; and he is stated to have been convinced "that as the theory of the ancient extension of glaciers in Europe is gradually coming to be accepted by geologists, so will the existence of like phenomena both in North and South America through the same period be recognized sooner or later as part of the great series of physical events, *extending over the whole globe.*" "Indeed," he asserts, "when the iceberg period shall be fully understood, it will be seen that the absurdity lies in supposing that climatic conditions so different could be limited to a small portion of the earth's surface. If a geological winter existed at all, it must have been *cosmic;* and it is quite as rational to look for its traces in the southern hemisphere to the south of the line as to the north of it."

Throughout the strata thus formed the traces of existent life are very scanty; so much so as to elicit expressions of astonishment from one like Lyell; but we shall have to look at this directly. The statement just given, upon the warrant of men who may be considered of the most unexceptionable authority, show at least a state remarkably approaching the waste and desolate condition of the earth announced in the second verse of the first of Genesis; and such a condition can scarcely be found in connection with another period of the earth's history, as known geologically, so long as life has lasted upon it. Exception will no doubt be taken to the view that the glacial phenomena indicate either an entire submersion of the earth or an entire extinction of life. These are the points we have to look at more narrowly. But it certainly should be enough to produce serious inquiry when we find such correspondence of fact with a statement of so ancient a document as confessedly we have in the book of Genesis. Let us now address ourselves, then, to the examination of such points as these.

Geology itself had first taught us the occurrence of breaks in the life-history of the globe from the beginning. "The older geologists held," says Prof. Nicholson, "what probably every one would be tempted to believe at first, that the close of each formation was characterized by a general destruction of the forms of life in that period;

and that the commencement of each new formation was accompanied by the creation of a number of new animals and plants destined to figure as the characteristic fossils of the same." His answer to this is not one which, according to his own account, science necessitates so much as a certain hypothesis which is widely influencing men's minds. He says, "This theory, however, not only invokes forces and processes, which we can in no way account for, but overlooks the fact that most of the great formations are separated by lapses of time unrepresented *perhaps* by any deposit of rock, or represented only in some particular area, and yet *perhaps* as great or greater than the whole time occupied in the production of the formation itself. Nowadays, most geologists hold that there was no such sudden destruction of life at the close of each geological epoch, and no such creation of fresh forms at the commencement of the next period." That, it must be confessed, *is* what most geologists hold. The question of why they hold it is another matter. The facts remain the same as they ever were. No longer ago than the date of Agassiz's well-known "Essay on Classification" it could be stated by him that "the number of species still considered as identical in the several successive periods is growing smaller and smaller in proportion as they are more closely compared. I have already shown, long ago, how widely many of the tertiary species, generally considered as identical with the living ones, differ from them; and also how different the species of the same family may be in the successive subdivisions of the same great geological formation. Hall has come to the same results in his investigations of the fossils of the state of New York. Every monograph reduces their number in each formation. Thus Barrande, who has devoted so many years to the most minute investigations of the trilobites of Bohemia, has come to the conclusion that their species do not extend from one formation to the other. D'Orbigny and Pictet have come to the same conclusion for the fossil remains of all classes. It may well be said, as fossil remains are studied more carefully in the physiological point of view, the supposed identity of species in different geological formations gradually vanishes more and more. So the limitation of species in time already ascertained in a general way by the earlier investigators of their remains in successive geological formations is circumscribed step by step within narrower, more definite, and also more equable periods. . . . . The facts do not exhibit the gradual disappearance of a limited number of species and an equally gradual introduction of an equally limited number of new ones; but on the contrary, the simultaneous creation and the simultaneous destruction of entire faunæ, and a coincidence between these changes in the organic world and the great physical changes our earth has undergone."

Such a statement in the present day will perhaps provoke an almost scornful rejoinder; but there can be no question of the competency of the men who made such statements, and the facts remain practically little altered by any new discoveries since their time. The alteration is entirely one of men's minds, with regard to the facts. Just about the time that the essay on classification was published, or but shortly after, Mr. Darwin's views of the origin of species were given to the world. Hypothetical as they were and are, their wide-spread acceptance is now a matter of history. Evolution will not admit of these breaks in geological series. The facts must suit themselves to these altered views. The gaps remain, but they must be gaps *in our knowledge*, not in fact. Here, as so often, our ignorance is successfully pleaded as the basis of knowledge; and an unbroken life-series from the beginning is what has come to be every-where affirmed.

With regard to the glacial period, especial exception will be taken to any view which represents it as a period of universal extinction of life. It may be confessed also that on many accounts, which may easily be specified, it is hardly possible to arrive at present at all the facts of the case. The "drift," so-called, in North America is especially marked by the absence of life; fragments of semi-fossilized wood being all that is found in it. In Europe, however, things are differently stated; although here also Sir Chas. Lyell remarks, as already said, upon the scantiness of life which, he notices, the extreme cold of that period is *not* sufficient to account for. It is well known, however, that the very names given to the various tertiary formations are based upon the supposed identity of living mollusca with those existing as far back as the Eocene itself. In the Eocene, about three and a half per cent. of species were believed to be identical with recent forms. In the middle tertiary or Miocene, ten to forty per cent.; and in the later Pliocene, fifty to ninety per cent. Dana, however, states that in the Eocene the species are *all* extinct, and that these formulæ are not capable of general application. It was in face of Lyell's statement that Agassiz made his own contrary one, which has been given from his essay; and with regard to the standard of calculation adopted by Lyell, it would seem as if it were not very happily chosen. Prof. Carpenter says, "The softness of the entire body of the mollusk prevents us from recognizing the form and structure of the animal after death in any other way than by the shell; but upon this, it must be remembered, entire reliance cannot be placed, since it is liable to great variation in accordance with the circumstances of the individual, whilst it is by no means certain that there are constant differences in its form in distinct species." D'Orbigny's manual, to which Agassiz refers, is in complete opposition to Lyell in this matter, who, as the head of the uniformitarian school, had already his own hypothesis to influence him in his view of the facts.

With regard to the fish of the tertiary epoch, we have again the statement of Prof. Agassiz as to their difference from those now living. He says, "They are so nearly related to existing forms that it is often difficult, considering the enormous number (about eight thousand living species) and the imperfect state of preservation of the fossils, to determine exactly their specific relations. In general, I may say that I have not found a *single* species which was perfectly identical with any marine-existing fish, except the little species, *mullotus villosus*, which is found in nodules of clay of unknown geological age in Greenland." This statement of Agassiz is quoted without objection by Prof. Owen and Dr. Page.

With regard to higher forms there is again diversity of judgment. "Prof. Owen tells us that certain quadrupeds found in the tertiary rocks, such as moles and shrews, hares, rabbits, voles, and other rodents, are not distinguishable from the species that still exist; but he expresses himself with great hesitation and caution upon the subject of the identity of the tertiary with existing species. He does so in consequence of the meagreness of the data on which such judgments are formed." Many quadrupeds, however, are asserted to be preglacial and to have survived this period,—the elephant, for instance, among others; but the question here has difficulties peculiarly its own, which we must shortly consider. Thus far, that is, as far as regards the preglacial and present species, we have very competent authority for their almost entire difference.

As to the glacial and related strata, there are several points to be considered which will naturally influence our acceptance of many statements that are current. First, it is to be remarked that such a period as we are now considering is one which would involve, by its very character, a mixing of material such as would be very hard to disentangle. In considering the question of the identity of species between any two formations, we have to take into account what seems very much forgotten, that the latter of these is formed, generally speaking, by the disintegration of the former. It is natural, therefore, that the species of a prior formation *would* be, to some extent, mingled with those of the one following it. Thus, in carboniferous rocks have been found pebbles containing Lingulæ of the Potsdam sand-stone from the lower Silurian; and Lyell observes that "many of the fossils found in the red crag have been washed out of the older tertiary strata, especially out of London clay;" and again, in the same page of the well-known "Elements," he remarks, as to certain fragments of the bones of Cetacea, "that they may be derived from the destruction of beds of another formation."

Where we have to do with results of ice-action, as admittedly we have in the present case, we have above all to take this into consideration. Ice is a great mixer. Page remarks this with regard to icebergs, which are the very things, as perhaps most geologists believe, which produced the mass of phenomena of the boulder-drift. "Many of the bergs which drift out to sea, having been the extremities of glaciers while in attachment to the coast, are loaded with large angular fragments of rock and other debris; and many of the floes, having been ground on shore-ice, lift with them immense masses of water-worn shingle and gravel. Thus, as both melt away, the bottom of the ocean must be strewed with very heterogeneous and curiously assorted material. Nay, icebergs have been encountered in the North Sea covered or interstratified with ancient soil, among which were the bones of mammoths and other extinct animals, still further confusing the nature of their deposits by mingling the remains of an existing fauna (reindeer, musk-ox, arctic-bear, etc.) with one of a much higher antiquity."

The matter is still more complicated by the assertion, made by not a few of the present day, and coming perhaps to be the most generally received opinion, that there were at least *two* glacial periods succeeding one another. Thus the products of a more recent one would have to be very carefully distinguished from those of an earlier; and I believe that there are evidences that some, at least, of the remains which are generally counted preglacial are rather to be considered interglacial remains, that is, that have accumulated between these two similar periods. These so-called preglacial strata are, moreover, found but scantily. The Cromer beds are considered the principal; and Lyell remarks that the plants of its buried forests "agree singularly" with those of the lignite of Duernten, which is considered to be interglacial.

The general idea which we gather from all these considerations is certainly in accordance with the thought of the present order of things, as dating from this glacial period. Traces of man's existence, it is acknowledged, have not been found before it; and the words of a well-known text-book, however much they may be modified in the writer's mind, nevertheless are quite suited to convey to us the thought of a new creation dating from this time. "In process of time," says Dr. Page, describing the close of the glacial period, "the land was elevated to its present level; another distribution of sea and land took place, and the glacial epoch passed away. A *new* flora and fauna suitable to these new conditions were then established in Europe; and these, with the exception of a few which have since become extinct, are the species which now adorn our forests and people our fields." He qualifies this, in some measure, directly afterward, but the broad fact he allows; and the question is, whether these facts really need to be taken with any abatement.

But we have now to consider a different question—as to what is the extent of the earth's surface to which these glacial phenomena are limited. Here we have to remember how much, unfortunately, geological researches have been limited to Europe and North America. Of South America we know little; of Africa, less; of large tracts of Asia, very little indeed. It is easy, therefore, to take, as geologists so often remind us for another purpose, the limit of our knowledge as the limit of the phenomena in question themselves. Yet, imperfect as research has been outside of the fields already indicated, even these have furnished us with some indications that, according to Agassiz's own belief, the glacial winter was *cosmic*. The boulder-drift upon Lebanon, the boreal shells noticed by Sir Chas. Lyell as occurring in the Sicilian seas, the drift found on the Himalayas, with Agassiz's observations (if admitted) of similar phenomena in the valley of the Amazon,—all point in one direction. We have also very clear testimony to the fact that even for long after, many parts that are now dry land were submerged. In Asia, Siberia, and the extent of ground covered by that "northern Mediterranean," of which the Caspian Sea and the Sea of Aral are the present remainder; in North Africa, the Sahara, which is still covered with recent shells. Siberia and northern Asia have been, in fact, rising apparently to the present day, and the large mass of the northern Asiatic continent gradually drying up. Europe, according to the evidence, was to a comparatively late geological period a cluster of islands rather than a continent, and the scriptural designation of the "*isles* of the Gentiles" would seem to be the record of a historical fact. All these things point to a submergence, the extent of which, indeed, they do not indicate. But if we follow in the direction to which they lead us, it is natural to ask ourselves, Supposing that the full extent of what Scripture indicates were admitted to have taken place, what proofs should we be likely to have more than just such proofs as in fact we have? As to the occurrence of ice, the Scripture-narrative, in fact, says nothing. The strictly glacial phenomena may have been limited to either side of forty degrees from the equator. The question would still remain, Supposing a complete submergence, what proofs should we expect to find of such a condition?

The existing evidences are of two kinds only:—The first, the occurrence of sea-beaches as the land rose, more or less intermittently, from the ocean; the second, the occurrence of marine shells or other evidences of sea-life. In a condition corresponding to the waste and desolate time indicated in the first of Genesis, *neither* of these evidences could be expected to be found. If life were absent, this of course would be wanting, save only as it might consist of traces of a condition which had then passed away. *Sea-beaches* could not exist when the sea was every where. Thus, as it would seem, all that we expect to find would be the evidences of a condition *prior* to or *succeeding* one of complete submergence. Just such marks we do assuredly find.

There is another question that might be raised here,—whether in fact the land sank, or the water rose. It is a little difficult to imagine the sinking of a large mass of whole continents, nay, of all the northern portion of the northern hemisphere altogether, and this with a similar state of things apparently in the southern. Whether strictly contemporaneous or not, we of course have no means of deciding. Hitchcock has remarked on the singularity of the existing sea-beaches of North America being so perfectly horizontal as they are, and inclined apparently on this account to believe in the rise of the water rather than the subsidence of the land. It must have been, in fact, a singular force, apparently unknown to geology, which could lift a large part of a continent out of the deep in so steady and equable a manner. With the thought of a rise of water, Scripture, as we have seen, is in complete accordance. Whether it necessitates such view or not is another question. If, however, the water rose, it follows of necessity that the whole earth was covered, and thus the condition indicated in Scripture would be fully made out.

Upon these facts, such as they are, we may at least rest the conclusion that the six-days' work of the first of Genesis was in fact the renewal of the earth after the close of the glacial period, and the repeopling with the forms of life which at present exist. As to the most of these, there can scarcely be a question that they date, so far as the evidence goes, from the glacial period; and upon no other ground than that of evolution could the conclusion be possibly escaped that creative power was here for the last time displayed. Creation may be unknown to Science; in fact, we do not *expect* her to know any thing about it. The traces of it she can only find in the sudden appearance of the *products* of creation. Science assuredly knows no more of evolution than it does of creation. The only difference is, that in the matter of the origination of life from combinations of mere matter, and in that of the alleged transmutation of species, all the facts of the existing world are confessedly against it. If former periods were unstable, we have a most remarkable *stability* as the present result of it, and the efforts to obtain some proof of evolution have only succeeded the more in bringing out this. But between evolution (that is to say, natural causation) and creation there is no middle ground. Science, therefore, so far as it can be expected to testify, testifies in favor of the latter and against the former. With this we may have abundant reason to be content. With men's hypotheses we have nothing to do. Arguments derived from our ignorance, and from those regions which are beyond the reach of the microscope or the chemist's tests, we may safely leave, as proving the animus of the reasoners rather than the capability of reasoning. On the other hand, we must not expect geology to do duty for revelation. We accept the statement of the latter on the ground of the abundant proof we have of revelation itself. All that can be demanded is, that the facts of science should not manifestly contradict the statements of revelation. But here we must remember that theorists, alas! can even manufacture facts, when only the will is sufficiently strong to demand it. Mr. Lewis, a most unexceptionable witness, for instance, will tell us "the psychological law that we only see what interests us, and only assimilate what is fitted to our condition, causes the mind to select its evidence;" and that he only hopes for the reception of his views by those "who by previous culture and native disposition have been prepared for a sympathetic attitude . . . . Unless the attitude of mind be sympathetic, there would be stubborn resistance to what otherwise would be clearest evidence." So Prof. Tyndal also remarks, "The desire to establish or avoid a certain result can so warp the mind as to destroy its power of estimating facts. I have known men to work for years under a fascination of this kind." But for such considerations as these we need scarcely appeal to any class of writers. We all of us know how the head is influenced by the heart; how, according to a common proverb, "where there is a will there is a way," in almost any direction. The facts to which people often so undoubtingly appeal have therefore to be questioned, not only as to how far they bear out the views for which they are appealed to, but even as to how far the views may be the parents of the facts; and this without any conscious dishonesty, nay, with the greatest desire, apparently, for nothing but truth. I conclude, then, once more, although it is but a conclusion, not at all admitted as upon the same ground as the positive statement of Scripture, that the present state of things dates back to its beginning in that period which, as a scientific writer believes, occurred seven thousand years ago; a time sufficiently near to Scripture chronology, when the glacial period came to its end. I believe that in this, Scripture and science are really harmonious, although it would be idle to affirm that the evidence, as we have it at present, is altogether unconflicting.

I would close with one or two considerations drawn from the study of the geological record itself, and in which it seems to me to harmonize, in the most distinct way, with some teachings of Scripture. First, it is evident from geology alone that the earth is found in a more developed condition the more we approach the historic centre from which man originally came. No naturalist doubts that the general character of the fauna and flora of Australia is lower in type than that of America; but even in America we find still the marsupials which pertained to a former condition of things in Europe, long since passed away. Thus Australia, America, and the great continent of Europe–Asia are allowed to illustrate three successive stages of geological progress, while the last alone seems to have furnished man with his domestic animals, and with his principal means of subsistence otherwise. The whole earth does not seem thus to have been got equally ready for his reception, but a special part of it only; and with this announcement of geology Scripture accords in the fullest way.

It teaches that man was placed under probation on earth, and as the head of creation, which depended upon him for blessing or for curse; and that accordingly *not* the whole earth, but paradise alone, was as yet prepared for him. Had he stood, the whole earth might have become a paradise; but, apart from all speculation, it is plain that the whole earth was not Eden, but only the place where man was put; and this is quite in accord with this, that at further and further distances it should be found still less and less developed. Here, certainly, is a remarkable and unexpected coincidence between the teachings of science and the inspired Word.

But it by no means ends here. As already noted, there was an apparent return of the cold to a considerable extent after man was upon the earth, and along with this, a 'brief period of submersion also, which so good an authority as Principal Dawson conceives to correspond with the biblical deluge. After this, the land rose, the climate became milder, and the so-called glacial period passed away.

Here, again, is a witness of geology to Scripture; for it is evident that according to the latter as to the ground after the deluge—in that world which came up from the waters, with which God entered into covenant anew— there was an amelioration of a former condition. "This same shall comfort us," says Lamech, alluding to the name of his son just born, "concerning our work and the toil of our hands, because of the earth which the Lord has cursed." And after the flood, when God smelled in the sacrifice a "savor of rest," He says, "I will not again curse the ground for man's sake; while the earth remaineth, seed-time and harvest, and cold and heat, and summer and winter, and day and night, shall not cease." How remarkably appropriate such language at the close, not of a deluge only, but of a glacial period which had forbidden seed-time and harvest and summer-heat to a large part of what is now man's pleasantest abode!

Let us close with the adoring remembrance that fruitful seasons are now not alone, or principally, signs of God's goodness; He has given His Son. In Christ His love has been manifested in such a way that all vail is forever removed. If the glory of Christ be hidden to men, alas! "the vail is upon their hearts."